TRI-CONTINENTAL JEW

A 20th CENTURY JOURNEY

Ernest Stock

TRI-CONTINENTAL JEW

Ernest Stock

Production: Mendele Electronic Books Ltd

MENDELE
Electronic Books

For online purchase:

Cover by Adlai Design

ISBN: 978-965-565-127-0

For Bracha

Contents

Introduction

S ome years ago, I was asked by the editor of the Princeton alumni publication to contribute an article on how the trauma of *Kristallnacht* which I underwent as a 14-year-old in Nazi Germany had affected my experience as a student at the university. In working on the piece, it occurred to me that the editor had identified two crucial turning points in my life, seemingly unrelated until then, and prompted me to make the connection between them.

I am appending some excerpts from the article to this introduction, both because they allude to themes that the book deals with at greater length, and also because they shed light on the motivation for my later move from America to Israel.

Through that move, which occurred in 1961, I joined the exclusive roster of individuals who escaped the holocaust and experienced all three types of Jewish existence in the twentieth century:

1) as a member of a community under a totalitarian, anti-semitic regime;
2) being part of a community under a free, democratic government; and
3) living in the world's only sovereign Jewish state.

I offer this memoir as a contribution to the speculation on the nature of Jewishness, which has become such a timely subject, one fraught with political implications. I would not, however, see it as leading to a single definition of Jewishness. The latter's character, as I perceive it, changed radically with each shift in location. In my native Germany, it was formally religious: Jews defined themselves as German citizens of the Mosaic faith. This held true until the Nazi government decided that the Jews were a race, and eventually formalized its decision in the infamous Nuremberg Laws. These excluded Jews from every level of national life – social and political, cultural and professional. The resulting ghettoization at first strengthened communal solidarity, along with individual Jewish consciousness, but this turned out to be a short-term delusion. No communal structure could withstand the government's determination to rid itself of its Jewish population. Still, in my own case the forced transfer, in third grade, from a public to a Jewish parochial school laid a solid foundation for what was to come. Upon leaving Germany, I came well prepared to play my part in Jewish life in Alsace, France, where I spent the first eight months of my exile. The encounter with new types of individuals and institutions in the bracing air of freedom led me to look upon Strasbourg Jewry in particular as the optimum to which a non-sovereign Jewish community might aspire. Alas, the outbreak of war in September 1939 brought the idyll I discovered across the Rhine to a sudden end.

Part One, then, *Escape from Europe*, consists of recollections of growing up as a Jewish child in Germany; of the escape to France after *Kristallnacht*, and from there on to the U.S.A. via Spain and Portugal, in flight from the German army.

In Part Two, *Becoming an American*, five separate phases of my experience during the ensuing two decades are described, with emphasis on the Jewish aspect in each: early employment; service in the U.S armed forces (including the return to Europe in 1944); university studies; coincidences, and work in the organized Jewish community (preceded and interrupted by exploratory stays in Israel).

In the first three, anti-semitism again reared its head, which came as somewhat of a surprise to me. Perhaps I was naïve to think of it as an exclusively German blight. But I was always aware of the crucial difference: in Germany Jew hatred was sponsored and promoted by the authorities, in America a social variety of anti-semitism targeted Jews as individuals, while discriminatory policies were practiced by private institutions such as country clubs, resort hotels and universities, rather than the state.

In retrospect, I realize that my initial three years in America before being drafted into the U.S. army were spent almost entirely in Jewish surroundings. My first employers were German Jews like myself. At my second job, at Loew's-MGM, the motion picture company, my colleagues were mostly American Jews, with non-Jews in the minority. It was only in the army that I found myself in a predominantly Christian environment. The same holds true, of course, for the Princeton campus. Together, the experiences related in these two chapters probably laid the groundwork for the move to Israel, though there were other factors at work as well.

The decision ripened during my first visit to Israel in 1949-50, which came early enough to find me caught up in the excitement of the emergence of the state. But it took twelve more years, and a second temporary stay in Israel on a Ford Foundation research fellowship, (as well as marriage to a *sabra*), to be implemented. The intervening period saw my transformation from a German Jewish refugee into a *bonafide* American, not only by citizenship but also by outlook and personality.

As part of that process, I count among the "other factors" that led to the decision a measure of intellectual curiosity. More specifically: after taking up the post of Consultant on Overseas Studies at the Council of Jewish Federations, I began studying for the Ph.D. in the Department of Public Law and Government at Columbia University. My major interest was in international relations, and particularly in the behavior of small states as actors in the state system, an area which had been relatively neglected. I became engrossed by the question of whether and how Israel's Jewish character would influence its relations with other powers. This quest also finds expression in my doctoral dissertation, *Israel on the Road to Sinai: A Small State in a Test of Power.*[1]

Concurrently, my research focused on the relationship of Israel with Diaspora Jewry. Here, too, I drew on work I had done in Israel on the Ford Foundation project, and on the dissertation. The subject in all its facets has remained a lifelong interest for me; I see my main contribution to it as twofold: 1) analysis of the complex institutional structures involved[2]; and 2) exposing the asymmetry in the relationship, and its implications.

But it would be wrong to leave the impression that my years in America were dominated by the Jewish element. Much that was novel and even fascinating in my day-to-day life was totally unrelated to it. Even the army service, despite the hardship and occasional anti-semitism I encountered, was a positive and formative experience, resulting in admiration for my new homeland's principled yet pragmatic power. Then the two and a half years I spent studying at Princeton had a lasting effect on my intellectual growth. I did a prodigious amount of reading in my course assignments, and there were numerous intangible benefits, such as the development of a critical attitude in the political and ideological realms.

Part Three, **Israel**, consists of two sections:

a) *Conversations with my Son*, in which I attempt to justify the move to Israel to a skeptical adolescent; and also respond to his questions about the country's existential dilemmas. Actually, these are not verbatim records of conversations, but rather summaries of talks we had over several years. The table of contents pertaining to this section lists some two dozen topics, many of which relate to Jewishness in the Israel environment.

---

1. Published as *Israel on the Road to Sinai 1949-1956* by Cornell University Press, 1967
2. See my *Partners & Pursestrings*, University Press of America and Jerusalem Center for Public Affairs, 1987

Others draw on my personal and professional experience, which included twelve years as director of Brandeis University's undergraduate program in Jerusalem.

b) an epilogue, in which I discuss problems of citizenship and also relate the conversations to current realities.

From the web site of the Princeton Alumni Weekly

Princeton Alumni Weekly

PAW Home > > After Kristallnacht

After Kristallnacht

Ernest Stock '49

Posted on November 5, 2008

The GI Bill of Rights, with its subsidized tuition and living grants, famously brought a new type of student to the Princeton campus: older, more mature, sobered by the war experience. I was one of them. I presented course credits from New York's City College (Evening Session) which I had earned before being drafted in 1943, and which added up to the equivalent of the freshman year. The evening part was born of necessity: After I arrived in the U.S. from Europe as a 15-year-old in July 1940, I promptly looked for a job to help my mother with the finances.

At the end of the war I was shipped back from Europe and was waiting at Ft. Sam Houston, Texas, to be discharged. While there, I happened to read in the *Stars & Stripes* that the army was administering its own college entrance exam. I took the test, which lasted an entire day, and my score was high enough to get me admitted to Princeton. Then the army released me in time to start the spring semester of 1946 as a sophomore there.

I shall always be grateful to the anonymous official who decided to admit me on the basis of the army-administered test, and to the Congress which passed the G.I. Bill, without which I would have gone back to evening college. Instead, I had the awakening charm of the Princeton campus in early spring awaiting me when I got off the train. The two and a half years that lay ahead turned out to be among the happiest and most meaningful in my life.

The mood on campus that spring semester was quiescent and soothing, as though the war had been little more than an unpleasant interlude. There was scant interest among the student body in discussing it or its aftermath. I found myself gliding willingly into this state of mind and saw no need to make an issue of my own background and experience. Devoting myself to full-time study for the first time since I left Germany eight years earlier, I threw myself with enthusiasm into the course work and reading.

I did not plan it that way, but it turned out that Princeton played a part in furthering my education as an American Jew.

When I first arrived on campus, I did not know anybody and was assigned a room by lottery. My roommate, a war veteran like myself, and I got along well together. But at the end of the spring semester he announced that he would be moving out. "My father wouldn't let me room with a Jew," was his somewhat embarrassed explanation.

Although taken aback, I took it philosophically. I knew that my roommate was no anti-semite himself, and I tried to understand the environment he grew up in. His father had, in all likelihood, sent him to Old Nassau not least for the social connections, and a German Jewish refugee was not a great catch.

As a major I chose SPIA (School of Public and International Affairs) which involved courses in History, Politics and Economics. It was the period the Palestine problem was before the U.N., and some of it was being re-enacted at our school's Conference on the Near East. I was a passionate advocate of Partition (now the two-state solution), but I also learned to understand the Arab case.

The domestic policy conference at SPIA that year dealt with the House Un-American Activities Committee, which practiced an early version of McCarthyite tactics on Capitol Hill. Perhaps it all came together when, while in charge of Brandeis' overseas study program in Jerusalem in the 1960's, I wrote a book on Jewish-Arab relations in Israel and later, together with a few like-minded colleagues, founded the Israel Association for Civil Rights.

Ernest Stock was among the first recipients of a Ford Foundation Near East area training fellowship in 1952 and later received a doctorate in International Relations from Columbia. He directed Brandeis University's undergraduate program in Jerusalem and taught in the Politics Departments of Brandeis and Israeli universities. Among his books are "Israel on the Road to Sinai" (Cornell) and "Partners and Pursestrings" (University Press of America). He also served as Executive Director of the European Council of Jewish Communities, based in Paris. Dr. Stock now lives in retirement near Tel Aviv.

PART ONE

Escape from Europe, 1940

Chapter One

A Jewish Childhood Under Hitler

My father left school at fourteen to go to work, as did most boys who grew up in villages or small towns in Germany. I always felt sorry for him when he reminded me of this, and not only because he had to get up at five every morning and walk half an hour to the train in freezing weather or summer heat to be on the job in the big city at eight. He had a fine mind and many interests, and I thought it was a shame that he had to stop his formal schooling so early. Little did I suspect then, as a boy of ten or twelve, that soon I would have to leave school at fourteen myself. After *Kristallnacht,* the "Night of Broken Glass," November 9-10, 1938, the Jewish school I attended in Frankfurt closed down. A few weeks later I left Germany forever, with my ten-year-old sister Lotte in tow. My mother stayed behind, waiting for her husband to be released from the concentration camp where he had been taken that night by brown-shirted thugs who had broken into our apartment and dragged him away.

We knew Papa was alive and well because he managed to send us a postcard from the train that took him to Buchenwald, the infamous camp near Weimar. He threw the card through the toilet bowl, hoping that someone would find it on the tracks and put it in the mail. This is exactly what happened: soiled but still legible, the card was delivered to our mailbox with the unfailing efficiency of the German postal system.

Our family was not to be reunited until almost eight years later. Only in 1946 was Papa to leave Holland, where he had been in hiding with a Dutch couple throughout the war, to join his wife and children in America. But during the long separation I rarely stopped thinking of him. A half century later, when I was asked to speak about the events of my childhood to a group in Jerusalem on Holocaust Day, I described him as one of the three heroic figures that remained in my memory from those years.

Another of my heroes was the gym teacher in my school, Emil Stelzer. A German "Aryan" himself, he was married to a Jewish woman. The Nazis gave him a chance to leave his wife before deporting her to her death, but he chose to stay with her until the end.

The third heroic figure was my classmate and best friend, Karlheinz Schweber (about whom more shortly). His parents were Polish Jews who had settled in Germany after World War I. They had the foresight to get out before Hitler decided, in October 1938, to ship all the Jews with Polish citizenship back to Poland. At first the Polish government refused to admit them, and they were forced off the trains to camp in no man's land at the border. Many of them died of exposure. It was an act of shocking inhumanity, and it set off the chain of events which culminated in the pogroms of *Kristallnacht.* A young man named Herschel Grynszpan, who lived in Paris, stood by helplessly as his aged parents were expelled from their home in Germany and dumped at the Polish border. Determined to draw the world's attention to their plight, he entered the German Embassy in the French capital and shot the first official he saw. The death a few days later of the diplomat, Ernst vom Rath, was the pretext the Nazi government had been waiting for to launch its wholesale pogroms on the entire Jewish population.

By getting out in time, the Schwebers were spared the suffering of Grynszpan's parents which drove their son to desperation. They moved to Thann, a town in Alsace, the province of France across the Rhine River from Germany. Karlheinz' father was a food engineer, and he had been offered a job in a bouillon factory located there. The evening after the Crystal Night, there was a long distance telephone call for Mutti. On the line was Rosa Schweber, Karlheinz' mother. She knew my mother casually, the way mothers of school friends know one another. Once she had invited our family to eat in the kosher restaurant which she ran on the *Weserstrasse*, near the railroad station. She was an excellent cook, but more than the meal she served us, I remember the shiny white table cloths which gave the rather bare dining room a festive atmosphere. Until then I had seen the tables mostly from below, as Karlheinz and I liked to race toy cars on the floor between meal times.

Now Rosa Schweber told Mutti on the phone that she and her husband had decided to invite me to join them in Thann, where I could continue my studies in the local *lycèe* together with Karlheinz.

My mother hesitated. Rosa Schweber told her to think about it and let her know. Then, wavering, my mother said something about not wanting to stay alone with Lotte, my ten-year-old sister. Rosa Schweber did not hesitate. She told Mutti to send Lotte along.

Mutti later told me that the decision to let us leave for France was the hardest she ever had to make. She had to make it on her own, because there was no way of consulting with Papa in the concentration camp. And indeed, when Papa came home on being released, after the two of us had left for France, his first question was: "where are the children?" I still don't know whether or not he approved of Mutti's decision, but at the time he had no choice but to accept the situation.

Mutti's main hesitation, I assume, was about sending Lotte, who was not yet eleven, and entrusting her to the care of her brother, who had just turned fourteen. Lotte (she would soon be called Charlotte in French) was a lively and intelligent girl who made friends easily, but she had never been away from her parents. The Schwebers were strangers to her, and if the match didn't work out, there would be no way back. At the time the German government was willing to let its Jews leave, but would not let them return.

As for myself, I not merely approved of the idea of leaving, but actually begged my mother to let us go. I had been away alone on vacation more than once, and had always enjoyed being away from home, on my own. And I was eager to leave Germany. In fact, I was annoyed with Papa for taking so long to realize that there was no future for us Jews. He was deeply rooted in German culture, and probably apprehensive about having to start life anew in a strange country. In an article about his first impressions of America he wrote, in 1946: *"If I had realized soon enough how relatively easy and painless this new start comes, even to a man in his fifties, I would have taken the decision to emigrate in 1933, when Hitler first came to power."*

The event which at last made Papa decide to leave was the deportation of the Polish Jews. As for many German Jews who were still hesitating, the fate of their Polish Jewish neighbors was a clear signal that their turn, too, would soon come. My father hurried to the American consular office which, faced with a sudden onrush of visa applicants, handed out numbered slips on a first-come, first-served basis. Papa was among the early birds, and his low number entitled our family to be processed for the visa at the Consulate General in Stuttgart a few weeks later. By that time the Affidavit of Support, the *sine qua non* for every would-be immigrant, should have arrived, sent by my Uncle Arthur in New York. Within two or three months, we could be on board a ship leaving Hamburg or Bremen for the United States.

That was the scenario. In real life, things happened differently.

A few days after Papa was given his number at the American consular office, his cousin Hugo Heyum rang the bell at our apartment. Hugo was a tall, serious-looking man who had recently lost his job as a high-school teacher of mathematics in the nearby town of Neu-Isenburg. All Jews teaching in the public school system had been dismissed, and there was nothing left for him to do but emigrate. It had been a hard blow for him; his wife was not Jewish, and he had hoped that, as a mixed couple, they could stay on. But the Nuremberg laws were quite adamant: he was still a Jew and as such not fit to teach German youth. Moreover his daughter, Ursula, blonde and fair-skinned like her mother, as a *Mischling ersten Grades* (mixed blood of the first degree) would also have trouble continuing her schooling. So he, too, had planned to call on the American consular office in Frankfurt to get a number. But his train was late that afternoon, and he had just missed the consulate's office hours. He would have to come back another time.

My father had always admired Hugo, who was the only one in his family with an academic education and (until recently) a highly respected position. Now, faced with his dejected cousin, he made a characteristic gesture. "Take my number," he said to Hugo. "I'll go get another one in the morning." This little act of generosity was to have dire consequences for our family. I don't know whether Papa called on the consulate the next morning; he may have had more urgent business that day and got there only the following week. But the result was that there were now hundreds of people ahead of us on the waiting list, and the new, higher number meant that our turn at the Stuttgart visa office would come only weeks, maybe months, later than with the original one. Many years afterwards I heard Mutti say that she could never forgive her husband for giving that number away: his foolish empathy had torn our family apart. But for now there was only resignation, not despair. A few more weeks of waiting for the visas to America, so it appeared, was not the end of the world. But then came Crystal Night, and our world did come to an end.

In future years I heard people, especially in America, express surprise that Mutti was ready to part with her children with such apparent ease. But I for one never had the least doubt about the rightness of her decision. I instinctively understood the mixture of apprehension, uncertainty about the future and fear of missing the opportunity to send us to a safe haven, which brought it about. Moreover, she was convinced that the separation would be temporary and brief. We would, she believed, soon be reunited in America.

Until the *Kristallnacht,* almost all the Frankfurt Jews who emigrated did so as a family; few children left by themselves. One of those few was my cousin Arnold Hirsch, the only child of Aunt Rika (my father's sister) and Uncle Heinrich, who had been Papa's partner in the food wholesale firm Hirsch & Stock, before 1933. Arnold was a year older than I, but we were good friends. Early in 1938 his parents sent him to stay with his uncle Alfred Stock, my father's younger brother, in Buenos Aires. Alfred, who lost an arm in World War I, had emigrated there with his wife Erna and son Fritz a year earlier and was ready to take Arnold in until his parents could follow. But they never did, and Arnold grew up an orphan. His parents remained in Frankfurt until it was too late, and they were deported and murdered.

In my class, Karlheinz' family had not been the only one to get out in time; almost every week another seat became vacant. And after the "night of broken glass," the Jewish schools were shut down altogether. Sitting home was not an enticing prospect for the long term. The idea of leaving, even without parents and in charge of my little sister, was far more attractive.

The school where Karlheinz Schweber had been my classmate was called the *Philanthropin.* It was the pride of the Frankfurt Jewish community, which had established it back in 1806 as a humanistic, secular institution where religious subjects were also taught. (It was probably significant that its founders gave it a Greek instead of a Hebrew name, the translation of which was "Love of Mankind.") After Hitler came to power in 1933, Jewish children all over the city transferred from the neighborhood schools they were attending to one of the two Jewish schools, the *Philanthropin* or the Samson Raphael Hirsch *Schule*, run separately by the Orthodox Jewish community. This was a gradual process at first, which accelerated with each passing year. I had entered first grade in a municipal school in 1931; at that time my parents did not even consider sending me to a Jewish school. But in 1933, after Hitler's rise to power, there was a drastic change. I was molested by other children on the way to school, and my homeroom teacher, a Mr. Habig, made matters worse with anti-semitic remarks in class. It didn't help that he was the head of the National-Socialist (Nazi) Teachers' Union in Frankfurt.

The transfer thus came as a relief to me and my parents. Moreover, the *Philanthropin* was an excellent school, both at the elementary and secondary levels. As throughout the whole German school system, the division between the two stages came early, at the age of ten. At that point the more gifted pupils were promoted to the *Gymnasium* (high school) while the less favored ones continued in the *Volksschule* until 14. Each *Gymnasium* class (as all over Germany) had its own color velvet cap, which contributed to the class spirit. There were separate classes for boys and girls, and between classes the two groups played in different parts of the school yard. Although there was no crossing over while school was in session, nobody could keep boys and girls from walking or riding bicycles home together. There were two or three such couples in our class; Karlheinz and his friend Marianne were one of them. I was not among the lucky ones. I could well understand it when Karlheinz preferred Marianne's company to mine on the way home, and I tried hard not to let on that I was jealous. .

The girls sometimes watched us boys play soccer from their half of the yard, and then I sought to impress Marianne with my skill with the ball – far superior to Karlheinz', who was short and not very athletic. But I don't think she paid any attention.

The *Philanthropin* had many first-rate teachers, and the subjects they taught included German, math and foreign languages, Hebrew, Bible, history, biology and physics. (Latin and Greek, the traditional *Gymnasium* subjects, had recently been replaced by English and French, to better prepare the student body for emigration). But the teacher who made the strongest impression on me was the gym teacher and sports coach, Emil Stelzer. He was one of the few members of the faculty who were not Jewish, yet we never felt that he was not one of us. Except perhaps that his external appearance was so unmistakably Aryan. Blond, ramrod straight, with steel blue eyes, tanned from being out of doors, his was the type the Nazis idealized. He taught us gymnastics on equipment, as well as boxing and wrestling, and also trained the school's teams for competition among Jewish sports clubs. As I mentioned already, he was murdered along with his Jewish wife.

Just how good an education I received at the *Philanthropin* was made clear to me two years later. When I enrolled in evening courses in New York toward a high school diploma, I was asked to submit my German end-of-year reports for evaluation to the State Education Department. It seems that my records made such an impression there that I was granted credits that enabled me to graduate in less than two years.

I must confess – childish as it may sound – that I was not altogether unhappy when the school did not reopen after Crystal Night. About a week earlier, my class was given a test in Biology, which was not my strongest subject. I got worse grades only in Music; perhaps because both my parents were tone-deaf. This time I was sure I had done poorly on the test - something that had never happened to me before, and which would leave a permanent stain on my record as the class' *Musterschüler* (model student). So that for the past week I had wandered through the school's corridors with a vague hope that something would happen to stave off the dreaded day when the test results were announced. Then came November 9, and neither I nor anyone else would ever know whether I passed or flunked biology. Except for the teacher, Dr. Max Selig, who was among those deported.

I mention this to show that the mind of a 14-year-old still is likely to function along intensely personal lines, rather than in terms of the larger events swirling around him. Crystal Night meant the end of German Jewry; the burning of the synagogues, which I witnessed from a window on an upper floor of my school, was barbaric and shocking; and the deportation of the adult Jewish males to concentration camps presaged much worse to come. But here I was, with my chief worry the grade on my biology test.

Actually, daily life at school had rarely been disrupted by the political turmoil that threatened Jewish existence in Germany. There were sports events, theatrical shows and concerts put on by the students, and even excursions. I recall an outing, with my class, to the site of the new Rhein-Main airport then being built on a clearing of old pine forest to the south of the city. It was to become, after the war, one of Europe's busiest airports, but at the time of our visit there were no runways yet. However, the field was already home to a huge craft which needed no runway to soar into the sky. It was the brand new airship *Hindenburg*, successor to the older, smaller *Graf Zeppelin.* The *Hindenburg,* one of the wonders of the world, was just being readied, in a cavernous hangar in a far corner of the field, for its maiden flight to the United States. The year was 1937, and I make mention of it because I remember how proud we were, pupils of the Frankfurt Jewish community school, to see this symbol of German industrial and technical skill overfly the *Philanthropin* a few days later as it began its transatlantic voyage. It was recess time, and we waved frantically from the school yard to the low-flying craft, eager that the crew and passengers in the gondola should take notice of us and wave back. How proud we were then, and oh, how grief-stricken when the great ship burst into flames as it came in for a landing three days later at Lakehurst, New Jersey. Somewhere deep down, so it seems, we were still German patriots.

I went back to the Philanthropin in April 1945 when I passed through Frankfurt as an American soldier. I wrote a little piece about my feelings then, which is worth recalling:

Whenever I think back to my old school, I see myself on that cold, clear November day in 1938, standing with a little group of classmates by the window in the long corridor on the top floor, silently watching the nearby synagogue go up in flames. A few fourth grade girls, those brave enough to come to school that morning, were walking from their empty classroom towards the stairway. When they passed us we saw that some of them had tears streaming down their faces.

The few minutes we stood there without speaking, our eyes glued to the thick column of smoke rising into the clear blue sky, seemed like hours. Then, slowly, I turned away and went into my classroom, for the last time. On the blackboard were the new words from yesterday's English lesson, with their German translations. Underneath, in my own handwriting, the proverb we had learned to memorize: EARLY TO BED AND EARLY TO RISE - MAKES A MAN HEALTHY, WEALTHY AND WISE.

I started up at the shrill sound of the bell. The ten-second sound seemed endless as it reverberated through the deserted hallways. By the time it was at last still again in the school, I had grabbed my books and was running down the broad stairs, taking two and three steps at a time.

I did not stop running until I reached the door of my parents' house. Only a few yards behind me was a gang of Hitler Youths, yelling "Jew" at the top of their lungs and trying to hit me with rocks and broken glass. Shaking with fear and exhaustion, I managed to get upstairs. Being the track star of my class had saved me from suffering anything more serious than a few bruises.

In April 1945 I came back to my old school. More than seven years had passed since the day I heard its bell ring for the last time, ringing to a close a chapter in my life. Now I could feel my heart beat against the inside of my steel helmet as I drove my jeep along the ghostly streets of Frankfurt. They were the same streets 1 had walked every day on my way to school. Then I was laughing and chatting with my pals, but now the street seemed dead, littered with the rubble of the proud buildings that had once lined it. Barely a wall was standing of my parents' house, and a crater marked the place where a bomb struck near by. As I came closer to the school, the scene around me grew more desolate. I could not even find the grocery store where I used to do the family's shopping. There was the Hebelstrasse and there it was, standing unscathed amidst all that destruction, exactly like the picture I had kept in my mind during all those years. But the large brown building with the ivy climbing along its walls was no longer a school. The red tiles on its roof had been shuffled around, and a huge Red Cross on a white field had warned our bomber crews that the building was a hospital. Now an American flag was waving way up there, and wounded GI's were looking out of the window of the room where I had first learned to say: "I am, you are, he is...."

I was glad my school had been spared.

Lotte and I were able to leave Germany by joining a *Kindertransport* consisting of the eighty orphan children who were being cared for at Frankfurt's Jewish orphanage. Its director, a Mr. Marx, was a friend of Papa's, and Mutti heard that he was making arrangements for his charges to leave for Strasbourg, France, where the Jewish community had offered to find alternate placement for them. Mr. Marx readily agreed to have the two of us join the group, which was scheduled to leave for

Strasbourg on December 6. He would himself escort the children and supervise their placement.

The farewell at the railroad station, its glass arches emerging from the wintry Frankfurt dawn on the day of departure, marked the end of the German chapter in my life. Mutti could barely suppress her tears when she embraced us for the last time, but for me the thrills of the journey soon superseded the sadness of the parting. Strasbourg was less than four hours away, but it was going to be the longest train ride I had ever taken. My travel until then had been mostly limited to twice yearly trips to my grandfather's house in Eberstadt, barely 45 minutes from Frankfurt on a slow train. It was the same route my father had taken every day after he left school and began to work as an apprentice in the big city.

I remember my grandfather Hermann Stock as a patriarchal figure with a white beard, who presided over meals at which children were not allowed to talk and had to finish every last bit of food on the plate. On the street level of his house there was a grocery store which was connected by a door to the living room-dining room where the family sat around the table. Sometimes the bell would ring in the store while we ate our meal; then my uncle Salomon, Hermann's oldest son who managed the store together with the old man, would jump up to serve the customer and thus assure that his father could finish his meal in peace. Salomon lived with his wife Herta and their twin daughters, Margot and Ruth, my cousins, on the second floor of the house, where there were also rooms for the guests. These rooms had no running water, only a bowl and water jug with which to wash. Under the bed there was a chamber pot, instead of a toilet. The outhouse was across the yard, next to the dung heap, in a low structure which also housed a stable with two or three goats. In cold weather, one had to put on warm clothes to get there, especially at night.

Before he opened the store, Hermann Stock had made a living dealing in straw. He bought straw from the farmers in the village and collected it from their fields on a horse-drawn cart which he rented for the purpose. Then he re-sold it, using the same horse and cart to deliver the straw to businesses in the area that used it to wrap their merchandise. Papa told me that his father often talked, with pride, of the time he had sold straw to a Darmstadt carpentry workshop where they were working on an order from the Czar of Russia. To think it was his straw which had been used to prepare the Czar's furniture for shipment to his palace in St. Petersburg! That was before the War, of course; after the revolution there were no more orders from Russia. Also, the use of straw for packing and shipping went out of use, and Grandfather switched to dealing in hay. He stored bundles of hay in the barn in his yard, which he sold to dairy farmers in the winter.

Uncle Salomon shared with his father responsibility not just for the store, but for the household as a whole, including the animals and the barn, as well as the orchard planted behind the house. There were cherries and plums, apples and peaches, in line with the season, and his wife Herta baked delicious pies with them all, which in themselves were worth a visit. When we picked apples (or plums) from a tree, we had to bite into them carefully, to make sure that there were no worms. Pesticides were not yet in use, and as often as not a fruit that looked ripe and succulent from the outside had a worm eating away at it from within.

Salomon Stock had a reputation as an excellent gymnast; he was still a leading member of the *Turnverein* (Gymnastics Club) of Eberstadt; in his younger years he had brought home quite a few medals from competitions in the area. Once I saw him wearing a *tricot* with the motto of the gymnasts all over Germany on it: the letter F printed four times back to back, which stood for *Frisch, Fromm, Fröhlich, Frei* (fresh, religious, cheerful and free), the ideal of sports-loving German youth in earlier times.

My grandmother, Malchen (Amalia) died when I was less than a year old. There is an entry dated 1 April 1925 in the diary my mother kept of my childhood years in which she writes (adding the Hebrew date, 2 Nissan 5685, as a sign of piety): "Regrettably, mourning has entered our house. My husband's mother has died after a brief illness. She was a woman who enjoyed her work and sacrificed herself for her children. It is too bad that she had to leave her grandchildren so soon. (Malchen Stock, née Heyum)."

The Stock household in Eberstadt was run by my aunt Herta, assisted in the kitchen by Malchen's younger sister, Tante Jeanette, a small, hunchbacked woman with a thin, squeaky voice who had never married. Whenever I saw her, she always wore the same grey skirt and black apron, both reaching almost to the floor; only the blouses, always tightly buttoned at the neck, varied in shade. Jeanette also took care of feeding the chickens, which ran around freely in the farm yard behind the house.

I was surprised to learn from my father on one of these visits that there had been a third, older, sister called Dorchen (Dorothea) Heyum who was Grandfather's first wife and Papa's mother. She died in 1896, when my father was four years old. Hermann then married Malchen, his late wife's younger sister. Malchen became a devoted mother to his three children by Dorchen (Salomon, Leopold – my father – and Frieda) and bore him three more of her own (Hannah, Alfred and Rika).

The Heyum clan was one of Eberstadt's oldest Jewish families. When Hermann Stock, a distant cousin, married Dorchen in 1888, he moved to Eberstadt from Lomersum, a village near Cologne. The marriage was arranged by the families, as was the custom among rural German Jews. I don't know much about the history of the Lomersum Stocks, except that Hermann's father was named Nathan Stock, his mother, Esther Herz (Stock).

Papa once told me his was one of only two Jewish families by that name in all Germany.

About the Heyums quite a few documents have survived, the oldest going back to 1723. I came across some of them when, together with Mutti, I rummaged through old family files to find the papers showing that Papa had been awarded the Iron Cross in the World War, and also that he had been wounded three times and was entitled to wear the German equivalent of the Purple Heart. In a postcard he sent from the camp, he had asked for these documents to help him obtain his freedom. And indeed, together with proof that Mutti had obtained an English visa for him so he could leave the country, the fact that he was a decorated war veteran brought about his release. The Germans still took account of such distinctions at that time, but not for much longer.

The First World War, and Papa's role in it, played an important part in the lore and imagination of my boyhood. Sometimes they mingled with the Jewish aspect, as when I heard and read, time and again, that 12,000 Jewish soldiers fell for their *Vaterland*. This was one of the main arguments used by the official organs of the community to defend the rights of the 600,000 German Jews, even after the Nuremberg Laws of 1935 had already effectively stripped them of their citizenship. Or when Papa told me how, as an infantryman in the trenches at Verdun, he had slightly raised his rifle when it was time to aim at a French soldier in the trench opposite, in case the bullet might hit a Jew.

The social group my parents belonged to during this period was the *Reichsbund Jüdischer Frontsoldaten,* the Federation of Jewish Frontline Soldiers, which also arranged festive events, such as Purim and Hanukka parties, for its members' children. The Federation published a monthly, called *Schild* (The Shield), which at one time announced a contest among the veterans for a piece describing "my most powerful experience" of the war. Papa's contribution, when it appeared in print, made a lasting impression on me. After fighting on both the eastern and western fronts and being wounded three times, he was taken prisoner by the French in 1917. They did not release him after the armistice was signed in November 1918, but kept him as cheap labor for more than a year longer. He came home only in February 1920.

The strongest experience of the entire war, he wrote, came the moment he walked through the gate of his parents' house in Eberstadt. His mother, Malchen, was feeding the chickens at the far side of the yard. When she saw him, she simply said, *"Da bist du ja!"* (So there you are!) *"Ich fuehlte mich unendlich gluecklich und geborgen,"* he concluded his account (I felt immensely happy and secure.)

In spite of the rather primitive conditions there, I always looked forward to my visits to Eberstadt. I could tell that my father, too, still felt very much in his element in his parental home, which had hardly changed since his childhood. His sense of humor seemed to flourish in these surroundings, with the local dialect making his jokes sound even funnier. One day as the family sat around the table, waiting for Tante Jeanette to serve the roast chicken, the smell of which wafted through the kitchen door, my father turned to me: "Do you like to lick chicken legs?" I nodded yes, eagerly. "Then go out and grab yourself a chicken from the dung heap, and lick its legs." Only Mutti did not join in the roar of laughter. She didn't much care for this kind of earthy humor, and perhaps she was afraid that father's next joke might be at her expense.

Among the documents Mutti and I came across in our search there was a petition, handwritten in an elaborate script on brittle, yellowing parchment, for permission to marry; another to practice a trade, in this case selling vegetables and fruit. Jews needed special permits for such privileges from the *Gross-Herzog*, the Archduke who ruled over the province known as Hessen-Darmstadt before Germany was united by Bismarck in 1871. The Jews had to pay steep fees for these favors; in return they enjoyed the Archduke's protection.

After he had settled down in America, cousin Hugo Heyum, who was somewhat of an amateur historian, put together a family tree which he prefaced with an essay, "About the Heyums." In it, he attributes the family's connection with Eberstadt to an anti-semitic incident in the 17th century:

The first Salomon Heyum, whom I assume is one of our fore-bears, was living at Eschollbruecken, a little hamlet 3½ miles to the west of Eberstadt. Both villages belonged to the Landsgrafschaft (principality) Hessen-Darmstadt. The time was the early 1620's, and anti-semitism was rife in German lands. At Frankfurt the Fettmilch riots a few years earlier cost many Jewish lives; at Worms at the same time numerous Jews lost theirs in the uproar of the mobs of the trade associations which were indebted to Jews. At Darmstadt, the reigning Landgraf banished the Jews from his capital.

At Eschollbruecken, the cow of the Jew Salomon Heyum, which earlier had been grazing placidly with all the other non-Jewish owned cows on the village common pasture (All-mend), was no longer allowed to graze there. Salomon Heyum complained in a petition to the government in Darmstadt. The outcome was that the authority suggested he move to Eberstadt.

Until Hitler came to power, the thirty-some Jewish families who lived in Eberstadt were an integral part of the population, just as the synagogue belonged by right in the center of the village. When, in 1913, it was time to replace the centuries-old structure with a new building, the mayor himself signed the appeal for funds. (The document announcing the opening of the campaign was also in the file; it reads very much like a modern fund-raising flyer). The relationship between the Jewish community and the non-Jewish population in Eberstadt was probably as close as anywhere in Germany, yet there's no denying that a faint whiff of anti-semitism emanated from it. The strange customs to which the Jews clung with such tenacity, such as keeping kosher, not riding or working on the Sabbath and going to synagogue instead, carrying the blue velvet *tallis* (prayer shawl) pouch, while everyone else observed their day of rest on Sundays, kept the Jews permanently apart on the level of folk and family. There was no intermarriage.

Outwardly, Eberstadt's Jews looked no different from their non-Jewish neighbors. It was as though living in the same rural landscape for generations, breathing the same air, had somehow shaped their physiognomy in parallel ways. I was given a somewhat unsettling indication of this while at play with some neighboring boys in my street in Frankfurt. My father appeared in the doorway of the house, on his way to somewhere. One of the boys was eager to impress me with his knowledge of "*Rassenkunde*," the Nazi racial theories, based on a primitive anthropology, which they were being taught in the Hitler Youth. "I can tell by your father's face and the shape of his skull that he comes from Hessen," my friend boasted, much to my astonishment.

After Hitler rose to power, the whiff of anti-semitism in Eberstadt became stronger. There were Nazi cells in the small towns and villages whose members kept a watchful eye on their fellow citizens. They had better be careful, not to be too friendly with Jews.

Crystal Night and the day following it brought about the end of the Jewish presence in Eberstadt. The events of those days are described in a report by a local historian, a high school teacher, with whom I carried on a correspondence. He based his account on the record of the trial of some of those who burned down the synagogue and then proceeded to destroy the homes of the Jewish families still living in the town. The trial took place in a Darmstadt court in October 1946; my informant complemented the record by the testimony of eye witnesses whom he himself interviewed twenty years later. My grandfather had died by that time, so he didn't have to witness what his fellow-citizens did to their Jewish neighbors. My uncle Salomon and Aunt Frieda, who both lived in Eberstadt, had emigrated to America with their families by this time. Only Aunt Rika, Papa's youngest sister, did not get out in time and was deported from Frankfurt with her husband and murdered.

After quoting the trial record on how the SA leader in Darmstadt received the order to blow up or set fire to all fifty synagogues in the area, and how this order was carried out in Eberstadt, with the fire brigade prevented from intervening, our historian reconstructs the events in the town. These are some excerpts (my translation):

*"As in many other localities in Germany, so in Eberstadt as well, there were attacks on Jewish townspeople all during the day until late into the evening. Groups of SA and Hitler Youth whose composition was constantly changing broke into the homes and apartments of the Jewish families. Hangers-on followed them, and curious onlookers joined in. Not only the synagogues were set afire. In Alsbach on the Bergstrasse (*the picturesque mountain road which begins just behind Eberstadt*) the funeral chamber of the Jewish cemetery was blown up, and centuries-old documents were destroyed. Tombstones were turned over; everywhere, crowds flocked to watch the spectacle. What followed now, from early dawn until late at night, was a series of acts of violence paired with a blind urge for destruction. The SA men and Hitler Youth, partly in uniform and partly in civilian clothes, who had broken into the Jewish homes, beat and manhandled the Jews, destroyed furniture, tossed clothes and linen into the street, and broke dishes, glass and crystal."*

The author then quotes from eyewitness stories about the attacks on five families, of whom two were Heyums:

"At the house of Hermann Heyum in the Pfungstaedter Strasse, four men broke down the door with their shoulders. A woman who happened to be visiting her mother nearby, witnessed this and later testified in court: 'Just afterwards I heard terrible cries coming out of the apartment of the Jews. And later she repeated: 'I must say again, that this shouting was very loud and terrible.' Although the synagogue arsonists came from outside of town, the perpetrators of these crimes against the local Jews were mainly from Eberstadt. Even women took active part. In the Heyum house, a woman slit bed covers and dropped the feathers out the window. "

The report then describes how Moses Heyum (an uncle of my father) was taken from his house and led to the Muehltal (Mill Valley) a scenic spot. Together with Max and Ferdinand Reinheimer and other Jews he was pushed into the River Modau. Later he told an acquaintance he had been terribly beaten. On the way back he was led through Church Street and again badly mauled. He had a wound in his skull, two broken ribs and a fractured wrist. The Reinheimers were close friends of my family. The author writes about them:

On Crystal Night a mob stormed into their house and up the stairs. The old man fled with his wife to the attic. The intruders searched the whole house and finally found them. The apartment was systematically ransacked and demolished; even the sink in the bathroom was smashed. After Ferdinand Reinheimer was badly beaten, he was led to the Mill Valley and thrown into the river. His front teeth were bashed in... A witness, who was watching from the courtyard and was able to look into the lighted room through the open window, saw how they made Ferdinand Reinheimer get up on the table and read from a prayer book. 'Every time he finished reading a sentence (which nobody understood, by the way), K.L., who was then about 18 years old, gave him a blow on the head, so that his skull hit the wall.'

And another witness testified in court: 'So I saw the Jew Ferdinand Reinheimer, whom the intruders had put on a hot stove and shoved a top-hat over his head (worn on the Sabbath to the synagogue). They forced the hat all the way down over his ears. A Nazi played on the piano, the melody was "Püppchen, du bist mein Augenstern (Little doll, you are the apple of my eye"), *and the Jew Reinheimer was forced to dance to it.'*

Our historian adds, *"A few weeks later, the Jew Ferdinand Reinheimer, who had fought as a German soldier in the First World War, died of his injuries. His wife was murdered some years later in a concentration camp."*

The report notes that the Nazi thugs were shouting *"Juda Verrecke"*, while perpetrating these cowardly and repulsive crimes.

This slogan, known well to every German Jew, is surely one of the most obscene expressions in any language. The verb really cannot be translated into English, which is too civilized a language to express what is meant here, namely, the slow death of a human being in the manner of an animal. It's the kind of death that the Nazis dreamt of inflicting upon the Jews, and eventually did inflict upon them in the gas chambers. The word, 'Juda', while literally meaning Judea, is a collective noun for all the Jews (*Juden*, in German).

In Frankfurt, the feeling of isolation, that as a Jew I no longer belonged to the larger surrounding community, came more gradually. For quite some time after I had transferred to the Jewish school in 1933, I was still playing with the neighbors' children in our street. It was only when, one by one, my playmates joined the Hitler Youth and began to wear its uniform on certain days, that I began to feel left out. We not only played hide-and-seek and "tags" together, with the street as the play-ground (there was very little traffic) but also regularly engaged in military close-order drill. A wiry, red-haired boy appoint-ed himself as the drill sergeant and put his troops through the paces. Erich Koch was smaller than most of us, but he had the authority of a natural-born leader. He rose quickly in the ranks of the Hitler youth, then became an SS officer and was killed on the Eastern front.

A few years later, when I was a new recruit in the U.S. mil-itary, we learned to march in unison to the commands that are part of an infantry soldier's basic training: "Forward, march!... to the rear, march!... column right, march!..." Suddenly the pla-toon sergeant blew his whistle and bellowed, "At ease!" Every-thing stopped. He came over to where I stood and asked me, menacingly, if I had served in the German army. "No," I said, rather stunned. "Why do you ask?" His answer: "Because you do these exercises the way the Germans do!"

Soon after the Nazis came to power, my father had to close down his wholesale food business, and there was sometimes real penury in the house. I was nine years old at the time and did not notice it much, but I did understand that our telephone was cut off because we could no longer afford to pay the bills. However, the line remained in the apartment, running along the bottom molding of the walls. In those days the wires were em-bedded in a lead casing. It so happened that I had a passionate interest in lead soldiers at the time, playing for hours with my friend Carlo with the brightly colored models. To save money, we stopped purchasing the soldiers in toy shops and instead bought forms in which we could cast the models ourselves, and then paint them. All we needed was some lead, to be melted down on the gas flame. Carlo pointed out to me that our phone line was no longer needed, and it was easy to pry it from the wall. I don't recall whether we ever got to play with these sol-diers; I do remember how furious my father was when he asked the telephone company to reconnect the phone, and there was no longer any cable.

Carlo and I also shared an interest in electric trains. He had quite an elaborate setup, which he was allowed to display in the living room once a year between Christmas and New Year's. At that time of year I would spend hours in his house, playing with the trains (I didn't have a set of my own). He often sat on the sideline with a sketchbook and pencil, drawing amazingly realistic pictures of the locomotives and the trains. Carlo's last name was Demand (pronounced Daymand), which was not your typically German name, and in fact his father was a native of Alsace. With his jet black hair and olive-colored skin, Herr Demand did look more French to me than German. Carlo sometimes travelled to Strasbourg on vacation, and his French cousins came to Frankfurt for return visits. Frau Demand was a fine cook, and she often made me taste her cookies and other delicacies.

All of us boys on the block played with marbles, which we carried around in little cloth bags of fifty or more. The game called for a hole in the ground, into which the marbles were rolled from a distance. The best place for the hole was the soil of the plane tree in front of our house; except that our landlord, Herr Knorr, disagreed and regularly filled in the hole after we went home at night. This went on for some time: we dug the hole and Herr Knorr filled it in, until Carlo and I decided to teach him a lesson. We took away the mat from in front of the door to his apartment and hid it in the basement. Knorr found the mat and put it back, three times in a row. On the fourth day it was my turn to hide the mat. But when I lifted it carefully off the floor, there was a noise on the other side. The door opened and Herr Knorr leaped out, his face livid with rage. He had attached a string to the mat and tied a bottle to it inside; so that when I lifted the mat, the bottle fell to the floor and the noise alerted the landlord. Carlo and I had to apologize, and we moved our marbles game to another tree.

Carlo was two years older than I, and his drawings were remarkable in their realism and detail. I was proud to be his friend, and I had the feeling that our little conspiracy against the landlord had cemented our friendship. But then Carlo came to our door one day and told me, with evident embarrassment, that he could no longer play with me. His leader in the Hitler Youth had warned him against being seen with a Jew. Not long after that, we moved from the house at Helmholtzstrasse 35, where the Demand family and Herr Knorr were our neighbors, to Baumweg 57, which was a mere five minutes' walk from my school. My friends from then on were all Jewish.

There was one other non-Jewish family in Frankfurt which I felt very close to. Frau Dr. Weyrauch and her daughter Margot, a nursing student of 18 or 19, were neighbors in the stately apartment building at Luxemburger Allee No. 4, in which we were tenants before the decline in Papa's fortunes forced us to move to more modest quarters. Frau Weyrauch, a dignified, somewhat old-fashioned doctor's widow, invited me to celebrate with them on Christmas Eve, and to find my present under the festively decorated Christmas tree. She and her daughter were deeply religious as well as outspoken anti-Nazis. As for me, I felt not the slightest guilt about singing "Silent Night, Holy Night" together with them. It seemed entirely natural at the time for Jews to celebrate the holiday with their neighbors.

My mother corresponded with Margot after the war. I found a postcard from her, postmarked Frankfurt, December 29, 1961, in which she thanked Mutti "for the understanding she showed to us Germans, in spite of the Eichmann trial!" She wrote, "My mother herself barely escaped being sent to a concentration camp. After we were bombed out, she was denounced to the Gestapo because she spoke freely about what was on her mind."

As for Carlo Demand, there is a postscript of sorts. In 1959, when I was married and lived in New York, the phone rang in our apartment one afternoon. It was Carlo on the line. He was in New York and would like to come visit me. Somewhat confused, I blurted out that we were about to leave the house (which was true), could he call back tomorrow. He never did. Perhaps he concluded that I did not want to see him. Later, I saw covers of books drawn by him in bookstore windows; Carlo had become an illustrator with a worldwide reputation who specialized in drawings of trains, cars and World War I fighter planes. When he died there was an obituary in the New York Times.

Chapter Two

Strasbourg - Thann - Strasbourg

Before our train crossed the River Rhine, which formed the border with France, the German customs officers thoroughly searched our luggage to make sure that none of the eighty Jewish children in our group were smuggling any currency abroad. Each was allowed to take with him ten German marks. On the other side of the bridge, as the train rumbled slowly into the Strasbourg station, no one bothered to check our luggage. Even the youngest of us suddenly felt that he was breathing the air of freedom.

On the platform, women volunteers awaited us with cocoa and a warm lunch, and then helped the children board buses to take them to their new accommodations. Mr. Marx, the director of the Frankfurt orphanage who had escorted us on the train, took the two of us aside and introduced us to one of the women, Mme. Andrée Salomon. She assured him that she would personally see to it that we got on the train to Thann, then took us to the station restaurant for some more food. She asked me to keep in touch with her after we got to the Schwebers and gave me her telephone number. She was a woman of about thirty, with dark curly hair, speaking German fluently as well as French and the Alsatian dialect, and she seemed to smile at us with her eyes. Suddenly I felt no longer alone.

Night was falling when we got off the Strasbourg-Basle express at Mulhouse, where we had to change for the local train to Thann. It was cold on the open platform, and a light drizzle was turning to snow. As we clambered off the carriage, Karlheinz spotted us and came running over. He embraced us warmly, then carried our luggage to the train on the next track. The ride to Thann took only twenty minutes, but it was long enough for me to realize that we had grown apart in the year since we were classmates at the *Philanthropin*. It was no longer my old friend Karlheinz who had met us at the station but Charles, a French *lycéen* (high school student*)*. He wore his *béret* at a rakish angle and looked every inch a young Frenchman. At his home I soon found that he was deeply absorbed in his studies and also had a new circle of friends. When he asked me to join the group on a hike to a nearby peak in the Vosges mountains, I went along but felt all day like the outsider that I was.

Lotte began attending elementary school immediately after our arrival. There was a problem at first with the language, but it didn't take her long to catch on (the German accent remained, but most of her new classmates spoke French with a thick Alsatian accent as well).The main culture shock for her was that it was a Catholic school, and all the teachers were nuns. She was excused while all the other girls studied their catechism and was allowed to come in an hour later. But she actually envied the others and often sneaked in to listen. Like all the girls in her class, she wore a black apron to school.

My own situation was more complicated. I applied to the *lycée* that Karlheinz attended but was told that no new students were admitted during the school year. Also, my French was not quite up to *lycée* standards; compared to Karlheinz' mastery of the language I had a long way to go. What this meant was that my formal education had, for the time being, come to an end.

I began to look around for an alternative, and found a job of sorts. It turned out that the first money I ever made was by way of the stock market. Through an acquaintance of the Schwebers' I was introduced to a blind elderly gentleman who was looking for someone to read stock quotations to him from the financial pages. He owned a portfolio of securities and was anxious to keep up with their daily fluctuations. I spent two hours with him most weekday mornings, for which he paid me ten francs a session.

The paper from which I read these quotations was the *Neue Zuercher Zeitung,* and since Thann was not far from the Swiss border, it was delivered early enough for my employer to have his breakfast while I read to him from the stock tables. Sometimes, when his shares had gone up, he offered me a *croissant* from his plate. Although Mr. Heidenheim was quite old and I was young, he was wealthy and I was poor, we did have something important in common. We were both recent refugees from Nazi Germany, and we both hoped to get to the United States. I don't recall just why the old man had chosen Thann, of all places, as his temporary refuge. But it became more and more clear to me that it was not the place for me. The job began to bore me, and I looked for an alternative. I could not expect further help from the Schwebers, beyond the hospitality they so generously offered to us. Mr. Schweber was busy producing bouillon cubes; Karlheinz was so preoccupied with his studies he had time for me only on Sundays, and Rosa Schweber did all she could to be a surrogate mother to Lotte, for which I was grateful.

Clearly, it was time to think more seriously about what our teachers at the *Philanthropin* had warned us all along: there was no assurance that we could continue our studies abroad, and that we should begin learning a trade to support ourselves. The Frankfurt Jewish community had begun to offer vocational courses for young people to attend after school hours, and in the months before leaving I had taken up lettering and sign painting. A kind of elementary graphic design, this was looked upon as a skill that could be useful in any language and required a minimum of materials and equipment. At the time, I found that I was fairly good at it. But now I realized that drawing letters and painting posters was not really what I wanted to do for the rest of my life.

There was, however, another subject I had pursued as a hobby, and that I could see myself exercising, with a bit more training, as a vocation: photography. I had owned – and used - a camera ever since my Aunt Bella had brought me a red Kodak box camera when she came on a visit from America in 1931. I was seven at the time. Sine then I used a more sophisticated 35-millimeter camera. With the aid of black-out paper, I had converted a corner of my room in Frankfurt into a darkroom where I developed my films and also operated an enlarger. The results, as collected in several albums, were quite creditable. The more I thought about it, the more I liked the idea of becoming a photographer. But here, too, Thann was not the place where I could exercise, or rather learn, my new occupation. Then I recalled that when we stopped off in Strasbourg, Mme. Salomon, the volunteer social worker who received us with such warmth at the station, had told me to phone her anytime I ran into a problem.

Before long I was on the phone to Andrée Salomon and told her of my predicament. She responded with the speed and resourcefulness that were characteristic of her. With the help of friends and acquaintances, she 1) found me a place as an apprentice to a Strasbourg photographer; and 2) had me admitted to a boarding school for Jewish boys from outlying areas. The *Ecole de Travail* was a rather remarkable institution of the Strasbourg community. In addition to room and board, it offered continuing instruction on Sundays and evenings to youngsters who had finished their formal schooling at age 14 and were now learning a trade in the city. (I was to learn French and math there, in addition to Jewish subjects).

Within a week I was on the train to Strasbourg, leaving Lotte behind with the Schwebers and the nuns. It was the beginning of January, 1939. Looking back now on my departure from Thann, I am not at all sure that I was acting in the spirit of the promise I had made to Mutti not to let Lotte out of my sight.

As for myself, the chapter in my life that began with my second arrival in Strasbourg promised to hold a lot more interest than anything Thann had to offer. I found myself in a new and stimulating environment. There was, first of all, Mme. Salomon herself and her family. When it turned out that the place she had obtained for me at the *Ecole de Travail* would not become vacant for a few more days, she simply put me up as a house guest in the tastefully furnished home she shared with her husband, Tobie. Andrée had no children of her own, and I had the vague but not unwelcome feeling that she looked upon me as a son. I quickly became part of the extended family. When the vacancy at the *Ecole* was delayed further, I was moved around the corner to the apartment of Andrée's mother, where there was ample space. A matriarchal figure with a delightful sense of humor, Mme. Sulzer made me feel equally at home as her daughter. Through her, I learned a great deal about the recent history of the Jews of Alsace and of the Sulzer family's share in it. On the same block was the home of Andrée's younger sister, Yetti, whose husband, Jules Weil, was a lawyer and leading figure in the Jewish community. After I eventually moved to the *Ecole de Travail*, I continued to be a guest for *Shabbat* lunch at the Weils, discussing current affairs with Jules and playing on the floor with their five-year-old son, Jackie. I had much admiration for Yetti, who possessed a great deal of charm, dressed stylishly (I still remember the wedgie shoes she wore, at a time when these had just made their appearance) and was also a first-rate cook and housewife. Now I can admit that I envied Jules, especially when I fantasized about the love-making of the young couple.

I spent altogether eight months in Strasbourg, until the war broke out and I had to leave the city, together with most of the civilian population. Living at the *Ecole de Travail*, I spent my working hours as an apprentice to a photographer, Charles Spehner. He submitted his work for publication in magazines, especially in Switzerland and the U.S., and his American agents would eventually become my first employers in New York.

Perhaps the most meaningful aspect of my stay in Strasbourg was the impact it made on my self-perception as a Jew. From the distance, I realized how badly hurt the German Jewish community I'd grown up in had been by the Nazi regime, psychologically as well as physically. The years of humiliation left their mark on the individuals who were part of it. For me, the freedom of living in a democracy now included the freedom to be Jewish, and it was exhilarating. The people among whom I moved wore their Jewishness naturally; they were neither "proud" nor did they try to hide it. As a part of their personality, it seemed to blend well with the part that was French and the part that was Alsatian. I admired the ease with which my new friends switched from the Alsatian dialect – still the every-day language in Strasbourg – to French or to high-German. I saw it as a sign of French liberality that throughout Alsace, German was still recognized as the official language alongside of French. Strasbourg's main daily newspaper appeared simultaneously in both languages. No attempt was made to suppress German and impose the use of French when the province reverted to France after the First World War.

Probably the most powerful single factor reinforcing my Jewish identity was my membership in the Jewish scout movement, *les Eclaireurs Israëlites de France, EIF* for short. Andrée Salomon introduced me to *Chameau* (scouting nickname of Dr. Frédéric Hammel), the regional Commissioner of the movement. He in turn saw to it that I found my place in the hierarchy (which was at the bottom). I was sworn in, was entitled to wear the scout uniform with the Baden-Powell hat, and took part in the meetings of my *troupe* and *patrouille*. As do scouts everywhere, I learned to tie knots and build a fire, to pitch a tent and to find my way out of a dark forest with the aid of a compass. I took the twelve articles of the scout's oath with the utmost seriousness, and to this day can recite three or four of them in the original French: *L'Eclaireur fait chaque jour une bonne action* (the scout does a good deed each day); *l'éclaireur est loyal et fidèle* (the scout is loyal and faithful); *l'éclaireur est propre dans ses pensées et ses actions* (the scout is clean in his thoughts and his actions) – the latter not always easy for a 15-year-old to observe.

When not out hiking in the countryside or camping in the Vosges mountains, our troop held its *réunions* at the *Mercaz* (Center), the community-owned building which served the EIF and other Jewish youth movements as a meeting place. The *Mercaz'* director, Leo Cohn, was another in the series of role models which Strasbourg Jewry supplied to its impressionable visitor in such ample measure. Among his many accomplishments, Leo conducted *Shabbat* morning services at the *Mercaz* in a way that made me want to attend them -- something that had never happened before. On *Shabbat* afternoons he gave talks or led discussions on Jewish topics that caused his audience to clamor for more. A tall, gaunt figure in his early thirties, Leo was both a brilliant talker and a natural-born leader. Instead of the academic career which was no doubt open to him, he chose to devote himself to his work in informal education. Like others of his generation the war found him active in the Jewish *maquis* (underground) which evolved from the EIF; he was caught by the Nazis and tortured to death.

The high point of the scouting year was the annual summer camp in a remote part of France. In 1939, the site chosen by our *chef de troupe,* Jean Lévy, was a fishing village called Camaret in the Finistère Peninsula, at the Western tip of Brittany. I spent three thrilling weeks there, together with my comrades, camping on a cliff overlooking the Atlantic Ocean, hiking through the rugged countryside and also practicing my scouting skills. On our outward journey in early August we traversed Paris by bus from north to south as we changed trains from the *Gare de l'Est* to the *Gare Montparnasse,* and that first nighttime view of the City of Lights, glistening in a gentle summer rain, was nearly as exciting as the camp experience itself.

But the bliss of those weeks was short-lived.

Chapter Three

The Outbreak of War

On our way back from Brittany, passing through Paris again, one of our scout *chefs* bought the *Paris Soir* at the *Gare de l'Est*. The evening paper's huge black headline screamed that Hitler had made a deal with Stalin. The date was August 23, 1939. The Molotov-Ribbentrop Pact, as it became known by the names of the foreign ministers who signed it in Moscow, enabled Hitler to launch his attack on Poland a week later by securing his Eastern flank. The young scouts in the compartment understood the ominous meaning of the event, and they became suddenly quiet with foreboding as the train sped through the night.

Back at Strasbourg, the scent of war was everywhere. Monsieur Spehner, the photographer to whom I was apprenticed, had been called up to his unit in the air force. He was a photographer in a bomber squadron based not far from the city. I worked by myself in the laboratory, doing odds and ends under Mrs. Spehner's direction. (She worked part-time in a bakery owned by her brother, which was located downstairs in the same apartment house, 37 rue Oberlin). Two days later my boss came home on leave. He had a piece of sensational news for me. Before he let me in on the secret, he made me swear that I would never divulge the source of the information. His squadron was under orders to bomb Frankfurt as soon as war was declared! He told it to me so that I could notify my parents to get out of the city. I was frantic, close to despair. I did not dare use the telephone, which was functioning but probably tapped by both sides. There was only the foreign mail, which was still going out but subject to censorship on the German side. I had to be careful about what I wrote, lest I got my parents into trouble. I knew my father was about to leave for Holland; and I could get him arrested again. So I phrased the letter with such circumspection ("I would go on vacation away from the city, if I were you") that my parents couldn't make out what I had in mind and ignored my advice. It was just as well, because the French never did drop any bombs on Frankfurt. By the time the Americans and the British did, much later in the war, both my father and my mother were long gone.

I often wondered afterwards whether there actually were such plans or whether my boss played a cruel hoax on his apprentice. I could not get myself to believe the latter because I felt Mr. Spehner genuinely liked me, and after the war even sent me an album of his pictures on "Strasbourg's Sufferings at the Liberation" with a personal dedication. He moved with his family to the south of France after the war and I never saw him again, so I could not ask him point-blank. It's quite possible that the bombing mission was actually planned but never carried out. In fact, there were no armed hostilities at all between Germany and France from the time war was declared on September 3, 1939 until the Germans invaded Belgium and Holland on May 10, 1940. The period soon became known as the Phony War; in French, *la drôle de guerre* (literally, the funny war). The French felt fairly safe behind their network of concrete fortifications, underground bunkers and tank traps known as the Maginot Line, named after the general who planned it. For most of its length, the "line" faced the Germans across the Rhine in Alsace, and there was every chance that the province would become a major battlefield. The French high command therefore decided to evacuate the civilian population to the interior. Those unable to make arrangements on their own, were directed to an area in central France known as the Périgord, with the city of Périgueux as its capital.

The *Ecole de Travail* was about to close, and I was faced with a major dilemma. Where should we go, Lotte and I? The community was sending some of the Frankfurt orphans who were still in the Strasbourg area to Périgueux; others were being absorbed by Jewish institutions in the Paris region. I was on the phone with the Schwebers, and they offered to take us along to Nice, where Papa Schweber's employers had a plant, and were offering him employment there. There was still another alternative: its name was Vaucresson, a suburban community about 10 miles to the West of Paris. Vaucresson was the home of Willy Reiss, who had once been landlord – and friend – of my Uncle Martin in Frankfurt. Martin Marx, my mother's brother, now lived in New York and had written to Willy Reiss from there to ask whether he would be willing to take in his nephew and niece temporarily, if the need arose. Mr. Reiss answered graciously that he had four children of his own; and there was room for another two. Then the war broke out, and the need did arise. I chose Vaucresson over Nice or Périgueux.

I packed my few belongings and left Strasbourg in haste for Thann, after wiring to Willy Reiss in Vaucresson that we were coming. (He had no telephone). There was no time to take proper leave of my friends, who were all in the process of mobilization (if they were men of army age) or "evacuation" in any event. I had the feeling the Schwebers were relieved that we were not coming with them. It's hard enough having to leave home abruptly with one's own family, without having to care for other people's children in a strange place. It was a tearful farewell nevertheless, especially for Lotte who had grown attached to her foster parents. Karlheinz and I exchanged a long handshake – neither of us suspected that it was the last time we would see one another.

Karlheinz was gassed at Auschwitz; his parents survived, and when I visited them in an old-age home near Nice after the war, they told me how he died. He had been a member of the *maquis*, the French underground and, having found a job as an interpreter in a German army headquarters, was able to pass on valuable information to his comrades. The Germans, not knowing that he was Jewish, valued his talents and placed full confidence in him. But he was betrayed, and arrested.

In Frankfurt, in these final days of August, Mutti was at last able to persuade Papa to make use of the British entry visa she had obtained for him while he was in Buchenwald and to leave Germany for Holland, on his way to England. He had resisted leaving her behind by herself, for as long as there was a chance that they might get the American visa and leave for the U.S. together. But with war so close, it seemed foolhardy to wait longer. And indeed, just as he was about to embark on the ferry for England at the Dutch port of Vlissingen on September 1, the British government announced that it would no longer admit holders of German passports.

Mutti accompanied Papa as far as the border on September 1 and then returned home on her own. She spent a lonely winter in the Frankfurt apartment, waiting for her visa to the U.S. and preparing our household goods for shipment. The fact that Papa did not reach England but was given asylum in Holland instead turned out to be a blessing. Whereas the war interrupted all communication between England and Germany, Holland remained neutral. Postal connections with both Germany and France were maintained, which meant that Papa could function as the hub for our correspondence.

Chapter Four

Vaucresson

Although I had only just turned 15 – my birthday was on August 6 - I was getting used to making decisions on my own which are normally made for children by their parents. Lotte, now 11, was too young to consult with; she usually accepted my judgment without question, the same way children accept their parents' judgment in vital matters. What I still lacked at that age was the capacity to look ahead and predict or estimate the results of my decisions, something which comes only with experience. But this relative innocence also kept me from pondering the pros and cons, the way adults often do, before deciding one way or another. I suppose it was sheer luck that most of my decisions at the time proved correct in that they helped me achieve the goal of reaching the United States.

But at this time all this was in the dim future. When I decided to seek refuge near Paris I had no inkling that nine months later Paris itself would fall to the Germans and that we would find ourselves in flight from them on the road, along with many thousands of others.

There was probably another side to the way I arrived at decisions, which might be called the adventure factor. Which path was likely to be more adventurous, more promising in terms of new experiences. Now the thought of being in (or near) Paris excited me, and it overshadowed the sadness of leave-taking and the uncomfortable six hours spent standing up in the corridors of a crowded train. I had been to, or rather through Paris only ten days earlier, on the way back from the scout camp in Brittany. Now I was on another train, with my sister sleeping on my shoulder, again heading toward Paris. I had the strange feeling that my wanting to be in Paris so badly, ten days ago, had played a part in putting me on that train. Once again, it seemed that wishing something badly enough helped make it come true.

When we arrived at the *Gare de l'Est*, this time at sunrise, the station, with its sweeping glass arches, reminded me of the railroad station in Frankfurt where we had said goodbye to my mother. Our luggage was a bit too heavy for lifting onto a bus, so I took one of the taxis in the line outside the station. The destination was the *Gare St. Lazare,* where we boarded the suburban electric train for Vaucresson, the home of our new hosts. Following the instructions Monsieur Reiss had sent us, we got off at the town before Vaucresson, which was called Garches. There was no taxi line at the station here, so we had to make our way on foot. The two pieces of luggage with which we had left Germany, a black suitcase and a green Rucksack, were still with us as we made our way uphill to the Allée St. Cucufa, where the Reisses lived at No. 37. Monsieur Reiss' map showed a shortcut, a footpath named *Chemin des Vignes*, which was rather steep and, because of the two bags, heavy going. It was a Sunday, the 31st of August, and an unusually hot day. It took us over half an hour from the station to the house, with a brief rest stop every hundred yards or so. At the top of the hill, where a highway separated the two *communes* of Garches and Vaucresson, there was a yellow mail box, with *République Française* embossed on it. In the months to come, this box was to be the recipient of the many letters that kept me in contact with the world, and above all with Papa in Holland. On the Vaucresson side of the highway a blue street sign read, "Allée St. Cucufa". We were sweaty and out of breath, but we had arrived at our destination.

The Reisses – all six of them – did their best to make us feel at home immediately. They showed us to our rooms, henceforth known as *la chambre à Charlotte* and *la chambre à Er-*

nest. The house, which was rented from an old couple who lived next door, was spacious, the furnishings old-fashioned and well worn. The plumbing especially was out-of-date; it reminded me of my grandfather Stock's house in Eberstadt, except that here one didn't have to walk across a cobbled barnyard to reach the toilet. (At the Schwebers, the house and rooms had been smaller, but the plumbing more modern.) The Reiss boys were aged four to ten, with two-year intervals. Their names were (starting with the oldest) Albert Michel, Herbert Ludovic, Edouard Robert and David William. These names sounded much too solemn for the exuberant personalities of the boys. Papa Willy, who no doubt wanted to honor certain of his ancestors or relatives in naming his foursome, was apparently aware of this and gave each son a nickname. I can still hear him calling in the direction of the wooded area at the other end of the *Allée*, which was the boys' favorite playing ground, with his hands cupped to his mouth, "Abi, Erfi, Mimi, Nène!" when it was time for supper. Not that there was much response, the first time around. None of the boys showed much respect for his father, sad to say, perhaps because he did not know how to apply discipline. Cajoling was his main mode of communicating with them, then came reasoning and finally appealing to their goodwill. Mme. Reiss (Marthe, but no one ever called her by her first name) tried appealing to their common sense. While Papa Willy would often wring his hands in despair, Marthe remained rather detached, always preserving her dignity. Her deeply lined face reflected a certain melancholia, as if she knew that little could be done. In return, the two middle boys – Erfi (8) and Mimi (6) - called their mother *folle* (crazy one) behind her back and sometimes also to her face. Abi was more of a gentleman, but he did nothing to restrain his siblings. David, at four, was too young to count.

Meanwhile, it was still a "phony war." In the afternoon of September 3 Vaucresson's fire engine had raced through the

Allée St. Cucufa with its siren screaming, to announce that war had been declared. But there was no immediate follow up. The children went back to school, and after a week or two left their gas masks at home. Only poor Monsieur Reiss, who had chosen France as his adopted homeland, had to report, with a small suitcase in his hand, to Maisons-Laffitte, a suburb widely known for its race course which had been turned into an internment camp for enemy aliens. I was lucky to be under sixteen, which was the cut-off age for internment. Instead, I merely had to report to the police in Garches once a week to have my provisional identity card stamped.

Lotte suffered from being "German." Shortly after the war was declared, the school children came home with gas masks in metal canisters which had been distributed in the classroom. To all but Lotte and the two older Reiss boys, that is, who were denied the benefit of the mask because of their nationality. While those three were all born in Germany; Mimi and Nène, the two youngest, were French-born and therefore eligible for the mask. Lotte was disconsolate about being left out; and I found it difficult to explain the intricacies of the situation to her. I think she was more distressed about the stigma of not having a mask to bring to class than about the dangers of poison gas.

When Willy Reiss was interned, I suddenly found myself in the role of *pater familias*. Without her husband at her side, Marthe Reiss would have had a hard time coping with her daily chores without me. These included managing her offspring: feeding them, seeing them off to school and helping them with their homework, getting them into bed and in general keeping them out of mischief.

I had enough time for my new role: while Lotte left home with the boys for school in the morning, I once more found myself ineligible for admission to the *Lycée* and spent most of my time sitting in M. Reiss' study, teaching myself English. My attempts to find work with a photographer in Paris, on the basis of my Strasbourg experience and the intervention of the Paris EIF office, came to naught. My German nationality, and the fact that I did not have a working permit (neither of which had deterred Monsieur Spehner), made potential employers hesitate.

I did rather well in assuming authority in the household. Where the boys had ignored their father's pleas and called their mother names, they seemed to respect me and the rules I laid down. A main rule was, "no swear words in the house!" (*fou*, *folle* = crazy, idiot were among the milder ones outlawed). To enforce this rule and others, I devised the following tactic: whoever had not broken any rule at the end of the day was eligible for a *bon point* (coupon); the one who had the most coupons at the end of the month received a prize (such as a ball, or pump for the bicycle, financed by Mme. Reiss). There were some noisy scenes just before bedtime when the *bons points* were distributed; one brother would dispute the other's claim to good behavior and reveal that he heard him use a *gros mot* (swear word) under his breath. When the prize was awarded at the end of the month, there was triumph and disappointment. To avoid too much of the latter, consolation prizes were added for the runners-up. All in all, the atmosphere in the house became quieter, and more civilized. Mme. Reiss was grateful.

I took advantage of the boys' readiness to hear me out to teach them some basic Judaism, about which they knew very little. Willy Reiss was the scion of a well-to-do assimilated Frankfurt family and had received an excellent education, but Jewish subjects were not part of the curriculum. His wife, who had been his secretary in the office he worked in, came from Schwarzwald (South German) peasant stock. To this day I do not know whether she converted to Judaism before marrying Willy Reiss. The question never came up during our stay.

It might well be that the strong sense of Jewish identification of the two older boys in later life was instilled by the lessons

I gave that winter. I remember particularly how impressed all of them were by the story of Hanukka, the heroic fight of the Maccabees against the pagan Greeks, and the rededication of the Holy Temple in Jerusalem with the flask of oil that lasted fully eight days. We lit the candles that commemorate the occasion (as I had done in my parents' house) and for the first time the house on the Allée St. Cucufa had a *Menorah* in the window.

While her husband was in the internment camp, Mme. Reiss made me her confidant as she wrestled with her financial problems. The French government had not only deprived Willy Reiss of his liberty, it also made it extremely difficult for him to support his family in wartime. This was because his bank accounts were "sequestered," which means blocked, as enemy alien assets, and only small amounts needed for the bare necessities were being released from time to time. Being a prudent man, M. Reiss had placed some of his funds in London, but the British authorities applied the same procedure against German citizens as the French. Even in Palestine, where M. Reiss also kept some money, the British authorities promptly "sequestered" it. (In 1949 when I visited Israel for the first time, Mme. Reiss asked me to locate a lawyer in Jerusalem who could help her gain access to the funds. By then the money had lost much of its value through devaluation.)

In addition to studying English, I taught myself how to type on the family's old Underwood, with the help of a "teach yourself" booklet. Soon I was able to help Mme. Reiss with her correspondence with various lawyers and banks. Moreover, having recently acquired some knowledge of the financial world through reading the stock quotations to the blind old gentleman in Thann, I thought myself qualified, now and again, to offer Mme. Reiss some advice, in addition to typing her letters.

Mme. Reiss later showed her appreciation in her own way.

On June 13, the morning of the day we left the house, she let me in on a secret she had previously kept to herself. Before being interned, her husband had given her a purse of gold coins. She had exchanged one from time to time into francs when she was short of cash. They were small yellowish twenty Thaler pieces, the common currency in Prussia and other German states before Bismarck. She took out some for the journey, but thought it was too risky to take the whole hoard along. So she asked me to help her bury the remaining coins under the coal stove in the kitchen. I don't recall how many pieces there were; perhaps thirty or forty. Just before we buried the purse, Mme. Reiss opened it once more and took out a coin. She handed it to me. "Keep it until you really need it one day," she said, a wan smile lighting up her careworn face. I accepted the coin silently and put it in my pocket. There was no way anyone could suspect from looking at the stove that it held a buried treasure; only Marthe Reiss and I knew the secret. But when she returned with the boys to Vaucresson after the war, the gold was gone. So was the kitchen stove, and every piece of furniture in the house.

Meanwhile – this was winter, 1939 – my own financial situation was precarious. In other words, I had no savings or other resources to fall back on. In Strasbourg, Monsieur Spehner had paid me 50 francs, which was then about $10, a month. This was used up for train fares, phone calls, stamps and other necessities. The twenty German Marks (about four to the dollar) Lotte and I were permitted to take out of Germany were long since gone. Mother had never been able to provide us with money (sending money abroad was a crime in Nazi Germany), and with the declaration of war direct contact with her was broken off in any event. We corresponded regularly with Papa in Holland, but he had no extra funds to send us. My only steady source of income was an occasional dollar bill enclosed with a letter from an uncle or aunt in America. I carefully noted these receipts – as well as expenditures - in the calendar supplied by the Félix Potin grocery chain to its clients.

After my failure to find employment in Paris with a photographer, I was ready to do almost anything to earn a few francs.

The first opportunity that presented itself was to give German lessons to the daughter of a well-to-do family who lived at the other end of Vaucresson. This brought in ten francs once a week, and it also brought me into contact with a rather elegant household. Anne-Marie, the daughter, was 12, and her parents wanted her to make more rapid progress with her German than she did in her class at the Lycée. I found that I was adept as a teacher; my pupil liked me, and so did her mother. I flattered myself that I was becoming a friend of the family. But the relationship ended abruptly when the Bonichons disappeared from their home without notifying me long before the Germans approached the capital. They never paid me for the last lesson.

I had more luck with Mme. Mahieu, the dentist in Garches who treated the Reiss family members and also was the couple's counsellor and friend. She had two daughters, one older and one younger than me, and each one rather attractive in her own way. She also had a husband who drank a good deal but did little else, being content to let his wife be the family breadwinner. He used to take her dental work to the laboratory in Paris in his black *traction-avant* (Citroën front-wheel drive), but of late – as Mme. Reiss told me in strict confidence – his drinking made him unreliable as a driver-messenger. Mme. Mahieu asked me one day whether I had time to run these errands for her two or three times a week. She would pay me 50 francs a month (the same $10 I had earned working full-time for M. Spehner) plus the train fare. I agreed eagerly. It meant visiting my beloved Paris frequently, and getting paid for it! Often, when I delivered a denture to the lab, which was not far from the *Gare St. Lazare,* I was told to come back later for finished work, and this gave me time to explore the streets and alleys of the 9th Arondissement, where the lab was located. . Once I went to see a movie, *La Bête Humaine*, with Jean Gabin, based on the novel by Emile Zola. The St. Lazare station, which was just across the square from the movie house, where I took the electric suburban train back to Garches after completing my errand, formed the background to this powerful tale of a *cheminot* (locomotive driver) and his illicit love. I still remember it vividly, especially when I lived for a while on Emile Zola Street in Tel Aviv. As for my own romantic interest, there was very little of it at the time. It is true, I was aware of the many street walkers in the 9th District and other areas I explored, and I sometimes wistfully observed them luring a client. But at 15 I was too young to seriously think of using their services. As for the Mahieu daughters, I found that I had little common language with either of them. Altogether, the fact that I was not in a scholastic framework made me feel like an outsider with young people my age. In Strasbourg, the Jewish scout movement had catered nicely to my social needs, and also made me feel welcome.

The round trip fare from Garches to Paris-St. Lazare cost six francs, and each trip lasted twenty minutes. Because the conductor did not always come around to check the tickets on the short ride, (and I was so short of funds) I was tempted to cheat the railroad out of its fare. The scheme I devised went like this: the ticket, which was valid only on the day of issue, had the date stamped on the back, and it had to be surrendered at the exit from the platform. I had somehow managed to hold on to a ticket from a previous trip, which I handed to the man at the exit. I had noticed that, being kept busy by the stream of passengers, he had no time to look at the date. But this time there was only a trickle of people getting off the train, and I made the mistake of handing him the outdated ticket nevertheless. He looked at the date and caught my error (or swindle) immediately. He also caught me so roughly by the arm that I almost dropped my briefcase with the precious dental work to the floor. Still holding me by the arm, he left his post to take me to the station master's office. I broke into a cold sweat. What would they do to me? Send me to jail? Or deport me, as a foreigner, and an enemy national? I thought of Lotte, who depended on me; of Mutti, all alone in Germany, and of Papa in Holland. And of our plan to be reunited in America. Would all this now come to naught? I regretted bitterly that I had risked so much for so little, a paltry six francs. The station master looked at me sternly and said: "Do you know that travelling without a valid ticket is a serious offense?"

Fortunately, I had an alibi. I did have a valid ticket, which I had bought to show the conductor (had he come through the car to ask for it, as he sometimes did) and which I had planned to save for the next trip. I now pulled it out of my pocket, saying that I had handed over the old ticket by mistake. The two men seemed surprised. The station master decided to let me go. But he warned me: "If we catch you again, you won't get away so easily." I've travelled with valid tickets ever since.

Chapter Five

Visas

Uppermost in my mind, in this bleak winter of 1939-40, was obtaining the immigration visa to the United States for Lotte and myself. Since our family was split into three parts, each fraction had to deal separately with the local American consul to complete the formalities.

Potential emigrants in the Paris area trying to deal with the bureaucratic pitfalls in the migration process could receive help at the offices of *Hicem*, a migration service operated jointly by the American *HIAS* (Hebrew Immigrant and Sheltering Society) and the local Jewish community's *Comité d'Emigration*. *Hicem*'s main mission was to assist refugees like ourselves get out of France. I spent many hours in its offices, where our case was being handled rather clumsily. The combination of an incompetent agency official and a rigid, unfeeling consul (probably acting on instructions from Washington) proved almost fatal in our case. But at the time I was not aware of this; I had implicit trust both in the competence of the *Hicem* staff and the good will of the American consular personnel. Ironically it was Mutti, now all by herself in Nazi Germany, who was the first to overcome the bureaucratic hurdles and get the consul to issue the coveted American visa to her. Papa was next, but he literally just missed the boat.

The job of a consul in issuing visas is to administer the U.S. immigration laws, and the regulations the Immigration and Naturalization Service (of the Department of Labor) has set up to interpret these laws. One of the few areas where he is given some leeway is in deciding whether the proof furnished by the applicant's sponsors that he will not become a public burden after arrival in the States is sufficient. That proof is contained in a so-called Affidavit of Support, which the sponsor swears to before a notary public and then submits to the consul. In our case, the sponsor was my Uncle Arthur, a brother of my mother's who had been living in the U.S. since 1927. But my uncle was a man of modest means and income; the Great Depression had kept him from rising beyond a presser's job in New York's Garment District. Moreover, he had already provided affidavits to both my parents, who applied for visas separately at the American consulates in Stuttgart and Rotterdam. One way he tried to get around the problem was to ask his employer to sign a supplementary affidavit, to guarantee that Lotte and I would not become a public burden. This man, Singer by name, was not a member of the family, which in itself weakened the case. If there were another depression in America (the consul might reason) would Mr. Singer have sufficient means – and incentive – to support us, who were not his relatives? And who would pay for our passage?

These questions and others might come up at the forthcoming interview at the consulate, and the *Hicem* official in charge of our case tried to prepare us for them. If asked about the tickets, he told us, I should say that *Hicem* would pay for them.

This turned out to be a serious error.

The connection with Mme.Mahieu, the dentist, and the frequent trips to Paris that came with it, made my contacts with the *Hicem* easier. Instead of roaming the streets while waiting for the work of the lab to be ready, I would take the métro to their office on the rue Vaugirard to hear if there was any news .Another reason for my visits to the agency was that, wherever fees were involved, the *Hicem* was ready to reimburse. This was very helpful in our situation.

At one time I thought that the process could be speeded up if we joined Papa in Rotterdam, so we could all get the visa there and leave for the U.S. together. He was now living with a Jewish family, van Messel by name, and they apparently had room for us too. It would also mean that we could be in close touch with Mutti in Frankfurt, since Holland was still neutral in the war. I made inquiries at the Dutch consulate in Paris about getting a visa and even filled out an application for the two of us, while the *Hicem* investigated the possibilities through their office in Rotterdam. In the end, nothing came of the scheme; the Dutch consulate informed us in February that the visas had been refused. It was probably just as well; we might have been stuck in Holland together with Papa when the Germans launched their invasion in May.

For the Reiss family, the year 1940 had started out happily: Papa Willy was released from the internment camp. I never found out whether his good luck was due to his age (he was 55) or because he was nearly blind, or because someone realized that it didn't make sense to intern Jews, even though they were German citizens. This is probably the least likely, because a few months later, when the real shooting war began, they locked up the poor man all over again.

Meanwhile Monsieur Reiss' return relieved me of some of my more mundane duties, such as lighting the coal stove that heated the house. (Mme. Reiss tried to set an example for all of us by taking a cold shower every day throughout the year, but Lotte and I preferred to wait for hot water for the once - weekly bath). I took up one new task in the household after Monsieur Reiss' return, and that was reading to the couple in the evening after the children were in bed. We sat around the dining room table, the three of us, with Mme. Reiss darning the boys` socks from a large basket, and her husband, delighting in the comforts of his home, leaning back in his rocking chair and smoking a pipe. They subscribed to a German-language émigré journal which appeared in Paris called *Neues Tagebuch*; its editor, Leopold Schwarzschild, each week presented his readers with a searching analysis of the international scene. His stinging anti-German editorials provoked the ire of the Nazis; when they eventually caught him they made him pay the price. Among the refugee authors then in Paris who contributed regularly to the weekly there were names who meant nothing to me at the time but were later to become famous, such as Hannah Arendt and Walter Benjamin. We also listened to the radio together; the evening news bulletin always began with the day's army communiqué, which nine times out of ten consisted of a laconic *"Rien à signaler"* (nothing to report).

It was Mutti, who had herself kept a journal of my childhood from the day I was born, who made the suggestion, relayed by Papa, that I keep a diary. In fact, my first entry, dated February 25, 1940, reads that "in Mutti's letters, which Papa sent me today, she wishes that I make a few notations." Until then, I had used the calendar with recipes supplied by the Felix Potin grocery chain in Paris to keep track of my daily receipts and expenditures, and also to keep a record of the letters I sent and received. From that date on I also used the calendar – actually a hard-cover book - to summarize and reflect on the day's events. There were about a dozen lines on each page which could be used for that purpose, but sometimes there was so much to report that my handwriting spilled over into the margins.

I am still grateful to Mutti for her suggestion; the diary is in front of me now, the ink a bit pale but still clearly legible, and it helps me recall the events of the time in great detail. Mutti's purpose in asking me to keep a diary was to let her and Papa later share our experiences during the separation, which she was sure would soon come to an end. Often there was *rien à signaler* in our little world as well. Sometimes Lotte broke the routine by misbehaving (as noted in the first entry).

But the visas figured inevitably every few days. I'll let the diary speak (my translations from the German):[3]

Monday, Feb. 26. *I went to the dental technician in Paris for Mme. Mahieu, after that to the* **Hicem**, *where they refused to give me the paper Papa asked for, until they get a reply from the Committee in Rotterdam. Lotte is well again. She behaved outrageously to Monsieur Reiss at table, whereupon I gave her a slap in the face and sent her off to bed.*

Tuesday, Feb. 27. *During the night, an air raid alarm, but as usual we stayed in bed. In the morning, errands in Paris, followed by a stroll in Montmartre. The Netherlands consulate, where I phoned, told me there was no reply from their government as yet*

Wednesday, Feb. 28. *Papa wrote unfortunately that our Holland trip won't come off, which depressed me greatly. Now it means waiting again. Went again to the Hicem to ask if their Rotterdam committee replied. The answer was negative. These visits are very tiring, as I have to leave here at 8 o'clock to get a place in the line. There are always a lot of people. Then, after a half hour's boring métro trip, you have to wait for an hour. Thank God it's not too expensive, because I always combine it with errands for Mme. Mahieu, who pays for the trip.*

---

3. The full text of the diary, in the original German, can be found in my *Jugend auf der Flucht: Die Tagebuecher von Ernst und Julie Stock,* published by Metropol Verlag, Berlin 2004. The book has an introduction by Prof. Edward Timms, then director of the Centre for German - Jewish Studies at the University of Sussex, UK.

Friday, March 1. *Papa wrote that he and Mutti now practically are assured of the tickets for the voyage. In the afternoon I accompanied M. Reiss to St. Cloud, where he has to report to the police every Friday.*

Saturday, March 2. *In the morning, after making the beds etc., I did the necessary shopping at the market like every Wednesday and Saturday when I'm not in Paris. Lotte comes home with the news that she is number two in the class. Then I give my German lesson. Even though I have to walk half an hour, it's worth my while for ten francs. The girl already speaks quite fluently.*

Sunday, March 3. *The Sunday goes by like every other day; on those days when there's nothing to do, one yearns most strongly to be away from here, for the parents and for a regular life, full of work. In the afternoon, a disaster. Monsieur Reiss goes walking with all the children in the woods, along with the son of a neighbor, Jean Delmas, who has a new bike. He wanted to let Lotte use it, but M. Reiss forbade it. When she took it nevertheless, she landed in a ditch and the bike was kaputt. Monsieur Reiss said he doesn't want to see her any more, and she came home crying inconsolably. But Mme. Delmas was not angry and forgave her; and said she'll have the bike repaired at her expense.*

Monday, March 4. *I was once again at the Hicem where – enough to drive one crazy – I had to wait fully three hours, only to hear that there was no answer from Rotterdam. I had no choice but to wait for the American papers. The Hicem is not much of a help; one has to take care of everything oneself, until one can tell them, "okay, this is it," and then they pay for the ticket. Papa sent a postcard; the two days without mail seemed like an eternity.*

Tuesday, March 5. *Again a day without mail. In the morning, I went to the Netherlands consulate, where they were so nice in the beginning. The visa has been refused provisionally, for the reasons we know. Mme. Reiss paid for Lotte's shoe repair, so that I show 28 francs less in expenses. Also mine, which cost 33 francs last week, she wouldn't let me pay. Today I was in Paris twice, in the morning and evening. At night, when the children are in bed, I read the paper to M. and Mme. Reiss until 9:30 – 10 o'clock.*

Sunday, March 10. *An eventful day! After I gave my lesson at 8 a.m., I travelled to Paris where I met Chameau, who was very happy to see me. He invited me to spend the day with him. We ate in a kosher restaurant in the Jewish quarter, and in the afternoon went to the Comédie Française, where Cyrano de Bergerac was playing. It was wonderful, and afterwards we still had an ice cream together.*

Tuesday, March 12. *This morning I went to the American consulate, where I was told that the papers did not arrive yet. …When I came home I learned that the mailman had a registered letter from America and will come back with it tomorrow. This means the papers have arrived!*

Wednesday, March 13. *For sure, it was the expected letter with the papers, and full of joy I went at noon to the Consulate. But, sad to say, they told us to come back next week and didn't even look at the document. We are used to this sort of thing, and we can forget about leaving this month.*

Sunday, March 17. *Only one more day, then we'll find out at the Consulate where we stand, this is what preoccupies me today …. After lunch I played a bit with the children, then Mr. Reiss wanted me to go for a walk with them, but I told him I* *first wanted to teach Lotte some English, which I did. After-wards they seemed to be insulted, because when I did want to walk with them, Mme. Reiss wouldn't let me and went herself.*

Monday, March 18. *Again a day lost. How stupid of me to go to the Consulate only in the afternoon, when no visa matters are dealt with. But they gave me a number for tomorrow morning. I had nothing to do in Paris the whole afternoon, since the denture for Mme. Mahieu was ready only about six. So I sat on a bench on the Place de la Concorde, opposite the Embassy, read the paper and studied English from one of the* **Langenscheidt** *booklets that I always carry with me.*

Tuesday, March 19. *Today I again got neither a positive nor a negative answer at the Consulate. They took the papers and said I would get a final decision within a few days.*

Wednesday, March 20. *Today my German lesson was especially successful: I translated some chapters from the English booklets, and that worked extremely well. I also give Lotte an English lesson every day.*

Friday, March 22. *Today I practiced on the typewriter; it's going pretty well. In the afternoon I worked in the garden; the soil has to be turned over completely at this time. With peeling apples the afternoon went by. On Easter or the following week I plan to go to the theater with Charlotte and Abi, so that they'll enjoy their vacations a bit.*

Saturday, March 23. *Today finally news from Papa. He wrote nothing new, but among other things that he had no heat in his room all winter long, which made me feel sad the whole day. The children were allowed to buy a football, and I played with them all afternoon in the garden.*

Monday, March 25. *Today general disappointment: after much to and fro the Reiss parents didn't want to let Abi go to the theater with us, it's too dangerous. Lotte made a terrific scene; to console her I went walking in the woods with her in the afternoon, and tomorrow will take her to a museum.*

Tuesday, March 26. *Today two letters came at once from Papa and Mutti, with Purim pictures of previous years which were fun to look at. But the main item was the news that the parents will leave from Antwerp on April 10. If we get our visas until then, Papa will try everything to take us along. Since we may be called to the consulate any day, we are postponing our visit to Paris for another two days, so as not to spend money twice.*

Thursday, March 28. *I finally kept my promise to Lotte and took her to Paris, where we visited the famous Zoo at Vincennes. It is fabulously laid out, without fences, the animals are on high rocks and separated only by ditches from the public. Then we walked about an hour and a half to the Jewish quarter, where we bought a sausage for Mme. Reiss. Then by Metro to the Pont de Sèvres and home on foot.*

Saturday, March 30. *Again, nothing to report. Papa wrote, however, that Mutti finally got her ticket, and he expects her soon with him.*

Sunday, March 31. *The Hicem sent a letter, I should come there as soon as possible. Tomorrow I'll go there, and of course am anxious to know what they have to tell me.*

Monday, April 1. *At the Hicem they had nothing new to tell me: they received a letter from Rotterdam inquiring how far our application had progressed. They will inquire at the (Dutch) consulate where we could get a visa.*

Tuesday, April 2. *Today was one of the happiest days of our stay here. Mutti wired from Rotterdam, that she was re-united with Papa. Now begins a new chapter in the migration history of our family. Tomorrow might be another such day; since tonight I went, on the advice of Mme. Mahieu, to see a gentleman in the neighborhood who is on the staff of the American embassy, in order to tell him about our case. He was very nice and said I should come see him at the embassy tomorrow where he'll try to help. Mutti wrote a very personal letter, still from Frankfurt.*

Wednesday, April 3. *This morning at the embassy the man gave me a note for the Consul personally, which caused him to grant me an audience. I explained our case to him, and he spoke with the vice-consul. Whereupon he told me he didn't think we could travel with my parents, but we would be get-ting a letter, probably still this week. It's strange, at the Con-sulate I have to act the opposite from the way I behave at the Hicem. Here I play the elegant young man with rich Amer-ican relatives; there I'm the poor refugee whose uncles are not in a position to pay for our trip.*

Friday, April 5. *Today Mutti's first letter from Holland came; probably also the last, since she left aboard a steamer for New York last night. Sadly, alone, apparently Papa didn't get the ticket as yet....*

Saturday, April 6. *Still no news from the consulate; it can drive you crazy.*

Sunday, April 7. *The mailman brought a huge bundle of letters; I already thought I saw the one from the consulate, but unfortunately there were only (!) eight letters for M. Re-iss and none for us.*

Tuesday, April 9. *Today is the blackest day we lived through since we are in France: the visa was categorically denied to us. At the consulate they returned all our papers together with a letter which says that the visa has been refused because of insufficient affidavit. We must obtain a new affidavit, and then we can make a new visa application. No need to say anything about the state of mind I'm in. Poor Papa also will have another big disappointment! For the Reiss family, too, it was a day of misfortune: they learned that, through a new high tax and the German invasion of Denmark they are losing a large part of their fortune and are close to ruin. Mutti wrote a card from the ship.*

Wednesday, April 10. *Today we have calmed down somewhat and become reconciled with the situation. Lotte didn't take it so tragically; she likes it in school, but she keeps accusing me: You see, we were supposed to leave in January, and now we'll still be here in May. Yesterday I wrote to Mme. Salomon I really wanted to take some kind of course, because living here for months without occupation would drive me crazy.*

The consul evidently concluded from the fact that a welfare agency was paying for our tickets that our sponsor either was not serious about having us join him, or else didn't have the money to pay for our passage, and therefore his sponsorship of us was questionable.

It is sad to reflect that such petty thinking motivated America's envoys at a time when lives were at stake, but the policy no doubt emanated from Washington. Also, the Paris Consul and his vice-consul were apparently too cowardly to tell me the bitter truth to my face and preferred to rely on the mail instead. Almost equally sad was the incompetence of the Jewish migration agency, which let us walk into the trap.

But help was on the way. There was reason not to despair. The U.S. immigration laws, which were so harsh and unbending when it came to quotas and affidavits, also made special provision for the minor children of American residents to join their parents in the States. They were issued so-called non-quota visas, which meant that no affidavits or waiting periods were required. The parents could be trusted to be responsible for their children's support without having to prove they had a bank account. And my mother arrived in New York almost at the very moment our visa application was rejected. The first thing she did, with the help of her family, was to apply for the non-quota visas for us, so we could join her. Already on May 1 I received copies of her letters to the Paris Consulate and to the Department of Labor (which was in charge of the Immigration and Naturalization Service) and which in turn cabled the Consulate to process our visas. On May 11 the mail brought the notice to call on the Consulate.

But this time our joy was mingled with despair about the fate of Papa, who was still in Holland which had been invaded by the German army the day before. He too had finally received his visa for the U.S. and was booked to leave Rotterdam on a Dutch vessel, the Veendam, on May 12. But the ship was sunk when the Germans bombed the port city and its harbor, and Papa had to spend the rest of the war in the Netherlands.

Later in the month, he was able to send this account of how he survived the bombing to Mutti in New York:

Rotterdam, 30 May 1940
My dear, dear Julie,
At last I can write to you, and thereby a great pressure is taken from me. Day and night I had to think of you, dearest, and the children: in what fear and disquiet you must have lived, and there was no possibility of getting in touch. You were probably already worried you might have to look around for another, but

it hasn't come to that! At least not in the next few years... I am just as healthy as you left me, and hope to be able to hold you in my arms very soon. The passengers of the "Veendam" will soon be allowed to travel via Italy. Let us hope for the best! Now I'm sitting here, completely in the dark about you, and especially about the children, and everybody else. Ernst has just written, full of hope. Now I only hope that the visa business succeeded.

The "Veendam" was due to leave on May 12, and then the war broke out on the 10th. I received my ticket a few days earlier and was going to cable once more on the day of departure, that I saved myself. You know that the Messels moved to another apartment on April 25, whereby I helped, and then I stayed alone in the apartment until May 1. Then I helped the Sterns move to the Botersloot and then moved in with them. Neither their old nor their new apartment are still standing. I was able to get away with my bare life, taking the two-year-old boy on my arm and running with him for ¾ hour into the open. Stern himself was, like most German Jews, interned. Everyone else, myself included, was not allowed to leave home since. Then, on May 14, the worst came over Rotterdam, and I'm lucky to be able to write this letter. Two valises which I still had with me, were burnt, and presumably also all the rest of the luggage which I had delivered to the Holland-America Line shortly before and paid 100 fl. for it. But it's also possible that part of it still lies buried under the ruins....

But no matter how painful the loss, I took a firm resolve not to mourn over it. Because you only feel how insignificant all earthly goods are after you escape from such a hell. In our neighborhood the bombs were raining down, and there was no way out because fires were burning on all four sides.

Write to me by return mail, also about the children (only in German); my wish is only that I can soon be with you, and that only three people come to meet me: Julie, Ernst and Lotte.

Sending you a thousand kisses, Your Leo

Chapter Six

More Dark Days

In the diary entry for April 9, the day the visas were denied to us, I called it the blackest day since our departure from Germany. But worse was still to come.

Friday, May 10. *Today events rushed headlong one after another. In the morning, the radio announced that the Germans had attacked Belgium and Holland. I was devastated. Monsieur Reiss actually wept and kept saying, "Terrible, terrible!" And Papa still wrote that he was going to sail tomorrow! All communication is, of course, broken off, and he certainly won't be able to get away. We sit near the radio all day long to hear news*

Saturday, May 11. *Amid all the misery and onrushing events today was a lucky day for us. The definite summons from the Consulate arrived, and there is no longer any doubt that we will be getting the visa. But our joy was not as it would have been ordinarily, since we are still unclear about Papa's fate. I phoned the Holland-America line to ask whether the boat left. They answered: we have no news, but we hope so. I was in Paris to apply for the certificates of good conduct* (necessary for the exit visas)

Monday, May 13. *The day started with two air raid alarms, at 1 and 6 a.m. and ended in a sort of catastrophe. At 8:30 p.m. the radio announced, that all German citizens between the ages of 17 and 55 must return to the detention camps im-*

mediately. Thank God this does not apply to M. Reiss, at least not yet, but it is a hard blow for all the refugees.

Mutti wrote us an airmail letter.

Tuesday, May 14. *Today I learned to my great horror that Papa's ship did not sail, and that he is therefore still in Rotterdam. He was probably arrested; let us hope that nothing will happen to him.*

The Hicem gave me the necessary money, so I could ask Lotte by telephone to come to Paris and go to the doctor, who took 100 francs to renew the medical certificates. (The Consulate requires a certificate of good health from an accredited doctor; ours had expired in the meantime and had to be renewed.) *Monsieur Reiss wrote the Belgian Consul and offered to take in a Belgian refugee child.*

Wednesday, May 15. *There was despair this morning when we heard on the radio that Holland surrendered! About Papa's fate we dare not even think. Today we got the good conduct certificate and will go to the Hicem tomorrow. The youngest Reiss boy had his birthday today; we gave him a chocolate bar and a little car.*

Thursday, May 16. *This morning I took Lotte to Paris already at 8:30, but because of the many errands for Mme. Mahieu our turn at the Hicem came only at 12:30. They were very nice and had the passports extended and reimbursed the $2 for the visa applications with no problem. Then we ate some lunch and went to the Consulate at 2, where they told us to our great disappointment to come back tomorrow.*

Friday, May 17. *At the Consulate they took the papers and told us to come back Monday at 11 with the twenty dollars. Then I put Lotte on the train, so that she could still make the* *afternoon class, and took care of Mme. Mahieu's business.*

Mme. Delmas will be leaving for Marseille tomorrow night, and I went to Paris again in the afternoon to get her tickets. The Committee sent M. Reiss 400 francs for our maintenance (at Mme. Salomon's suggestion) of which he gave me 100, for the many travel expenses because of the visas.

Saturday, May 18. Today I was again twice in Paris; in the evening I accompanied Mme. Delmas and Jean who are going to her parents in Marseille, in a taxi to the Gare de Lyon. After their train left, I looked around at the whole station traffic: the Simplon Express happened to be there, which goes through the Balkans to Turkey....

Sunday, May 19. Mme. Weil wrote a very nice letter from Brest and enclosed ten francs.

Monday, May 20. Today was the great event, yearned for so fervently these five months: we received, without difficulties, our American visa. Now the question is: will we be able to depart six weeks from now, given the present situation?

M. Reiss went with us to the Hicem and the Consulate, where we had to wait for two hours...

The *Hicem* promised to arrange our ocean passage after we had the visa in hand, but the best they could come up with was a sailing on July 6 from the port of St. Nazaire on the only ship of the French line still maintaining service to New York, the s.s. *Champlain*. The war between France and Germany which had broken out in September was still a "phony war," and the U-boats had not yet made the Atlantic unsafe. "It's too bad the visas didn't come through a few days earlier," our *Hicem* case officer said. "The *Champlain* just sailed yesterday. Now you'll have to wait until July 6."

Tuesday, May 21. *In the morning I went with my visa to the Hicem, where they promised to look after the passage, while I will have to get the French exit visas. I stayed the whole day for Mme. Mahieu in Paris; in the afternoon I called at Mme. Gamzon* (wife of national scout commissioner Robert Gamzon, and a community worker who took an interest in the children on behalf of her colleague, Andrée Salomon.) *She told me M. Reiss should register his children and us for evacuation. In the evening we were caught in Boulogne by an air raid alert and took shelter in a nearby basement. I read in a paper this evening that many Germans from Holland had arrived in France in sealed railroad cars and were imprisoned. This gave us much hope.*

Wednesday, May 22. *The whole country is in feverish excitement for days already, for the fate of the world is really at stake.* (The German army, having conquered Holland and Belgium, was now invading France from the North, bypassing the Maginot Line which was designed to resist an invasion from the East). *We are by no means safe here any more, and were rather disappointed to hear in Paris today that the children's camps are all full and we cannot be accepted any more. I wrote about this immediately to Mme. Salomon. Afterwards I went to Versailles for the exit visa, but the Prefecture was already closed.*

Thursday, May 23. *In Versailles they accepted my application; I can get the* (exit) *visa four days before departure. I also took along various items for the Belgian refugees which I left at the Prefecture. Mutti wrote a letter in which she enclosed five dollars she earned herself, for Mme. Reiss. Aunts Bella and Frieda each sent one dollar for us. Unfortunately the German lessons stopped, as the people, like many others, left for the provinces. They still owe me twenty francs.*

Friday, May 24. *Today was again a terrible day. I went in the afternoon with M. Reiss to St. Cloud, where he has to report to the police every Friday, and to accompany him to Paris from there. He came out with trembling steps: they told him he would have to check into the detention camp again tomorrow morning. What a blow! We went afterwards to Paris to see Mme. Gamzon about the evacuation of his children and us, but she cannot do anything either for the time being. She plans to visit Mme. Reiss Monday night; I should call for her. Then we went to see a man, at Mme. Salomon's recommendation, who should advise M. Reiss, but through a misunderstanding we didn't find him home. When we told Mme. Reiss the news of his re-internment, she was in despair.*

Saturday, May 25. *Today I accompanied M. Reiss to the camp at Maisons-Laffitte. He was calm, and his wife too was much calmer today. I took leave of him at the entrance to the camp and thanked him for everything, in case we should not see each other again. If only I could read what will be written on the still empty pages. For example on July 6, whether it will say, "today we sailed away," or whatever else will happen until then!*

Sunday, May 26. *Uncle Arthur sent a cable with reply paid for, to find out whether we got the visas or need additional documents. I cabled back, "reçu visas, depart 6 juillet."* (The authorities had decreed that all cables sent abroad be written in French only. I had to hope that Uncle Arthur would find someone to translate it to him.) *Charles* (Schweber) *wrote me a long letter.*

Tuesday, May 28. *Today was again an awful day, even though not for our own fate, but for that of the whole world, which one now takes to heart more than if it were something personal. The Belgian king has capitulated! Which of course* *makes the situation much worse. I am hoping all day long that Mutti, in view of the critical situation, can somehow scrape together $400 and will cable us, we should leave via Italy. If only that country will not declare war as well.* (Which it did in short order. So we had no choice but to wait for the July 6 sailing from France, to be financed by the *Hicem*.)

Wednesday, May 29. *We read in the paper today, that in England all German women were interned, together with their children. We are afraid, of course, that this might happen in France as well, and I wrote to Mme. Salomon to ask whether we might come to Clermont-Ferrand in that case.* (If Mme. Reiss were interned). *Mme. Reiss received a card from her husband; he started it with a big black dot, which means – so they had agreed – that things are very bad.*

Today I thought more than ever of Papa and Mutti, as we read a story, "Thoughts about the Parental Home." Another five weeks and two days until our departure.

Thursday, May 30. *Mme. Mahieu came back for a few days, and I had to resume my frequent Paris journeys. Afterward I went to the Committee to ask if it wouldn't be possible to sail on an American ship leaving Bordeaux on June 4. Nothing doing: (1) they cannot afford the fare; and (2) it's only for Americans. Concerning Papa, they are sending me to the Red Cross, which will try to find out his address. A ray of light!*

Friday, May 31. *This morning I left at 7 to bring M. Reiss a package to the camp. When I came home, I found a letter from Mutti, with an enclosure for Mme. Salomon, in which she asked whether we couldn't sail on an American ship...*

Saturday, June 1. *Mme. Salomon wrote that, in case we had to leave here for whatever reason, we could come to her* (in Clermont-Ferrand). *She also enclosed a letter to the Hicem which I should read and forward to them. She inquired whether we could not leave from Marseille and requested that we should sail as soon as possible. I sent her Mutti's letter with a few words of my own. Today I was at the Mairie* (town hall) *to pick up our ration cards.*

Sunday, June 2. *Today I met a 17-year-old boy at the post office, who will sail tomorrow night on the Washington from Bordeaux. He is an American and has been living in Garches for six years, his parents are still staying here. He asked me if he could take something for Mutti, but I couldn't think of anything, because I just sent a letter. I was very jealous of him.*

Monday, June 3. *Today was the first serious air raid alarm: The Germans bombed Paris for an hour and set factories on fire. Some bombs fell about 2 kilometers from here and a boy was killed.*

Tuesday, June 4. *We learned today through the paper and radio, that yesterday 240 planes dropped over 1,000 bombs and killed 50 people. In America there's supposed to be great excitement about this; I hope Mutti didn't get too upset.*

Friday, June 7. *Another day that brings us closer to our goal, that's all I can say about today. We now eat all our meals in the garden, morning, noon and night. After the meal I water the entire garden, then a half hour of steno, at 9:30 we listen to the news, and then to bed.*

Sunday, June 9. *We are very depressed by the continuing bad news which we hear on the radio. Who knows what the next few days will bring us!* (The French army was being overrun by the German armor, and resistance was crumbling all along the front. The occupation of Paris was only days away).

Monday, June 10. *This day, which began so happily – Mutti cabled that she had good news from Papa – ended with Italy's declaration of war. Even though we had been expecting it for weeks, it was still a hard blow. The Germans, moreover, are advancing steadily, and we are packing our suitcases to possibly travel to Mme. Salomon. We are thinking of taking the third Reiss boy along, so as to ease Mme. Reiss' burden somewhat.*

Tuesday, June 11. *It's impossible to describe all that happened to me today! In the morning there were no trains, and I had to stop a car to get to Paris. At the Hicem the offices were empty; they moved to Bordeaux. Mme. Gamzon also is gone; we are all alone. I went to the Gare de Lyon to get tickets, but there were such tremendous crowds that I had to give up after five hours' wait. I had changed $8 for the purpose. I also applied for my sauf-conduit* (certificate of good conduct) *in St.Cloud, without which we supposedly cannot leave. We are just about the only ones left in the street, everybody else left in their cars.*

Wednesday, June 12. *This morning I went to the market. There were only three or four stalls; the whole town is deserted, shops shuttered. We also took the decision to leave. At noon I had to go to Versailles to pick up the American visa* (with the exit visas) *at the Prefecture; since all traffic was paralyzed, I had to make my way on foot. On the way I asked everybody whether he had a bike for sale. I found someone who was willing to lend me his for 200 francs until the end of the war. I bought various accessories, had a new tube and tire mounted, so that the price came to almost 275 francs.*
At home the mood was terrible.

Chapter Seven

The Flight

Thursday, June 13. *This day brought about a turning point in our life. We left everything behind and rode, with a knapsack and a small valise, into the unknown. In the morning I bought a man's bike for Charlotte for 150 francs, with the intention of lowering the saddle. Mme. Reiss loaded the most necessary things for herself and the boys on two wobbly baby carriages, and at one o'clock the sad journey began. For a long time I couldn't decide whether we should travel by ourselves or together with them; then I resolved not to leave them.*

We were barely 500 meters from the house when a terrible cloudburst broke loose. The boys had left their coats behind, and Mme. Reiss asked us to ride back to the house to get them. When we returned - after having waited in the house for the rain to end - we did not find a trace of the group (two neighboring families had also come along). We looked for them for another half hour, then brought back the coats, ate something and rode off by ourselves. Lotte could not ride on her bicycle, so we took that of the oldest Reiss boy instead. We rode southward until about 7 o'clock, then the stream of refugees became so dense that we had to push the bikes. At 10 o'clock we lay down in the grass, wrapped ourselves in our coats and slept, although quite badly.

When we awoke at 4 a.m. it was June 14, the day an American historian, Norman Cantor described, because of the German entry into Paris, as France's most fateful date of the century. For the two of us the day was almost disastrous: I got separated from Lotte in the surging crowd on the road, and for a while thought I'd lost her for good. Just how it happened I don't recall (neither does she); all I remember is that I found myself on the bike coasting down a hill, all the time picking up speed. When I came to the bottom, I realized I was alone. I stopped and got off the bike; the others swept past me. Once again, I remembered how I had promised Mother to watch over my sister Lotte, and I felt like crying. But I couldn't afford to let my eyes cloud up; I had to keep looking out for her so that I wouldn't miss her if she came by. With each passing minute – and the hundreds of refugees passing by with it – I became more desperate. What would she do by herself? I tried to stop people to ask if they'd seen her, but they paid no attention. Everyone was in a rush to get on. I didn't know whether to join the stream myself and look for her down the road, or to stay where I was in the hope she might still come by. I chose the latter course, standing by the side of the road with my eyes peeled on the never-ending flow. To my immense relief I saw her coming down the hill, pushing her bike. She had not dared ride on it; the hill was too steep and the brakes felt unsafe. She did not seem too upset, being sure I was waiting for her at the bottom. I again felt like crying, but held back because of Lotte.

I'll quote from the diary again to tell about the remains of this "fateful day":

Friday, June 14. ...*At about 2 we got to Etampes, where the Germans had bombed three hours earlier. Dead bodies were lying around, covered with a cloth, wrecked trucks, etc. At the station people were gathering and saying a train would be leaving for Orléans. Sure enough, we were able to climb aboard a freight train, but on the cruel condition that we must leave our bikes behind in the station. All that money lost! The train travelled terribly slowly, stood still for hours*

on end, and we had to spend the night on it. This was dreadful, because German planes flew overhead all the time, and we expected to get a bomb on our heads any minute. A freight car just behind ours was loaded with explosives.

About noon we got to Orléans, but the train stopped so long a few kilometers from the station that we decided to get out and walk to the station, where we hoped to find another train. It was broiling hot, and I thought any minute I'd collapse under the heavy load. There were another two men with us, but they were carrying heavy burdens themselves. I cursed myself for having given up the bikes. We picked cherries off a tree and bought a few groceries. Almost every place was deserted; the next day there was heavy fighting here. Completely exhausted we arrived at the station, where we got on a freight train loaded with soldiers and refugees. It left soon enough, but stopped at every crossing to pick up more unfortunates. In the evening we arrived in Vierzon; on another track there was an express train. We got on it, it didn't go any faster, but we were in a second class compartment....

Even though the compartment was full, those in it were willing to make room for two more children. But then there was a tense moment. After the train started moving, Lotte began speaking to me with the German accent she had not managed to get rid of since arriving in France. The chatter in the compartment died down; the people who had been so friendly before suddenly became suspicious. Where are you from, they wanted to know. All Frenchmen had been warned there were German spies everywhere; could they be disguised as children?

"We're from Alsace," I said. "We're on our way to an aunt in Clermont-Ferrand." The whole compartment breathed easier. Everyone knew that Alsatians spoke French with a German accent. We gratefully took the chocolate they offered to us, but I still signalled Lotte to keep her mouth shut.

The fortunate fact that I myself spoke French without an accent I owed - I think – to my language teacher at the *Philanthropin*, the Jewish community school I attended in Frankfurt. Waro (a nickname made up of the first syllables of his name, Walter Rothschild) who taught us ten-year-olds both English and French, put great emphasis on pronunciation. The idea was to prepare us for emigration, meaning for real-life situations where the niceties of grammar were less important than making oneself understood. He would work with each of us individually, standing patiently by the boy's side while he tried again and again, until at last the correct sound emerged. This he did in both languages. I recall the particular care with which he made us pronounce the English "R", which has few equivalents in other languages and certainly not in German. He had each of us first enunciate the French "J" and then roll the tongue slowly backward along the roof of the mouth, so that an effortless transition sound resulted. Classmates whom I later came across in the United States all spoke an accent-free English, unlike Henry Kissinger, for example, whose high-school teacher was evidently not privy to Waro's technique.

But now we were still in France, my silent sister and I, in a crowded compartment on the way to Mme. Salomon in Clermont-Ferrand. The lights dimmed down, and the rhythm of the wheels seemed to lull everyone to sleep.

As for the Reiss family, this is their story as I later pieced it together:

After waiting in vain for some time for Lotte and I to return to the spot where we parted, they joined the flow of refugees southward. Leaving behind the baby carriage with their possessions, they managed to continue the flight by army truck and by train, much as Lotte and I did when we abandoned our bicycles. We compared notes after the war, and it turned out that our routes almost overlapped; we were all waiting many hours for a train at the Vierzon station at almost the same time. But Lotte and I were heading east from there, to join Mme. Salomon at

Clermont-Ferrand; the Reiss family continued southward and ended up in the small Pyrenean village of Cailhau (Aude). It was in the unoccupied zone of France, later also known as Vichy France, and the family felt safe there. Marthe found work as a household help, while the boys attended schools in the area. Father Willy, released from the French detention camp once more, was able to locate his family through the intermediary of Mme. Mahieu, the dentist and family friend who had kept in touch, and there was a blissful reunion.

The boys experienced a primitive anti-semitism in their place of refuge when the Cailhaud *curé* warned his parishioners not to let their children play with the Christ-killers in their midst. M. Reiss told his perplexed offspring to inform the priest that Jesus had himself been a Jew.

Then, in November 1942, the Germans moved into unoccupied France. Soon they began the hunt for Jews, using the French *gendarmerie* to help them carry out their policy. Non-French Jews headed the list of those deported, with the tacit consent of the Vichy government under Marshal Pétain. One day Willy Reiss was given a warning that the *gendarmes* were about to come for him, but he refused to go into hiding. He told his wife, "I have faith in the Maréchal." But he was arrested and never heard from again; the meticulously kept German records show that he was sent by train from Drancy (near Paris) to Auschwitz and gassed there.

The children were now in danger, and a French underground network placed the three older boys, with forged papers and identities, in Catholic boarding schools. The head of the network, a French army colonel named Henri Cordesse, was posthumously declared one of the "Righteous of the Nations" by the *Yad vaShem* Memorial Authority in Israel, upon the Reiss brothers' recommendation.

When they returned to Vaucresson at war's end, Marthe Reiss and her sons found the house on Allée St. Cucufa empty of all its contents; the neighbors, most of whom had come back during the occupation, pointed to German troops as the looters. But M. and Mme. Jean, the old couple next door who were their landlords, knew otherwise. They saw the neighbors themselves carry away furniture when it appeared the Jews might not come back. A great surprise awaited Mme. Reiss after the Jeans died some time afterward: in their will, they left her the house at No. 37.

When conditions were ripe, Marthe took a trip to Germany to visit her aged parents. She also found her younger brother at home, and he confessed to her that he had been in the S.S. She screamed at him, "You scoundrel, you are still alive and my husband had to die!" She slammed the door after her, never to return.

Chapter Eight

The Flight (continued)

On June 16, we were still on the train from Vierzon, with our destination the city of Clermont-Ferrand, where we hoped to find Mme. Salomon. The diary entry reads:

Another day's travel, with changing trains and waiting 5-6 hours in the stations, spent in stoic idleness. At 10 a.m. we arrive in St. Sulpice, from there to Montluçon, where we have to wait from 9 to midnight. We drink coffee, the first warm nourishment since Thursday. (This was Sunday)

I gave up entering expenditures for this month, since I cannot remember them exactly.

Monday, June 17. *At 3 in the morning we arrived in Gannat, about 40 kilometers from Clermont, but we found a train to take us there only at noon. We were furious when it stopped at a siding a few kilometers from the station, since Clermont could not absorb any more refugees. We decided to get off and march to the station on foot. A very nice lady walked along with us and helped us carry the luggage. In the end a military truck took us to Clermont-Ferrand. Mme. Salomon was delighted to see us and received us like her own children. We ate, then she went with me to the villa where the other refugee children from Strasbourg are lodged. I told her all kinds of things, then we went back, and I was happy to sleep again in a bed. Lotte was already asleep.*

The next morning, over breakfast, Andrée, Tobie Salomon and I held a kind of war council on our next move. Andrée had read, or heard on the radio, that ships were still leaving from the port of Bordeaux, and she thought this would be our best chance to get out. If not to America, at least to England, and to the States from there. I had implicit trust in her judgment and was ready to act on her advice, without questioning. When do we leave? Wait, Andrée said. In addition to wisdom and warmth, Andrée also had authority; and connections. Tobie, her husband, was a rather pale figure next to her, smoking his pipe somewhat enigmatically and not talking much. Andrée now picked up paper and pen and wrote two letters on the stationery of the *Caisse Centrale de l'Est*, the Strasbourg Jewish welfare organization with which she was still associated. One was to the Chief Rabbi of Strasbourg, now in Bordeaux, whom she asked to extend us assistance, and the other to a Dr. Lévy-Dreyfus, a prominent Strasbourg physician also resettled in Bordeaux, whom she asked to put us up while we looked for passage. The doctor and his wife were close friends of hers, and she was sure they would receive us accordingly. I carefully tucked the two letters into the secret compartment of my knapsack where I kept the American visa (which was stamped on one sheet for both of us, with the two immigrant green cards stapled on to it), and Mme. Reiss' gold coin.

Once the decision that we should leave for Bordeaux had been taken, Andrée's business-like side took over. Letters of recommendation, provisions for the journey; checking that papers are in order, warm clothing for cold nights. It was like leaving for summer camp (for which she had also prepared me as a scout in Strasbourg less than a year earlier). I could see that her no-nonsense manner had a soothing effect on Lotte, for which I was grateful. Two days after arriving in Clermont both of us were ready for the next stage, with renewed confidence and energy. Here I again quote from the diary:

Tuesday, June 18. *Since the Germans might occupy Cl-ermont any day, Mme. Salomon wanted us to move on to Bordeaux and to board ship there. She gave us letters to the Grand Rabbin and to the Hicem and provisions, and at 10 o'clock we left for the station. Another boy and little girl from Strasbourg went with us; to join their parents in Périgueux* (city in the Dordogne, along the route). *At the station there was a large crowd, and no trains were leaving. We were in despair, for we saw no possibility of getting away. Finally, at 4 p.m., a truck took us along, even though it was already chockfull. Because of the huge number of vehicles on the road, we travelled only 35 km. until 9:30 p.m. and then slept on straw in a barn.*

Wednesday, June 19. *At 3:30 in the morning we started out again and arrived in Ussel at 11. There we changed to an overcrowded freight train, and the old routine began all over again. At 10 at night we arrived in Brive, where all had to get off. The boy who was with us spoke fluent Alsatian and became friendly with two Alsatian soldiers who helped us get onto a train to Bordeaux which was meant for military personnel only, and to hide us there. I had to make believe I was Alsatian as well, and answered only curtly. Most of the time I made believe I didn't understand, so as not to give myself away.*

Thursday, June 20. *At 5 a.m. the train stopped at Péri-gueux, where the two Strasbourg children who had come with us got off. The 2 1/2 hour journey to Bordeaux took over twelve hours. Once we got there, we went straight to the Committee. The doorman received us rather gruffly, saying the* **Hicem** *was no longer there, and the Grand-Rabbin was not receiving anyone. We stood all alone in the rain, and if we hadn't had the address of the Lévy-Dreyfus family, we would* *have been really desperate. So we went there, and were very touched by the cordial reception we received from them. The son had also come home from the battlefield just two hours earlier; they had already given him up for lost. We got something warm to eat; then they let us take a bath and prepared a bed for us. We fell asleep right away.*

Friday, June 21. *We consulted what we should do, since there were no more ships leaving Bordeaux for the U.S., and the Hicem had closed down. A certain Mr. Klewansky, also a refugee, advised us to continue to Lisbon, since from there ships were still sailing. He helped us to get the Portuguese visa, which involved quite a few problems. In the afternoon we went for a walk in the city, which had been bombed two days earlier. We saw several destroyed buildings.*

Sometimes the diary is too laconic; the format of the Félix Potin calendar no doubt forced me to be so brief. Obtaining the Portuguese visas was a bit more dramatic than the entry lets on. Marshall Petain was about to sign the armistice with the Germans, and thousands were waiting on the square in front of the Portuguese consulate, desperate for visas. There seemed to be no hope of getting in. I did notice, though, that French army officers simply elbowed their way through the crowd and entered the building. I went back and reported this to Dr. Levy-Dreyfus, who promptly left the house and returned half an hour later with an army captain, who was a friend of his. The captain took our American visas and made his way into the consulate. Within less than an hour we had our transit visas. Then the doctor said: "You should leave right away, to try to cross Spain and get to Portugal. The Germans are going to be here in a few days."

There was one more problem. I was worried about running short of funds. Mme. Reiss' gold coin I kept hidden deep inside my knapsack as an iron reserve. Mme. Levy-Dreyfus had the solution. She had been the president of the Strasbourg chapter of WIZO (Women's International Zionist Organization, the European equivalent of Hadassah) and as such had been entrusted with the treasury. She now poured the bills and coins on the table from the velvet purse in which she had kept the cash and started counting. It came to 224 francs, or a bit over 50 dollars. She put it back and handed me the bulging purse. I signed a receipt for the amount, on WIZO stationery. Unless we started checking into hotels, our cash problems were solved for a while.

Saturday, June 22. *We slept late, ate a good lunch, and then the youngest son drove us to the Bayonne road, about a kilometer outside of town. He waited until a car stopped for us and took us along. We drove the 175 kilometers to Bayonne in three hours. There we were able to get on the last train to the border, thanks to our visas. In the train we met a Belgian Jewish family which was also travelling to Lisbon. They offered to look after us and were very nice. At 9 p.m. we arrived in Hendaye, 300 meters from the border, where we spent the night on a chair in a hotel lobby.*

Chapter Nine

Crossing the Spanish Border - Twice

Sunday, June 23. *In the morning from 6 to 8:30 we stood in the rain outside a military bureau, where they put a stamp on our passport so we could leave France. After the luggage went through customs we got on a train that took us to Irun* (Spanish border town). *There we had to show the Spaniards our papers, and when they saw that they contained no Spanish visa, they locked us, in spite of our protests, in a sort of cage. The Belgian family felt very sorry for us, and they gave us 100 francs. We were told we only had to go to the Spanish Consul in Hendaye, there we would get our visa and could continue our journey the following day. The fellows really sent us back to France, along with about 50 other unfortunates. There the authorities were, thank God, very nice to us. We spent the night again in the same hotel.*

Monday, June 24. *To be on the safe side, we went to the Consulate already at 6 a.m. so as to be among the first, but we were number 42. At 9 o'clock we were told that, because of the measures taken by Portugal, all visas were cancelled and no new ones would be issued. We nevertheless waited outside the Consulate and were also received 3½ hours later. The official confirmed what we had been told. We spent the whole afternoon in the rain in front of the station, until about 7 p.m. a woman drew our attention to an American van bearing the inscription: Foster Parents Plan for War Children. I applied to the man, told him our story, whereupon he said: I'll take you along to our colony. We drove to Biarritz, about 30 kilo-*

meters away, and there we were very kindly received at the Villa, ate a meal and then were each assigned a bed.

Tuesday, June 25. *There are mostly Spanish children in the colony; the staff also are Spanish, and we have trouble making ourselves understood. Biarritz is beautifully situated, has one of the best beaches in France, many luxurious hotels and elegant people. I wrote Mutti an airmail letter; the first sign of life, and asked her to send us money. The nice American consul will try to send us off with an American convoy, but first we should relax for a few days. We read, played ping-pong and went for walks.*

Wednesday, June 26. *Today we were at the Consulate; we must wait for about a week until the Americans* (repatriates) *have left, then it'll be the turn of the special cases. I don't have any idea how we will pay for the trip; when somebody asks about it, I say, "I am going to cable my parents to send me the money." In the end I believe it myself. Today we were at the beach and swam in the sea, it was wonderful. Since I don't have a bathing suit, I wore a regular pair of shorts; Lotte didn't have anything and was terribly unhappy.*

Thursday, June 27. *On one of our walks today we saw a car whiz by with a huge swastika on the hood and field-grey officers in it: the first Germans. Biarritz is in the occupied zone. Soon they were all over; they came with tanks and machine guns and motorcycles. But they were correct, paid for everything they bought and didn't do anyone any harm.*

Friday, June 28. *I spent the whole day at the beach and went home only for lunch. In the evening the Director told me he had spoken with the Consul, and we should try the following day to travel to Spain with the last American convoy.*

Saturday, June 29 ! (marked with !) *At last the longed-for day: we leave French territory for good! In the morning we leave Biarritz in a large station wagon with an American family, another man and a lady. But we were stopped on the way by the Germans, who told us that the road was closed until 4 p.m. We made it back to the colony just in time for lunch, and after a second goodbye we got started again at 3:45. At the border there were masses of Germans, women and children, Hitler Youth and B.D.M.* (Bund Deutscher Mädchen = Federation of German Girls) *who had come to make friends with the Spaniards. We got across all right. After having our papers stamped by both sides and changing money, we drove by taxi to San Sebastian, 30 minutes from the border. We slept in a small hotel.*

Sunday, June 30. *We had breakfast in the hotel: milk and very black bread, there is no other kind. Then we went sightseeing for an hour; the city is very modern. At 11:30 we boarded the train for Bilbao. The station was a one-story red shack, the train stands right at the door, old narrow-gage wooden carriages. A bearded old grandpa rang a rusty little bell, and the thing started moving. We rode for four hours through countless tunnels and the bloodiest battle fields of the Civil War; every second house is a pile of ruins. Everything gives the impression of a completely impoverished country.*

In Bilbao we went into a cafe, where we met a French-speaking man who recommended an inexpensive pension to us. The two of us have a huge room; the food is excellent, but I have no appetite as I fear that, with the bad exchange rate, the money won't last. Tomorrow I plan to cable Mutti about it.

Monday, July 1. *Today all our material worries were suddenly taken away. We went to the American consulate and spoke with a very nice man, who assured us that our tickets,* *as well as the pension and the trip to Lisbon, would b e financed by the American Red Cross. Nor do I need to cable; the Red Cross will cable the parents about our arrival. Our joy knows no bounds, and we imagine Mutti's reaction on receipt of the telegram.*

We wrote to all our French friends and acquaintances, who are less lucky than we, and to Mutti by air mail.

In these few brief diary entries our destiny was decided, one might say with hindsight. With a bit more hindsight, then, that Sabbath, June 28 was our journey's most fateful day, the date on which Lotte and I were able to cross the Spanish border, after a previous failed attempt, and leave German-occupied Europe forever. How did this come about? Was I really as nonchalant and even cold-blooded among those crowds of desperate Jews and others at the border who had reason to fear being caught in the Nazi vise, as those diary entries would have it? I don't remember what mood I was in at the time, although I do recall certain other details precisely, such as the hotel lobby where we slept, or the way the train rumbled over the little bridge separating Hendaye from Irun in Spain. I suspect that I was trying to keep up a brave front for my sister's sake, and that the writing style was kept deliberately sober and sparse, perhaps because of the limited space in the calendar. There is no doubt that the discovery of the American van was a piece of sheer luck, or the kind of lucky coincidence that from time to time seemed to push the course of my life in the right direction.

The few words I devoted to the American consul in Biarritz deserve elaboration. Following upon the driver of the van who turned us over to the children's colony, and the colony's warmhearted personnel, the consul was another essential link in the chain which made our escape possible. The pre-condition, of course, was that we had American visas in our *laissez-passer*. That gave him a basis for including us in a convoy of Americans whom the Germans had agreed could cross the border into Spain as repatriates. The U.S. at that time was not yet at war with Germany, and the Germans were also willing to guarantee safe passage for a liner that was to pick up Americans from Lisbon, Portugal. A basis, yes, but no obligation. His instructions were to arrange the border crossing for American citizens, and we were not in that category. He obviously went out of his way to help two stranded children, and not without risk to himself. Had the Germans checked and found out that he was smuggling two little German Jews across the border in the guise of Americans, there might have been unpleasant consequences. I doubt whether at the time I was completely aware of the generosity and humanity of the man's action, so contrary to the conventional image of the hard-headed consul whose first, and often only, concern is the letter of the law. Much to my regret, I did not note the consul's name in my diary, which might have enabled me to express my gratitude to him later on.

As for the children's colony in which we found refuge after the first aborted border crossing, it was operated by an American voluntary agency called Foster Parents Plan for War Children, whose purpose was to rescue child victims of the Spanish Civil War. The work was being financed by contributions from individuals who "adopted" specific children whose photograph and *curriculum vitae* they received in the mail, and to whose maintenance they contributed at the rate of $15 a month. By the time we arrived at the scene that war was over, but the colony in Biarritz was still being maintained to shelter Spanish children with no family to go home to. And after World War II broke out in full force, there was no shortage of "war children" waiting to be adopted. The Plan organization expanded, and after a while needed more staff to keep track of eligible children and maintain the connection with the foster parents. One of the new secretaries taken on by the headquarters office in New York was my sister Lotte, who by then had graduated from high school, with secretarial skills.

The first week in July brought in some ways a return to the kind of normal childhood I had almost forgotten existed. Judging by the entries in the diary, attendance at a bullfight (where the guest of honor was the German general for whom the border was closed on the day we left Biarritz) or fighting against giant waves at the beach took up most of our attention, with only an occasional thought left for Mutti and Papa or for those left behind in France. The diary entries, in that week, seem to report on events in another world:

July 2. *Today we spent the whole day at the beach with the boy from the pension and his Belgian foster mother, having taken food along with us. One has to ride more than an hour by tram, all along the port, where more than 60 ships of all nationalities were at anchor. Lotte had borrowed a bathing suit, and we had a great time in the giant waves.*

Wednesday, July 3. *We learned at the consulate, that we'll be leaving by train for Lisbon on Sunday or Monday. There we'll be able to board the Manhattan directly. Saturday I should come back with the hotel bill. We are having a good time here, only it's a bit boring. We already know the city inside out, but we have trouble making ourselves understood. The Spaniards are, thank God, friendly and pleasing people. At 10 in the evening there was a big fireworks display; altogether there seems to be no end of festivals. The day after tomorrow there is a bullfight, for which we already have reserved seats.*

On July 6, the diary notes briefly that, instead of leaving France via St. Nazaire on that day, we found ourselves in Bilbao. Although we are not yet on the ship, as we had hoped a month ago, in another four days we should be there. It was raining, and we stayed home all day, playing cards with Manuel, the boy from the pension, and reading.

The last diary entry reports:

Monday, July 8. *Since Lotte asked for it so insistently, I bought her a pajama. In the evening Mrs. Davis set her curls, and she now has a hairdo like a beauty queen.*

Mrs. Davis was the wife and mother of an American family evacuated from Paris who crossed the border together with us in the Biarritz consulate's station wagon. Throughout our stay in Spain, she and her husband treated us almost like their own children. It was my first contact with an American family, and I was enchanted by it. The casual but genuine warmth, the footing of respect and equality on which they met with children, the humor and affection which permeated relationships. There was no probing into the past or into our family background; only acceptance. If this was a foretaste of what America held in store for us newcomers, I was eager for more. Also, the contact with the American officials we encountered in Bilbao, both the Red Cross and consular personnel, opened up a new vista on the role of officialdom. It was so different from our experience in France, where such encounters often took place in an atmosphere of suspicion on one side and anxiety, if not fear, on the other. Here it was all smiles and helpfulness, making one feel that the official was there to serve the citizen, especially at a time of distress. In our case, Mr. Bain, the delegate of the American Red Cross, who had been sent especially to Bilbao to organize and assist in the departure of American expatriates via Portugal, went out of his way to ease our lot. He paid for both the hotel bill and the railroad tickets (first class, the only class available on the special train to Lisbon) for which we reimbursed Red Cross headquarters in Washington when the bill was presented to us years later. He also assured us that his colleague in Lisbon would lend us the money for the steamship tickets. But that turned out not to be necessary.

Chapter Ten

Stowaways

Manuel, the son of the owners of the Pension Baez, accompanied us to the station on the day of departure. We had become friends, and for some years to come exchanged correspondence. On the train, another member of the small group who crossed the border together in the Biarritz consulate's station wagon took a paternal interest in us. His name was Benjamin Protter, and he was a freelance journalist who had been based in Paris and was now returning to an uncertain future in his native New York. He offered to share the food he had brought along, told us a few things about American politics, and explained some of the features of the landscape we were passing through. The countryside looked withered and drought-stricken, even though it was only the beginning of summer. Everywhere there were traces of war and destruction, especially in the large cities on our route, Valladolid and Zaragoza. The trip took 30 hours, as the train made frequent and longish stops even though no passengers got off or on. Crossing into Portugal was like entering another world: smiling faces on station platforms; handsome, well cared-for houses, and many cars on the roads. Mr. Protter explained that Portugal was one of Europe's poorer countries, and yet the contrast with war-ravaged Spain was a striking one.

It was three o'clock in the morning when our train reached its destination. It had been shunted onto a special siding in Lisbon's port, and through the windows of our carriage we could see the s.s. Manhattan hulking over us, festively lit as if departing on a holiday cruise rather than on a rescue mission.

My heart leaped at the sight. She was huge! The largest vessel I had ever been on (or seen) was the excursion steamer on the Rhine river on which my parents had taken me for a trip as a birthday present.

We walked up the gangplank straight from the train; no one asked any questions. Instead, we were served sandwiches and tea, and then led to an area where public rooms had been converted into provisional dormitories. A cot with gleaming white bedding awaited each of the passengers. We were told that these were temporary accommodations until we could arrange for our tickets at the office of the U.S. Lines in the morning

We slept in our clothes as there was nowhere to undress. The next day, Mr. Protter rode into town with us. There was another Red Cross man, Mr. Brant, at the steamship company's office, ready to advance the cost of the passage to those who did not have enough funds. Signing a form with a promise to pay back was all that was needed. I recall that the cost of a third-class ticket to New York was $112. But in our case, there was a hitch. When Mr. Brant asked to see our passports, he was surprised and even upset. "You are Germans? For heaven's sake! The Manhattan was sent here to take Americans home. German citizens can't be allowed on this boat." He went out of the room and left us there, Lotte crying and I trying to console her. "Don't worry," I said. "We won't be stranded here." But this time I was not so sure. What worried me were rumors that the Germans would next occupy Spain and Portugal, and that the Manhattan was the last ship sent to take home American citizens.

Mr. Brant came back a few minutes later with more bad news. "I've spoken to the American consul," he reported. "Our government has assured the Germans that the Manhattan would only take on Americans; that's how she was given safe passage. We cannot take you along. But there'll be another ship. Go back on board, and come back here tomorrow with your things; we'll see what can be done." He wrote on a slip of Red Cross stationery: "Ernst and Lotte Stock are two little refugees traveling alone. Please let them sleep on board tonight."

Mr. Protter waited for us outside. He had figured that something was wrong. When I told him the story, he shook his head. "You are not leaving this ship," he said. "Just do as I tell you." When we got back to the Manhattan it was late afternoon. By then all the other passengers had arranged for their tickets and been assigned cabins, as well as places in a dining room. We had neither. But when we went aboard no one asked any questions, and on Protter's instructions we did not show the slip of paper to anyone .The cots had been removed from the lounges, and people sat around talking or reading papers. Departure was set for 11 the next morning.

It was Protter's plan that we should simply stay on board until the ship sailed, then show the slip and say we had planned to get off but realized too late that the ship was leaving the dock. Meanwhile, he stored our meager luggage in his cabin and fed us some sandwiches he had left over from the train and made room for us to sleep on the floor.

In the morning we sneaked out into the corridor and back into the third class lounge. Again, no one paid attention to us. Protter brought us some food from the breakfast table. We enviously looked at the menu he showed us. It was a tense wait till 11 o'clock departure time; we tried to avoid people who knew us so as not to be asked embarrassing questions. We also stayed away from the dockside railing, so as not to be spotted by the company or Red Cross people who had dealt with us. Protter was the only one who was in on our secret. The Davis family was in second class and was not likely to see us. Eleven o'clock came and went, but no sign of departure. Could the Germans have reneged on their agreement for safe passage? Lotte grew pale with nervousness. At last, close to noon, the gangplanks were pulled up, the hawsers unwound and a tugboat pulled us away from the pier. The engines started, and soon we were in the midst of the wide Tajo river, with the city receding further into the distance by the minute. Not far downstream there was the Atlantic ocean. Our mood was one of jubilation mixed with anxiety. What would happen when they discovered there were stowaways on board? Protter tried to reassure us: the ship would not turn around to take us back! But he had hardly finished the sentence when the Manhattan did stop in its tracks. A small craft, probably a police or customs cutter, pulled alongside and a man climbed up the rope ladder that was thrown down. Had they come to get us? I felt like hiding with Lotte in one of the lifeboats on the deck just behind us, but Protter held me back. We kept staring at the boat as it bobbed up and down far below. Soon the man climbed down the ladder again, the craft's motor started up and it was on its way, describing a wide arc around the Manhattan's stern, which resumed its glide toward the sea. A close call, but they obviously had not come looking for us. I could now explore the ship to my heart's content, after leaving Lotte in the lounge playing dominos with another girl.

One of my most startling discoveries – and there were many – was a door, unlocked, on one of the lower decks which led from the third class area straight to first class, without any transition. I was amazed at the opulence of the lounges there; at the wide, velvet-covered stairways, the elevators and, here and there through a half-open door, the elegant, spacious cabins. Yet the people didn't look much different than those in our part of the ship, and I wondered whether I would ever travel first class myself.

When I saw passengers enter the dining room I realized it was time to go back down to our part of the ship and consult Mr. Protter about the next move. I slipped through the secret passageway and found my way back to the third class lounge without difficulty. But Lotte wasn't there. Instead, the girl she'd been playing dominos with jumped up when she saw me coming, as though she'd been waiting for me. "Your sister got sick and threw up!" she exclaimed. "My parents wanted to take her to your cabin, but she didn't know the number. So they took her to lie down in our room. You'd better go down there!" I thanked her and turned around to look for Mr. Protter instead. Could Lotte have gotten sea-sick already? The rolling of the ship was barely noticeable.

When I told Protter what happened he decided it was time to turn ourselves in. "I would have liked to wait a bit longer till we're in the open sea, but you need a cabin of your own," he said. Then he took me to the Chief Purser's office, which was on the upper deck, close to the captain's quarters. "This boy and his sister were supposed to get off the ship this morning, but they were playing around till past sailing time," Protter told the Chief Purser. The man's weatherbeaten face was grave. He looked at me sternly. but I thought I could see a twinkle in his eye. "Tell me what happened," he turned to me. I more or less confirmed Protter's story, with a few embellishments, and showed him the slip from the Red Cross. The main thing, I told him that we had American visas, and that my mother was waiting in New York and would pay for our passage. "We'll find a cabin for you," was his verdict. "And now you better get some lunch." To Protter he said, "The whole thing is damned unpleasant for us. We had strict orders from Washington to take only American citizens."

The six days we spent on the ship made for a welcome transition from Europe to America: a preparation for life not just on another continent, but almost on a different planet. Not only geographically, but temperamentally, psychologically, and in many other ways. Once we were legitimized, shown to a cabin, and assigned to a table at the first sitting in the third-class dining room, we had suddenly left behind the sense of danger lurking around almost every corner; the feeling of being pursued by an implacable enemy that was the lot of the Jew, no matter how young, on the European continent. That feeling didn't leave us even after finding safety in Spain and then in Portugal, as we couldn't escape the apprehension that the Germans might decide to invade the Iberian peninsula and catch up with us. But once we were permitted to join the carefree life on board ship, all that was far behind. Games, sports, movies (I remember seeing "Anne of Green Gables," with Ann Sheridan in the ship's theater), but then life itself had suddenly become a kind of Hollywood movie. If the choices on the menu card we were presented with by white-jacketed waiters made up third-class dining, then what must second and first class be like?. There was also gambling: one of the friendly adults had staked me to some coins so I could try my luck with the "one-armed bandits" that tempted the passengers. Thanks to three oranges, I arrived in New York feeling rich, with a pocketful of quarters. I also learned that there was a more austere side to America: the pinball machines were covered up when the ship reached the three-mile limit.

But by the time the New York skyline and the Statue of Liberty came in sight, all our thoughts were focused on the reunion with Mutti. We had wired her from the ship about our arrival, and she was waiting for us at the pier. Would we be able to spot her among the crowd? Or she us, high up on deck along the railing? The closer the ship drew to its berth, the louder our hearts beat with excitement. And a bit of apprehension. It was just over a year and a half since we parted from her, but how much we had changed in that time! Perhaps Mutti too. Would we still get along with each other?

Since I picked her up at the Schwebers on the way to Vaucresson at the outbreak of the war, I had grown much closer to Lotte. We had been together every single day since, and the feeling of responsibility I felt for her made me take much more of an interest in her moods and emotions, little joys and suffering. She in turn had learned to talk with me, tell me what was bothering her. Still, I was glad Mutti was about to take over her rightful function again, releasing me from the responsibility.

Yes, we spotted her on the pier below even before the ship made fast; and we could see that she had tears streaming down her face. The two of us were also crying (at last!) and just waved and waved.

But there was one more hitch to overcome: we were not allowed to debark until our status was cleared up and the tickets paid for. The immigration officers who came on board decided to send us to Ellis Island , the place in New York Harbor where illegal immigrants were being detained ever since the 19th century. By the time this decision was reached it was late afternoon; the Ellis Island ferry had stopped running, so we had to spend another night on the Manhattan. When we shouted this news to Mutti, who was by now waiting all by herself on the empty pier, she was disconsolate. To be so close to her children and yet unable to hold them close! But then a little miracle happened. An official of the shipping line (or the immigration service, I don't recall which) decided that Mutti should be allowed to board the ship and spend the night with us. She was escorted up the gangway, and we fell into each other's arms at the top of it, where it meets the deck. Then we were led, all three of us, to a first-class cabin, where a white-uniformed steward saw to it that all our needs were taken care of. Even a room-service dinner was provided. True, the ship was lying at anchor and we were the only passengers on board, but I had realized my dream to sleep in first class much earlier than I could hope for.

Though the beds were soft and luxurious, none of us slept much that night. Mutti, underneath the smiles and tears of joy, looked careworn and gaunt, even more so than when we left her. In the dark, the sound of the water lapping gently against the side of the ship mingled with that of our voices.

The decision, taken by an anonymous official, to let Mutti stay with us overnight on the ship, was a humane and moving gesture, typically American. It caused us to look upon our new homeland with even more affection and hope.

About Mutti's feelings we learn from the entry into the diary in which she recorded the highlights of my life since the day I was born and which she turned over to my wife Bracha on the day of our marriage (Feb. 11, 1951): "A kindly Deity led them back to me, and the happiest night of my life was the night from 18 – 19 July which I spent on the ship Manhattan together with my found-again children. O God, how my heart was beating, it was as if I had given birth to both of them all over again." (*My translation from the German*)

The next morning my mother went to the offices of the United States Lines at One Broadway to pay for our passage, while Lotte and I were taken by ferry to Ellis Island. But our detention there was a mere formality. When mother appeared with proof that the tickets were paid for, we were no longer stowaways but legal non-quota immigrants. Our visas were stamped "Admitted" and we were free to leave. The date was July 19, 1940.

Chapter Eleven

Papa

The joy of being reunited with Mutti was mingled with sadness over the fate of my father, who remained behind in Nazi-occupied Holland. If we had known at this point that the separation would last six more years, the sadness would have turned to despair. Yet we could also count ourselves lucky: most of the Jews living in Holland when the war broke out perished in the death camps.

The pity of it was that Papa had come so close to following in the path of Mutti, who had passed through Holland in March 1940 on her way from Frankfurt to the U.S.A. But his American visa came through only a few weeks later, and so he had to see her off as she left by herself on the *Volendam* from Rotterdam for New York

Since Germany was not at war with the United States until December 1941, mail service was still functioning between the two countries and Nazi-occupied Europe (I don't know by what circuitous route). Which meant that we were able to keep in touch with Papa from America by correspondence. In the beginning, his letters were hopeful and optimistic; he rejoiced with us in our little successes and triumphs in adjusting to the new country, and also tried to play his part in his children's education by sending encouragement and fatherly advice. The three of us – Mutti, Lotte and myself – reported to him regularly on our daily routine and special experiences. All this came to an end with Pearl Harbor and the U.S. declaration of war on Germany: a letter Lotte and I wrote to Holland on December 7, 1941 came back, stamped "Undeliverable." For more than a year after that, all contact with Papa was cut off; only in 1943 did brief messages get through on forms of the Red Cross. By then Papa, in hiding, was using an assumed name, but his handwriting was clearly recognizable.

By the time the Nazis began rounding up Dutch Jews for deportation, Papa had gone underground. He disappeared from the address where he was registered with the authorities and moved in with an elderly couple in the city of Utrecht, where no one knew him. Just how he got to these remarkable people, who not only treated him like a family member and shared everything they had with him for three years, but also took a grave risk by hiding him, we learned only much later. There was a secret register of Dutch families willing to take in Jews, and Papa's hosts figured on that list. Most Jews who were thus hidden by the families on that list were saved, while of the tens of thousands of others who dutifully reported at assembly stations when their names were announced, few survived.

Papa was too restless to spend months on end hiding in his attic room at Spoorstraat 15, next to the canal. He ventured out from time to time for a breath of fresh air or to make small purchases. On one such excursion he was stopped by two Gestapo agents who asked him to accompany them to headquarters for identification. Papa did not lose his cool. He had been given his false identity papers for just such an eventuality. Flaunting them, he turned on the Gestapo men: "Aren't you ashamed of yourselves interfering with a German citizen, who came here to do business, not to be molested by the likes of you!" Looking for local Dutch Jews, the Gestapo agents were unprepared for my father's Frankfurt dialect. They believed his story and, somewhat sheepishly, let him go. He had to promise his hosts not to take any more unnecessary risks and, by staying in his hiding place, managed to escape the increasingly ruthless deportations.

Even without leaving the house, Papa led an active social life through the Kinkhorst's family and friends who came to visit. He learned to speak Dutch, and with his lively sense of humor, became a popular member of the household. In the darkest days of the war he forged some lasting friendships. Perhaps one reason he got on so well was that, from his earliest youth, my father had always had non-Jewish friends and acquaintances. But while in Germany the contact with non-Jews, no matter how close, often carried with it a slight disdain for the Jewish partner, among the Dutch there was a genuine respect for Jewish people as Jews, the people of the Book. When I called on the Kinkhorst couple on a visit from Israel many years later, I was surprised by their knowledge of Biblical Israel, and even more by their interest in its modern successor state. They could not hear enough details from me about daily life in the country; the topography, the kibbutz and the cities. It was not the expression of a naive fundamentalism, but of a much more intellect-driven faith in which the returning Jews were an indispensable instrument in the scheme of redemption. Their most fervent wish was to be able to see Israel for themselves; although ever since arthritis had forced Hendryk Kinkhorst to give up his trade as a watchmaker, they were resigned that this was not within their means.

Papa's encounter with the Gestapo was a typical manifestation of a trait in his character of which I was aware from early childhood, the kind of courage which has in it several parts of *chutzpah*. In retrospect, his refusal to leave Germany may have stemmed from the same trait of defiance rather than from meekness (he was quiet and retiring in company, never loud and assertive); he simply refused to accept the Nazi edict that there was no place for Jews in Germany. From his childhood and youth in Eberstadt, he was convinced that there *was* a rightful place for them in German society, and he would not let any brown-shirted rabble deprive him of it. One day, when I was seven or eight and was alone in the house, I gathered up enough courage myself to open the drawer in Papa's night table to see what he kept there. The most puzzling find was a small blue and yellow box labelled "Fromm's Akt" containing a set of strange-looking rubber rings, such as I had never seen before. The second, more ominous discovery was a revolver with a drum meant to hold six bullets, the like of which I had only seen in the movies. The drum appeared to be empty, but it was impossible to tell whether or not there was a bullet in the slot opposite the barrel. I preferred not to check further into it. The third item I came across in the drawer was a cudgel, or clout, of the type used by police to quell demonstrations. It was covered with leather, flexible, with a small steel ball at the end opposite the sling which served as a handle. I could imagine easily how it would be swung to land on someone's head and crack his skull. What I could not imagine was what possible use Papa had for these weapons. I obviously could not ask him at this point, as I would have to admit that I was rummaging through his drawer. But there came a time when he told me why he kept the weapons. We lived in a ground-floor flat, and one had to be prepared against intruders. I had the impression that this included the brown shirts as well; though when they did come for him on Crystal Night we no longer lived on the ground floor, and he did not make use of his weapons.

The sense of humor which helped Papa overcome such grim situations was reflected in his love of practical jokes. Mutti learned about this the hard way even before they were married. She was sometimes late for their dates, and kept him waiting at one of the round pillars for advertisements and announcements that are a feature of German cities. When he saw her approaching, he slouched to the other side of the pillar, and kept a few steps behind her as she circled around it, looking nervously at her watch. Before she gave up the wait in despair, he turned around and they bumped into each other. It cured her of her habit of being late. Many years later, well into the Nazi period, she once told him she was worried about not getting any mail from her sisters in America. Papa took an old letter, re-sealed the envelope and put it into our mailbox. Mutti found it there the next morning and, thinking it was new mail, could hardly contain her joy. But when she began reading, a puzzled look came over her face: it all seemed so familiar! Papa's face was beetle-red with suppressed laughter.

Papa and I sometimes differed about what was funny. Sex, for example, was not a subject for jokes, at least not for us children. I not only did not recognize the condoms when I opened his drawer; at age six or seven. I had only the vaguest knowledge about more elementary matters. The main source of information was an illustrated book my mother gave me about how babies are born. It was very beautiful and poetic in language, but uninformative when it came to the heart of the subject. The older boys with whom I played in the street decided one day to take advantage of my ignorance and taught me a question I was to ask my father at table: "Papa, did you fuck your wife today?" I had hardly opened my mouth when I got such a resounding slap in the face I almost fell off the chair.

This kind of physical punishment was part of every boy's upbringing in those days: I don't believe that I ever protested when my cheek burned from a slap (called *Ohrfeige,* or ear fig, in German). But rather I felt that I had it coming and rubbed my cheek quietly. There were other occasions when I deserved – and received - a fig on the ear. I recall one of them: In 1932 there were general elections and the *Helmholtz-Schule,* which was around the corner from our street, served as a polling station. The boys in my block, myself included, distributed flyers on the steps of the school, with the name of the party to vote for. I later brought some of the flyers home with me. It said Vote for List No. 8 – *National Sozialistische Deutsche Arbeiter Partei* (the Nazi Party). Even aside from being Jewish, I should have known better, because I had accompanied Papa to a mass rally of the SPD (German Socialist Party) in the *Ostpark* only a week earlier.

To conclude this chapter, I let the spotlight shift to another scene entirely. It is May 13, 1945, a few days after V-E (Victory in Europe) Day. The German forces in Holland have surrendered, as elsewhere in Europe, and a U.S. army jeep with a couple of GIs on board is driving back and forth on some Utrecht streets, near the canal. Here and there people stare at the two soldiers. With their Eisenhower jackets and round steel helmets they are the first Americans seen in this part of Holland, where only British and Canadian troops have been stationed. The two are looking for Leo Stock, but not at Spoorstraat 15, where he lives with the Kinkhorsts. No, Papa didn't write his real return address on those Red Cross messages he sent to his family, but another name and address, which the soldiers are looking for now. How did they learn about it? One of them held the Red Cross form in front of him, studying it, while the other, taller one, steered the jeep. The one with the letter was me. I saw my father sitting inside a ground floor window at the street address on the form. We stopped the jeep, and I got out. He looked at me with curiosity. He was much thinner than I remembered him. I took off the steel helmet and said, *"Papa, kennst Du mich nicht?"* (Don't you know me?)

(More about this encounter in Part II, "Becoming an American.")

A Letter to his Son, which Leo Stock wrote in Julie's Diary on Feb. 7, 1940,

(Translated from the German and abridged by Ernest Stock)

After your mother sent it to me to Rotterdam in January, I read most of the diary which she began to write on the day of your birth, for the first time. I was profoundly moved to realize that the diary, from 1933 onward, turned into a piece of living Jewish history, no less than a witness to Jewish fate!

What your dear, precious mother wrote down and collected in the diary these past few years will convey to you and others a reflection of the suffering, the pain, the sorrows and the humiliation to which we were exposed during all those years.

Dear Ernst, we are experiencing a return to the darkest Middle Ages, only more terrible in the results for us. We, meaning the Jews, are once again persecuted for our Jewishness, dispossessed, hunted down, tortured and murdered.

Your Mutti asked me to write something into your diary about my five months of exile.

My dear Ernst, in the age of technology everyone takes part in the war every hour, whether he listens to the radio in Europe, America or Australia; a few hours later the events are already overtaken by new sensations. However, the suffering and pain of the individual, as member of a family unit, is rarely mentioned in the news. Yet it is just this pain, this suffering which make of Hitler, and his war, the scourge of mankind.

Many thousands, even hundreds of thousands, lived through what I did, and worse; we were dragged from our homes and beds and torn from our families by the brown and black-shirted hoodlums. They paid no heed to the weeping and pleading of our women and children and loaded us like cattle onto the trains to the concentration camp. Many didn't see their loved ones again to this day. But even this was just another episode in the agony of the German Jews. But this event was the signal to all those who still hesitated to turn their backs on Germany. There was no time left to prepare carefully for emigration; getting out as fast as possible was the only response. That's how you children felt, too, and your mother, determined and quick-witted as she always is, went into action. So that when I returned from Buchenwald on Friday, December 9, I no longer found you at home. That was the greatest blow that Hitler dealt to me, and the greatest joy will be when I again have you with me, my dear children and dear Mutti.

After we will be reunited in good health we will gladly renounce, if necessary, much that is dear to us for the sake of living in freedom among free men.

My dear Ernst, continue being a good son, a dear brother to your sister and a helpful person, and you will also be a good Jew! May God bless you and keep you!

Rotterdam, Feb.7, 1940 Your Papa

(Three months later, Papa really lost everything in the notorious German bombing raid on Rotterdam and barely escaped with his life. E.S.)

PART TWO

Becoming an American

Chapter Twelve

Job Hunting in New York

L ooking back as I write this, some six decades later, I find that the most remarkable thing about my early experience in the United States was the speed with which I became an American. I don't mean the formal process of naturalization, which takes five years (in my case only three, because of the army service), but rather the adoption of American norms, manners, language and outlook, which went incredibly fast. I identified with the new environment uncritically, and was eager to learn as much about it as possible in the least possible time. And all this while contributing my share to our little household, which consisted of my mother, my sister Lotte and myself

The three of us spent the first few weeks after our arrival as lodgers in my aunt Bella's kindergarten. This made for a difficult situation, since our sleeping quarters had to serve as playrooms during the day. Finding an apartment of our own thus became the first priority. But this required money. The 30 cents an hour my mother earned as household help were not sufficient for the rent, which came to about $50 a month. The conclusion was clear: I had to go to work and contribute my share. I was not really upset by this. In Europe, many boys started apprenticeship at age 14, upon leaving elementary school. Continuing formal education after that age was the privilege of the well-to-do or the talented. My father had often told us how, after leaving elementary school, he had to get up at five every morning to catch the train to Frankfurt, where he was apprenticed to a wholesale food company to "learn the business." In my own generation we were prepared to go to work upon leaving Germany, rather than continuing our education. In my last year at the Frankfurt Jewish high school, the Philanthropin, I took an evening course in poster graphics at a community center to help me earn a living abroad. Then the apprenticeship with Monsieur Spehner in Strasbourg prepared me for finding a job in the field of photography.

There was one minor obstacle to my going to work immediately after arriving in New York, and that was my youth. The minimum age for leaving school was 16, and this was also the age when one could get a Social Security number, without which no employer was allowed to hire you. My 16th birthday was still some weeks away, so until then I decided to look for part-time work. Someone referred me to a bakery in the Bronx where they were looking for help. It was a short bus ride across the Harlem River from Aunt Bella's Kindergarten, our temporary home. The work was at night, when the baking was being done, and the pay $2 a shift. This might add up to S12 a week, more than grown men recently arrived from Germany were being paid at various menial jobs in Manhattan.

But my first night at the bakery was also to be my last. The place turned out to be hellishly hot.. I stripped down to the waist, and the sweat ran down my torso in torrents. There were no introductions; I was immediately handed a long stick with a board at the end to shove loaves of dough into the glowing oven, one at a time. In between, I used the same board to fish out other loaves that had been baking long enough. It meant being constantly on the alert, because if I waited too long a loaf would quickly turn a dark brown or worse, black. After an hour of this, I was exhausted and kept looking at my watch. Seven hours to go! Another hour, and my eves grew blurred. My body moved automatically, like a robot. But I was determined not to quit before the end of the eight-hour shift, both out of pride and because of the two dollars.

I found less strenuous work running errands for a pharmacy, delivering medicines in the neighborhood. The pay was only

20 cents an hour, but there were also tips which brought the average up to 30 cents or more.

In those days most prescriptions written out by a doctor were actually prepared by the pharmacist from ingredients he kept on shelves or in drawers, and it might take as long as an hour until the medication was ready. I noticed that often the pharmacist added to the time it took so as to make it appear that there was a complex and lengthy process involved.

Many customers preferred not to wait and to have the medication delivered to their home. That is where I came in. But the new job also had its drawbacks. The last thing I had expected was that in America teen-aged boys would chase after me in the street because I was a Jew, yet this is what happened! They called me a "kike" (a word I had never heard until then), and I was glad I was a good runner because I could tell they were serious about beating me up if they laid hands on me. When I told my aunt Bella about the scary incident, she muttered something about those damn Irish and told me to look for a cop if it happened again. The pharmacist thought the gang might be after me because I had invaded their turf and taken the job away from one of them. I quit shortly afterwards.

I realized that being a Jew had its downside also in America, even though in New York the problem was dealt with fairly easily: Jews circulated mostly among their own. They lived in Jewish neighborhoods, socialized in Jewish clubs and went to Jewish vacation resorts. In the case of the German Jews, the part of upper Manhattan known as Washington Heights had become their favorite residential area and was known jocularly as the Fourth Reich. I was not too happy about this self-segregation and attempted to break out of it. A few blocks north of the kindergarten on Fort Washington Avenue there was the Washington Heights YMHA (Young Men's Hebrew Association), a Jewish community center. On the sidewalk outside the building (which has since been torn down to make way for a bus terminal) teenage boys hung out on the warm summer evenings, talking animatedly. I tried to join one of the groups and take part in the conversation. Since my school days in Frankfurt I had not been in the company of boys my own age, and the prospect appealed to me. I had the advantage of speaking English fluently and without an accent, for which I had to thank the same teacher at the Philanthropin who had also taught me French. But the boys, after asking me one or two polite questions, went on with their chatter without paying attention to me.

The talk was mostly about sports, movies, and girls. I resigned myself to being left out, since I had little to contribute at this stage. My ignorance of baseball was particularly painful, and it followed me throughout my life as an American. I had simply arrived on the scene too late to play the game which every American boy learns in kindergarten, and also never caught up with the lore that surrounds it. The names of players and their teams, as well as the scores of games several seasons back, are basic items of information without which conversation is virtually impossible at that age level. There are two major leagues, the American and the National League. The playoff of the winning teams each year is called the World Series, even though the world beyond North America has not the slightest notion of what is involved. I myself was never able to share in the general excitement at World Series time, due to my inability to either play the game or master its theoretical intricacies

As for movies, I had seen American films in Frankfurt now and then, with or without parental permission. Also, I had been an ardent admirer of Shirley Temple's, even sending her a fan letter at one time to which I waited in vain for an answer. But this was not something to discuss with the boys outside the Y. On the other hand, quite close to Bella's apartment house, there was a movie theater which showed the most recent films. Loew's 175th Street covered the better part of a city block and was by far the most prominent building in the neighborhood.

The theater exuded cool air when the rest of the city was sweltering; reason enough to part with the twenty-five cents admission for the double feature. I vividly remember two of the films I saw at Loew's 175th Street that summer: the first was Charlie Chaplin's *Great Dictator*, which, having just escaped from the real dictator's clutches, I found straining too hard to be funny; and the other, *The Great Escape*, an anti-Nazi melodrama evidently designed to let the world know that Hollywood was not afraid of political themes.

Concerning my social life, I soon made contact with two of my classmates from Frankfurt who had arrived in New York a year or two earlier, Kurt David and Helmut (later Joe) Fath, and we resumed our interrupted friendship. Our families lived in different parts of the city, but this did not prevent us from getting together regularly. I never became a member of the Washington Heights "Y".

On my 16th birthday, I was entitled to a social security number, which made me legally eligible to look for a steady job. The number comes on a card somewhat smaller than a credit card (not yet in use at the time). It does not even have an identifying photo on it; only the name and number. There was no other identification anyone needed then (except for the army serial number, if you were a soldier.) Though usually forgetful and prone to losing things, I managed to hold on to that little social security card throughout my entire life.

At this moment, however, my thoughts were far from old age pensions or social security; I was first of all looking for a job, preferably one related to photography. The name "Three Lions" flashed through my mind. It was the name of the picture agency in New York to whom my photographer-teacher in Strasbourg, Monsieur Spehner, had sent a batch of his 8x10 glossy photographs from time to time, hoping that the Three Lions (derived from the German family name, Löwenherz) would manage to sell some of them to American publications.

I was the one who had put the prints in the mail. After Spehner selected those he thought would appeal to the American public, he handed them to me to wrap and take to the post office. Thus, when I walked through the door inscribed "Three Lions, Publishers" in the office building at 55 West 42nd Street, I already felt on familiar ground. And in fact, the two brothers who jointly headed the New York branch of the agency, greeted me cordially. I learned from them that the third brother, Heinz, who had been in charge of European operations out of Amsterdam, was trapped in Holland by the German invasion, like my father, and was desperately trying to get out (he never made it).

When I asked the brothers, Walter and Max, if they could help me find work with a photographer, they withdrew briefly into an adjoining room and came out to offer me a job in their office. The pay - $6 a week – was low even for one so young and so new in the country. And the work I was being asked to do could hardly be called photography, though it involved handling photographs. But I liked the idea of being connected with the publishing field, and of being initiated into the business world by people of my own background. The following day I was among the crowd of commuters in the subway on my way to work.

In the absence of television, there were a great many illustrated magazines on the newsstands. The job of supplying those magazines with photographs fell mainly to the half dozen or so picture agencies in New York, of which "Three Lions" was one. Most were in the hands of German Jews, who brought their stocks of prints and negatives with them from Europe. The newcomers quickly found their way around the editorial offices, and also maintained relations with photographers who supplied them with fresh material. The agency in turn suggested ideas for picture stories to its photographers.

To sell a cover photo to *Life* or *Look* (the two largest illustrated weeklies) was a major coup, rivaled only by a photo reportage placed in the *National Geographic*. Another important market was the rotogravure sections of the weekend papers; these would soon become my specialty. If I had stayed with the Three Lions, and the army hadn't drafted me into its ranks, I might well have become a picture salesman like my colleague Ido Forchheimer, who pounded the pavements with a briefcase full of 8 x 10 glossy prints, showing off his wares at magazine offices. Beyond that, my ambition was to become a picture editor myself. In the meantime, an older colleague, Walter Green, taught me how to write captions for the photographs, which often required some imagination.

The agency subscribed to 40 or 50 Sunday papers from all over the country, which were scanned for ideas for picture stories. These might be items about animals, or children, or unusual feats, or inventions, or out-of-the-way professions. If the story lent itself to be illustrated, a note went out to a photographer in the area, and before long another photo reportage landed on an editor's desk. One day Max had the idea of letting me take a stack of the weekend editions home to read and paying me extra cash for each item I found. Apart from the additional money I earned, those Sunday papers opened up the American heartland for me. From the *Dallas Morning News* to the *San Francisco Examiner*, from the *San Antonio Light* to the *St. Louis Post-Dispatch*, and from the *Atlanta Constitution* to the *Kansas City Star* — I carefully perused them all. And nearly 70 years later I remember their sonorous names, including some that have long since disappeared. The romance of the mastheads may not have been reflected in the papers' mundane contents, but my later fascination with journalism probably had its beginnings here.

Even though I now worked full time, my formal education was not over, unlike that of an apprentice in Europe who goes to work at 14. At the beginning of the school year, in September 1940, I enrolled at the George Washington Evening High School. I was as excited as a six-year-old entering first grade.

The classes were held in the imposing building of the George Washington High School, which was located on a promontory overlooking northern Manhattan. The evening students had the run of its spacious and well-equipped classrooms, corridors and assembly halls; only for use of the sports facilities there was not enough time. My schedule included courses in English, Economics, American History and Literature, most of it material that was quite new to me. The required reading I did partly in the subway to and from work, and partly at lunch hour on a bench in Bryant Park, across the street from the office.

One weighty tome I carried underground with me for weeks was Charles Beard's American Economic History. It was the text for a course which fascinated me not only because of its subject matter, but also because the teacher, Miss Branson, was a genuine American beauty, tall and blonde, who seemed embarrassed by the admiring way I stared at her. I had never had a female teacher before.

One of my fellow students at the evening high school was called Henry Kissinger. He lived, with his parents, quite close to us in Washington Heights and spent his days working in a brush factory. Another fellow student, Eric Lynn, also a recent immigrant from Germany, had a girl friend whose aunt was a dancing teacher. Eric took me along to one of her classes on a Sunday afternoon, and I eagerly enrolled. Somewhat to my surprise, I did rather well (I was not in the least bit musical) and even won second prize in a tango competition. Moreover, the dancing class was a good way to meet girls; in evening school there were mainly older women since most girls my age were studying full time. I still had not made contact with American youngsters, socially. All those attending Mrs. Peritz's class came from Germany. And the one girl there whom I really found to my taste was not old enough! I made a date to take her to the movies after class one Sunday afternoon, but her parents made her call it off. They decided it was too soon for her to go out with boys. I thought I saw real regret in Vera's eyes when she told me about it, but that was scant consolation. It turned out she was fifteen. But then Dotty, Eric Lynn's steady girl, was only sixteen, and *her* parents did not object. (Eric married her eventually).

A far greater calamity occurred on that Sunday, while we were learning the conga. The date was December 7, 1941, the day of the Japanese attack on Pearl Harbor. Within the week, Germany and the U.S were at war, which meant that our connection with Papa in Holland was cut off and any hope of a reunion indefinitely postponed. It was a bitter blow, and Mutti needed my support more than ever. I was now seventeen, and the thought that within a year I might be drafted into the army caused her sleepless nights. But then there was an unexpected development: In the spring of 1942 I played soccer in Central Park on Sunday mornings with a group of French-speaking youngsters whom I had met through one of my Jewish scout leaders from Strasbourg, who was now in New York. One Sunday I came home from the game with a pain in my chest, and Mutti insisted that I see a doctor. Dr. Rothschild had started an informal medical insurance scheme among the German Jews of Washington Heights; $1 a month was the premium he charged for a family to benefit from his professional services. He had hundreds of subscribers, but his clinic was never crowded. Most of his patients were a hardy lot who would consult a doctor only as a last resort. In my case, Dr. R. diagnosed a heart murmur, and he told me to stop playing soccer. Mutti, although worried about the heart, felt relieved: the murmur would surely keep me out of the army. I myself was not at all pleased; my ambition was to get back to Europe as an American soldier and look for my father.

Meanwhile I was still a civilian, working for the Three Lions by day and attending the George Washington Evening High School at night. And there was another school I attended of which there are no fond memories. A New York State law obliged boys and girls who went to work before graduating from high school to attend classes in a continuation school one morning a week The Three Lions, aware that the law applied to their new employee, insisted that I comply. I reported to a vocational school on lower Sixth Avenue and, along with a rather rough bunch of semi-literates, was taught a single subject, week after week: how to wire an electric bell. It was the only time I actually hated school, nor did I show any aptitude for the subject. And I never wired a bell again for the rest of my life.

As if to compensate, there was unexpected progress in my evening course. The New York State Education Department announced that it was ready to evaluate the records of newcomers who had attended high school abroad, and to grant equivalent credit toward the diploma. I promptly sent off my German report cards to the state capital, Albany. Not only were the grades almost all in the top category, but the subjects I had been taught in Frankfurt, from mathematics to physics and literature, must have impressed the evaluators. In due course I was notified that my German schooling counted for more than half the course credits required for the New York high school diploma.

Now I was eager to graduate as quickly as possible, so I could attend evening college and start studying towards a B.A. At George Washington a student could only take four courses a semester, but there was another school, Washington Irving Evening High, where one could take five courses at a time. I enrolled there for the following term, even though it involved a long subway ride, down to 14th Street at Union Square, and having supper at a nearby cafeteria rather than at home. It meant being on the go from 8:30 am, until 11 at night, but to graduate a semester earlier was worth the extra effort.

My grades were good enough to get me admitted to the tuition-free but highly selective City College in the spring of 1942 (again in the evening session, of course).

From the Three Lions to the Lion's Roar (MGM)

As a high school graduate and college student, I felt I was entitled to better pay from the Three Lions. When they turned down my request for a raise, I decided to quit. Looking at the Help Wanted columns in the newspapers, especially the listings by the many employment agencies, I was sure that finding another job at better pay would not be a problem. In addition to fast typing and fairly good shorthand, I now also had some actual experience to show. I began job hunting during lunch hour, without telling my employers about my plans. But then I made a startling discovery: in most of the places Jews were not wanted. This was true especially of banks and large corporations, as was explained to me with brutal frankness at some of the agencies where I filled out endless forms. They did not even bother to send me to be interviewed for the attractive-sounding positions they advertised, saying it would be a waste of time. I was glad I had not yet given the Three Lions notice of my intention to leave. Then I answered some "help wanted" ads directly, without going through the agencies, which charged a week's pay as commission. One elderly gentleman looking for a male secretary asked me to meet him at Schrafft's tea room on 57th Street. He was a writer, he said, and needed a secretary-typist. I must have made a good impression on him over tea, and he asked me to come with him to his apartment on Park Avenue. We took a taxi there, something I never did on my own.

There was a doorman who greeted him with respect, then an elevator man at the end of a long, dimly-lit lobby who took us to the 17th floor, and to an equally dark apartment. My prospective employer appeared to live there by himself. I passed the dictation test easily, and the pay he offered was tempting. But I felt uncomfortable alone with him in his study, and I said I would let him know. I was impatient for the elevator to come and take me down to the lobby, and daylight.

But the next day, while I was still pondering the pros and cons of Park Avenue, I found a message from one of the employment agencies to get in touch. There was an opening for which I was qualified. It turned out to be a job as an office boy with the New York office of one of the major movie companies, Loew's-MGM. Being Jewish was no problem here, as the motion picture business was mostly in Jewish hands. The pay was less than that offered on Park Avenue, but there was a chance for advancement. Suddenly, the movies seemed like a logical extension of my first passion, photography. I could see myself working as a film editor in Hollywood before long, after taking a course in editing which was part of the curriculum at City College.

In the meantime, the job at MGM was anything but glamorous. I was assigned to the Legal Department, which occupied the seventh floor of the 16-story Loew's State building on Times Square. My work consisted mainly of carrying manuscripts, books, plays and galley prints back and forth to the Scenario Department, on the 14th floor, or to literary agents' offices all over town. When a literary 'property' was being considered as potential movie material, the lawyers in my department went over it with a fine tooth comb to make sure that it contained no libelous or otherwise offensive material, and only after they gave their okay did the story, or novel, or play, continue on its way to the studio. If a book or story - or original screenplay - was accepted, the Legal Department negotiated and drew up the contracts with the literary agent and the writer involved. Or they drew up contracts with the actors and actresses who were being discovered and sent to Hollywood by the talent scouts. There was a lively traffic between New York and "the coast" (Hollywood) on the part of executives, producers, directors and other personnel, and I was sent to pick up their tickets at the Consolidated Railroad Ticketing Office on 47th Street. Almost no one flew by plane in those days; the higher ranking the passenger, the more luxurious the sleeper compartment he occupied for the journey. The ticket might easily be two feet long, consisting of a dozen or more stubs for the various portions of the trip and the several railway lines involved. The clerk behind the counter spoke with some mysterious party on the phone to confirm the reservations; then he filled in the stubs by hand, a procedure which could take the better part of an hour. My role in all this was that of a messenger boy, nothing more, but I nonetheless felt part of the business of America.

The highlight of the week came on Fridays, when Joan, the blonde from Bookkeeping, came around with the paychecks. Mine was one of the smallest on the floor - $14 - but still more than twice what I had earned at Three Lions. Joan carried all the checks in an open bundle, and after she handed me mine, she let me see how much others on our floor were being paid. The checks were all printed on the same yellow perforated paper, only the names and the figures varied. Thus Mr. J. Robert Rubin, the head of the Legal Department, earned $2,000 a week; Mr. William Orr. his deputy, made $1.500, and Mrs. Florence Browning, the departmental secretary, who freely walked in and out of Mr. Rubin's corner office, received a check for $250. It was common knowledge that Mr. Nicholas Schenk, who was the head of the New York operation and who sent me a personal letter when I was drafted into the army, earned much more than anyone else, but I never actually saw his pay check. Strangely enough, we office boys who made $14 or $16 a week were not at all jealous. True, we were still at the bottom of the ladder, but the way to the top was not barred to anyone. This was America.

Through the job at MGM I had a chance at a painless introduction to sex, but I chose not to take advantage of it. On the 11th floor was the Talent Department, staffed by some youngish and middle-aged men known as talent scouts. Their job was to discover young actors and actresses on and around the

Broadway stage who might be suitable for the screen; to arrange screen tests for them and then send some of them to the studio for further testing and possible acting careers. In the department's waiting room there was a large black leather couch, and it was here, so the story went, that the aspiring starlets had to pass their first test, after hours. We office boys on the 7th floor also had access to the couch, though not to the actresses. Our counterpart on the 11th floor was a girl called Betty. Betty would sometimes show up for work an hour early, and before the rest of the staff arrived would "fool around" on the casting couch with Henry, the senior office boy who was her friend. Henry, whom I remember mainly for his watery eyes, had taken a liking to me and offered to let me have Betty one morning, assuring me that she would let me "go all the way." I politely declined, mainly because I found her unattractive. But it may also have been shyness, or reluctance to show my inexperience. The initiation would have to wait until I returned to Paris as a soldier, more than two years later. The German Jewish girls I met at parties would at most play the kissing game, Spin the Bottle; and let themselves be held closely while dancing.

While waiting to be sent on errands, I read assignments for class, or the trade papers available to visitors in the reception area, such as *Variety* and the *Hollywood Reporter*. Sometimes I spent a few minutes in conversation with one of the lawyers, Jacob Weinstein, who took an interest in me. One day, when I delivered some mail to him, he asked me to stay for a chat. It was the first time since I began work at MGM that I had the feeling I was speaking with a Jew, someone to whom Jewishness mattered. This was the period when millions of Europe's Jews were being murdered by the Nazis, but at my place of work no one seemed aware of it. True, the newspapers had not yet begun to write about the mass murders. But in any event, everyone was so busy with their trivial pursuits that the events in Europe seemed far away. I can't say that I was an exception. At the City College (Evening) I was learning about the fundamentals of Freudian Psychology, and also found myself engrossed in Thomas Hardy and his tragic heroine, Tess of the D'Urbervilles. Then there was the course in film editing, which I hoped would eventually help me gain a foothold in Hollywood.

I thought I was coming nearer to that goal when I was offered a job as a typist in the Scenario Department, where I had been a frequent visitor. More important than the raise to $16 a week was the direct contact with producers and directors who dropped in from "the coast" in search of literary properties. Some of them actually found time to exchange a few words with me. Most of my work consisted of typing up the brief synopses prepared by readers in the department from advance manuscripts before the new novels or plays were published or reached the stage. Then the synopsis was itself condensed into a one-page outline of the plot and main characters, and finally that "top page" was summarized in a single sentence. The readers who did this back-breaking work, some of them failed or former writers themselves, were paid $60 a week. The two department heads, Mr. Olin H. Clark who was in charge of fiction, and Miss Julie Herne who headed the Drama Department, each earned about $250. They were the channel to the studio executives who sometimes came to visit, in search of material. I knew by then that people's importance was reflected in their salary checks, and that anyone making $250 weekly or more deserved to be taken seriously.

An unpleasant incident occurred when I let one of my new colleagues persuade me to join the labor union of which she was the representative. Alice Goodman insisted that I was not being paid enough, and that the union would fight to get me another raise once I signed up. I became a member of UOPWA (United Office and Professional Workers of America), but not for very long. Miss Herne called me into her office one day, her usual smile when she saw me giving way to a serious expression. She explained to me that the powers-that-be were very much opposed to having a union at MGM, and that joining it at this stage might jeopardize my future with the company. Alice was unhappy when I returned my membership card.

There was almost no Jewish content to my life then, except for the fact that most of the people I associated with, whether at work or at school, were fellow Jews. A minor key religious note was supplied by my grandfather, Jakob Marx, who had moved in with us after my grandmother died in October 1940. He belonged to one of' the neighborhood German-Jewish congregations, and I sometimes accompanied him to Sabbath services. The rabbi was rather young as rabbis go, with a great deal of energy. He needed it to attend to the needs of his community single-handed, as there was no other personnel in the congregation. Rabbi Koppel knew most of his elderly congregants intimately. Since he had been in the U.S. longer than most of them and spoke English fluently, he was able to help them with their problems of adjustment. These included employment and financial matters; in fact, the members of his flock admired their rabbi as much for his business acumen as for his godliness. Often it was the congregation which benefitted, as when he went into partnership with a cemetery in New Jersey to which he directed the burial business. Also, the hall where the services were held was a former movie theater, which the rabbi rented for the purpose. When the owners put the building up for sale, Rabbi Koppel launched a bond issue which he placed (in $100 denominations) among the membership. With the proceeds he was able to buy the movie theater. Later, upper Manhattan real estate rose in value, and the members were able to sell the bonds at a handsome profit. Unfortunately, the rabbi did not enjoy the fruits of his foresight; he was found murdered at the entrance to his Washington Heights apartment house. Rumor had it that some of his business partners were underworld figures.

Chapter Thirteen

Army Service

April 28, 1943, the date I was inducted into the U.S. Army, was a sad day for my mother.

As a first step, I was asked to report for a physical examination, where I would be either found fit or be rejected for medical reasons. It will be recalled that our family doctor had advised me, only a year earlier, not to engage in sports because of a heart murmur he had diagnosed. Mutti was hoping fervently that the murmur would cause me to be rejected, whereas I prayed just as fervently for acceptance. The army medical officer, after listening carefully to my heart, assured me that I was fit, and that the murmur was of no consequence.

It was an important turning point in my life. How could I, as a Jew, miss being part of the force that would fight against the Nazis and liberate Europe, I asked my mother (and myself). By the time I left for the reception camp at Fort Dix, New Jersey, ten days later, she had begun to see things my way, and I think she was even proud of her soldier son. She was prouder still when I showed up at home in uniform on a short leave before the week was out.

It was the second time in less than five years that I left home, but what a difference from that somber December morning in Frankfurt! Then as now, Mutti had to wave me goodbye without my father at her side. But now the thought that I might have a chance to look for him made the parting easier for us both.

The brief stay at Fort Dix was the first stage in the process of turning civilians into soldiers. It involved unlearning many of the habits that make up daily life in a civilized society, and learning instead a set of routines that are part of your new career in the military. You are taught to perform duties and tasks designed to keep you alive and functioning under stress, but which might well seem ridiculous and even absurd without the prior conditioning.

Fort Dix, so I reported in my first letter home, was like a city with roads and streets, except that here there were tents and barracks instead of houses, and jeeps and trucks in the place of cars. Sleeping in a tent, with all your belongings in a duffle bag under your bed and another eight men sharing the space, is the first step in the conditioning. When you wake up in the morning you are no longer the same private individual who arrived on the train the day before. Just to make sure, you send your civilian clothes home by parcel post after you are issued your uniform. The latter comes in two parts: o.d.'s (olive drab), which is for going out; and fatigues, everyday working clothes. Shoes, socks and underwear are also GI, or Government Issue; by the time the new soldier is fully clothed and equipped he has become a GI himself. He is also given an eight-digit Army Serial Number (ASN} that accompanies him wherever he goes. Meals are eaten from a metal mess kit, which is dipped in three pots of boiling water after use. "Today I worked with another boy cleaning the toilet in a warehouse," I wrote home. "It took us 1 1/2 hours, as it had to be shining."

I was thrown together with a group of men who reminded me of the electric wiring class in continuation school. Except that my fellow students then were New Yorkers, which made for relative polish, whereas my new tentmates grew up in the Pennsylvania hill country or the wilds of New Jersey and looked with suspicion on anyone from New York. They were all working class people, some of them stevedores on the docks of Hoboken or Philadelphia. Their language was rough and full of expressions foreign to me, most having to do with physical functions and excretion. They also made generous use of words the meaning of which remained unclear to me for some time to come, such as "cocksucker" and "motherfucker."

On Tuesday, May 16th, I broke a long-standing religious tradition: "Today I ate twice *trefe* (pork, in this case) I am sorry to say. For breakfast bacon and eggs, and two pork chops for lunch. They tasted quite good..." Thus my letter home. There were to be many other times. A rabbi had assured me that the dietary laws did not apply in the army, which made the whole business easier. I had always thought that I had an instinctive revulsion against the forbidden meat, but it wasn't so. As if to atone for the transgression, I went to the camp synagogue on Sabbath morning; it was a Reform service, very brief and for the most part in English.

The people who make up the rules at an army base are actually quite clever. Take this example: If you neglect to pick up your mail at the mail tent at night, it's handed to you at Appeal the next morning. But if K.P.'s are needed (Kitchen Police, the most dreaded assignment) those getting mail are the ones who are chosen. One letter equals 12 hours of kitchen duty. The purpose is to discourage you from getting mail at Fort Dix, which is a transit camp where the average stay is rather short, and forwarding mail causes complications. But it seems they want you to learn this by yourself, rather than telling you outright.

One rule you learn very quickly is "Hurry up and wait." Everything has to be done "on the double," such as getting shots and the uniform, and then you wait around, sometimes endlessly, for the next stage. There are loudspeakers all over the camp blaring forth announcements, starting with "Attention, I Company, rise and shine!" at six o'clock in the morning. "Let's go, on the double!" Still, after a few days of this, I could honestly write home that "I like the army so far." Perhaps the feeling that all decisions are made for you by someone else, relieving you of responsibility for your fate, is basically a comforting one.

No doubt the most important part of my stay at Ft. Dix was the interview for the Form 20. That was the form on which all one's educational and professional qualifications are recorded, and which accompanies the soldier when he is transferred from one unit to another. The information was elicited by a personnel specialist in a long *tête-a-tête* and entered on the form in a hole-punching code which was the most up-to-date classification system at that time. The aim of the interview – and of the form – we were told, was to help the army make the best use of our skills and qualifications. This certainly sounded promising, and it raised my hopes that on the basis of my experience in the movie business, as well as in the photographic field earlier, I might be assigned to the army's film studios in Astoria, close to home, or to the Signal Corps base at Ft. Monmouth, New Jersey, where they train combat photographers. But after another week of "hurry up and wait," my name was called over the loudspeaker one morning as part of a group of 30 men who were to leave that same afternoon for Camp Wheeler, Georgia, to start infantry basic training. The code that was punched on my form 20 to denote my future army specialty was 745, which stood for Rifleman. So that was the best they could come up with, I thought somewhat bitterly, after all the hole-punching and interviewing. Actually, the fact that my knowledge of French and German was recorded on the form, was responsible for landing me the assignment in Europe a year later which made it possible for me to look for my father in Holland. But this I had no way of knowing then. In the meantime, I found some consolation in the fact that the train which took us to Georgia was made up of Pullman sleeping cars, so that I enjoyed a pleasant 34-hour ride to what turned out to be the most arduous four months in my life.

Basic Training

If Fort Dix provided an introduction to soldiering, Camp Wheeler, which proudly styled itself the biggest infantry training camp in the world, taught the essentials of it.

At the core of the course was the use – and care – of the weapon, the M-1 Rifle in this case and later of such other basic infantry weapons as the machine gun and the mortar. The subjects were taught under calculated conditions of hardship, so that the soldier who emerged from the course was a far hardier specimen than the rookie who started it. Adding to the hardship was the oppressive temperature. I wrote to New York, "Thank God for the 10-minute breaks every hour – without them, the heat would drive us crazy."

I was proud of myself of the way I weathered these tests, and my letters home (which I found carefully preserved 38 years later, after Mutti's death) sounded a surprisingly upbeat note. Here is an excerpt from one dating from the early stage of the course:

Our platoon leader is a wonderful guy; he wants to speak to all of us individually, so as to get to know us. There are 50 men in one platoon, divided into 4 squads. Our training course is laid out according to an exact schedule, every minute is planned, and if we don't get through with something we still have to go on to the next point and try to catch up at night. This happened today, when we practiced making our field packs until 8 o'clock. The pack contains blanket, ½ tent, underwear, toilet articles, socks, mess kit, shovel, bayonet and raincoat. Then we have a gas mask and the rifle. Everything has to be in place and tightly packed, which is a lot of work. This morning we had a lecture on the wearing of the uniform, then we saw three training films, all very good. In the afternoon we learned how to take the rifle apart in order to clean it. It has about 20 parts, they all have names, and if one of them isn't in the right place the whole gun doesn't work. You have to pay strict attention, as you can imagine. Then we went to the drill field for an hour of drill.

Then we sat down in the woods for a lecture on personal hygiene by the medical officer. Then we came back and had

our teeth examined. Our training schedule for the week is post-
ed on the bulletin board, and I notice that tomorrow we'll see
more movies, pitch a tent, and go to the gas chamber to test our
masks. It's amazing how one gets used to the heat. It's much
warmer than it ever is in NY, but I work all day and it hardly
bothers me any more. We get salt tablets to make up for the salt
that leaves the body with the sweat

The movies we saw the next day were known in the army as
Mickey Mouse films; they were animated shorts whose subject
was venereal disease. AIDS was not yet known at the time, but
the army did its best to instill the fear of syphilis and gonorrhea
in its young recruits. Being shown the result of these scourges
in vivid technicolor was bound to banish any thought of wom-
en for days, if not weeks. But in case someone still succumbed
to the urge, "Mickey Mouse" demonstrated a preventive procedure called *prophylaxis* which was available wherever G.I.s
gathered. But the mechanics of it are too unpleasant to dwell
on.

There was no further mention of the films in my letters home,
but I did report on the visit to the gas chamber the next day:

Today we had four hours of lectures and visual material on
gases. We got to smell them all and can identify them; then we
were taken to a room full of tear gas, with the mask on. After a
few minutes we had to take it off, and instantly the eyes teared
and burned. This was to give us confidence in the mask. It is
the best in the world and 100% safe against all types of gas. We
have to carry it everywhere – rather awkward.

My fellow Jews in Europe were even then being led to real
gas chambers, with no masks to protect them against the dead-
ly vapors.

There was no getting away from the Jewish problem in the
army. I knew by now that anti-semitism was not confined to

Germany, but that it was endemic in Gentile society, including (though in milder form) the American one. In New York I had been little affected by it; working among Jews, living among them, going to evening high school and college with them and socializing among them. But Camp Wheeler was different. My platoon in Company D, 11th Training Battalion was composed entirely of non-Jews, except for two other Jewish soldiers and myself. Again most of the men came from areas of rural New Jersey and Pennsylvania that seemed to be specially infected by anti-Jewish feelings. I was amazed by the disdain, even contempt, in which they held the Jews as a group, even though most had probably never met one before. The fellow in the bunk next to mine, Elmer C., took a special delight in sounding outrageous, as when he calmly informed me one evening before Lights Out that he would "rather kill a Jew than a Jap any day." This was after we spent the day running our bayonets through stuffed puppets made up to look like Japanese soldiers. In the same breath, he assured me that he had nothing against me personally. "I don't agree with Hitler except for one thing," another buddy chimed in "and that's the way he took care of the Jews."

When I heard talk like that, I thought I was back in Germany again, listening to the harangue of a Hitler Youth. "The Jews owned practically all Germany, and it was about time the Germans got rid of them," Elmer would say. To argue with him, no matter how passionately I attempted it, was useless. I became exasperated at the habit, which others in the platoon shared with him, to counter all serious arguments with profanity. Whenever a dispute, or even a friendly argument, arose in the barracks, expressions so vile that I had not even suspected their existence were the common currency.

Sometimes, when I had those epithets hurled at me in response to an appeal to reason, I vowed never to speak to Elmer again. Yet I noticed all around me how men who at one moment sounded like bitter enemies, were buddies again the next. Perhaps it was my German background which made me recoil from such easy forgiveness. Still, I caught myself speaking to my neighbor again when, the day after he had launched a particularly vicious attack on the Jews, he offered me comradely advice on how to obtain a better polish on my boots.

It was the same Elmer C. who caused one of the two other Jewish men in the platoon to complain to the company commander. The rumor went around that the officer summoned Elmer to his orderly room and threatened him with disciplinary action if he continued his diatribes. From that moment on, he kept his thoughts to himself.

But as I said, there were others. One of them, John K. from South River, N.J., was as vehement in his attacks on the Jews in general as in his personal jibes at myself. Not only did he predict that, once the war ended, he and his buddies would "take care" of all the Jews in South River, but he let no day pass by without trying to needle me. I developed a hatred for this man such as I could not remember having experienced before.

Our training included a daily practice in "dirty fighting," the knowledge of which, we were told, was indispensable to the infantryman. The two opponents jumped at each other without the restraint of rules; only gouging of the eyes was prohibited. The fight lasted until one of the men tapped his hand on the ground, usually when his foe had him by the throat.

On August 6th, my birthday, there came an opportunity I had long waited for. In the line-up opposite our team, John K. glared at me. I was going to fight him! If I had fought for my life against a Japanese enemy, I would not have struggled more fiercely.

Every fiber of my being was bent on hurting and defeating him. For the first time I felt the kind of strength I had never realized was in me. The rest of the platoon circled around us; I became aware that they were rooting for me! They knew about the personal animosity which made our fight such a bitter one, but they had not expected that I would be a match for K. When they saw me put up a good fight, their sense of fair play made them cheer me on.

By the time it was over - the sergeant had finally declared the fight a draw – they came to pat me on the shoulder and shake hands with me, not only my friends but even those whom I had thought were my enemies. I suddenly felt a deep affection for them all, and for several days after the fight I was in a state of elation. Somehow K. was never the same again after that - he regarded me with a kind of distrustful respect and stopped making remarks about Jews.

I was disappointed in both of the other Jews in the platoon. Michael S. was a mature man of 35, whom the physical aspects of our training taxed severely. He was exposed to much ridicule because of his clumsiness, but for several weeks his name concealed the fact that he was Jewish. When he finally did admit to it, he became not only the object but also the cause of anti-semitism. I myself disliked the man for his lack of character: on Yom Kippur all three of us were excused from training to attend services, but Michael chose to play poker in the barracks instead. He refused to accept advice from me, a "young punk", and, although he was known as the worst soldier in the platoon, he believed quite sincerely that he was as good as the next man. All the little misfortunes that happened to him, and only to him, were mere coincidence: in his own eyes he was always the victim of circumstance. When he was the last one to fall out for formation, "somebody took my helmet,"… when he was the only one without leggings on, "I got back the wrong size from the laundry," and when he would know nothing about the mortar shell, "I was on K.P. the day we took it up." One after another, the non-coms caught on to his excuses, and when they openly showed their contempt for him, S. blamed it on anti-semitism. He was happy when the platoon sergeant, with whom he had often been at odds, was transferred to another company, but after two days he was in the same fix with the replacement. One morning, while the platoon was standing at attention, S. was still laboring to get his pack on. He couldn't seem to make it ride on his shoulders. The corporal called him out in front and asked if anyone could find anything wrong with Michael's pack. He had it on upside down!

A weaker man would have broken down under the constant ridicule, mockery, and outright animosity to which Michael S. was subjected. But he had a tough hide, and an acid tongue, and usually whoever tried to insult him drew back with burned fingers. One day, during the rest period after chow in the field, he was engaged in a violent discussion on a topic of economics, with four or five others taking the opposite view. I believe he argued that money was unnecessary. Although his position was hopeless, he would not give ground until he was entangled in a skein of illogic. To make his point, he kept raising his voice and everyone eating and resting in a wide radius was forced to listen. At this point Samuel Gouge, a sturdy farmer boy from Virginia, turned to a fellow soldier and said: "Do you blame Hitler for chasing the Jews out of Germany?"

Seymour T., the third Jew in the 1st platoon, was from Newark, 19, short, fat and not very intelligent. He was rather shy and good-natured when we first arrived at Camp Wheeler. In the course of the training cycle he lost some forty pounds, and in direct proportion to his diminishing waistline, he became more aggressive. Soon he could outdo almost everyone in the profanity that flowed from his tongue. He considered himself the close pal of Brady and Curry, two bullies who, by sheer brute force, were the self-appointed leaders of the trainees.

Seymour, so it seemed, had made a discovery. While he had been accustomed to playing a subordinate role in the social game all his life, it dawned on him now that, by associating with the powerful, some of their prestige might rub off on him.

So he kept following Brady and Curry around like a faithful puppy, trying to read their every wish from their lips before they even pronounced it. At first the two Irishmen were a little annoyed by his unsolicited attention, but soon they found that he could be of use to them. "Seymour, get me this… Seymour do that for me," they would call out in the barracks at night. Slowly Seymour worked himself into the esteem of the rest of the platoon, for who would not like to be friends with such an intimate of Brady's and Curry's?

Brady, too, did not like Jews, more as a general attitude than a specific dislike. T., on the other hand, was allergic to mention of the word Jew, and whenever Brady let off an anti-semitic tirade he discreetly disappeared. One day, while the platoon was standing at "rest" in the company street, Brady, well aware of T.'s weak spot, began teasing him. "So you're Jewish, eh Seymour?" Seymour shot back impatiently: "Why do you always have to bring that up?"

Then I asked him, "What, are you ashamed of it, Seymour?" He turned to me haughtily: "You mind your own goddamn business!"

But Brady took up the thread: "Eh Seymour, you're ashamed of it?" he asked mockingly, affecting a Jewish accent.

Once I had a fight with Seymour over some trifle, and I told him I would not let him drink again from my canteen. He always drank all his water during the first break on a hike, and then came running to me for more. He came begging to me again on a particularly hot day, and since my anger was gone, I couldn't refuse him a drink from my canteen. We became buddies again.

Nor could his underlying good nature be denied. At the end of the training cycle he was held over for a few days and hoped that he might not be sent overseas just yet. But when the movement orders did come through, Seymour T. took it bravely and with outward calm, like a good soldier.

As for Brady, he represented a type I had never encountered before. I dared call him a bully only to myself, because to speak up against him would have brought forth a torrent of threats and abuse. A dock worker from Bayonne, New Jersey, he was unable or unwilling to utter a single sentence devoid of cuss words. While at the beginning I felt only disdain for him, I gradually came to see that there was something wholesome in this boisterous Irishman; below the rough surface he had a sense of humor and a layer of decency. When Brady once helped me to my feet with a comforting word after a 10-minute break, I immediately regretted all the evil I had wished on him in the weeks past.

The plus side to being a Jew at Camp Wheeler I found in the chapel, where the Jewish chaplain had his office next to his Christian colleagues. Aside from conducting services on Friday evenings, he was available to soldiers who wanted to discuss specific problems with him. In barracks lingo, this was called getting a TS slip, where the TS stood for "Tough Shit." The implication was that the chaplain could do little more than commiserate with you, whereas actually he had real influence when it came to securing home leave for family reasons or similar matters. I never had any specific request of him, but I greatly admired the man and often stayed for a chat after the Friday evening service. I don't remember his name, but I do recall that after the war I went to visit him at his congregation in Teaneck, New Jersey. Meanwhile, he officiated at the wedding of a Jewish officer and his bride in the chapel one Sunday evening, to which the Jewish GIs were invited. The ceremony was simple yet beautiful, and the rabbi spoke movingly to the young couple. When it was over, our platoon commander, Lieutenant Rasmussen, turned to me and said, "That's some religion you've got there!"

I met the bridegroom again when I was on KP duty in the officers' mess, and I served him at table. I was a bit jealous of the way the officers were being treated like gentlemen, eating tasty food from real china and silverware, instead of chow from mess kits like the enlisted men. I thought of applying for officers' training myself at the end of the course. But I changed my mind when I found out that most of the fresh second lieutenants whom I served on porcelain dishes ended up as casualties later that summer in the Italian campaign.

While it was considered a special privilege to be doing KP in the officers' mess; most of the kitchen duty was performed in the enlisted men's mess. It meant being woken up half an hour early so as to get the mess hall ready for breakfast; the rest of the day was spent washing dishes, scraping pots, scrubbing floors and tables, and peeling potatoes. The mess sergeant insisted that all the ketchup bottles, salt and pepper shakers and whatever else was on the table (seven items in all) be lined up in perfect symmetry with those on the tables next to it, and so on up and down the entire mess hall. Two KPs used a string, like a builders' plumb line, to achieve the desired effect. If one item somewhere was out of line, there was "hell to pay" in the form of extra duty.

For the rest of the platoon, the day began at six with the sergeant's bellowing over the loudspeaker, "All right, first platoon, hit the deck!" When he was in a poetic mood, Sgt. Gondolfo might add a vulgar rhyme, such as "Drop your cocks and grab your socks!" Or else exhort us to hurry: "I want you guys to shower, shave, shit, shine and fall out with full field packs in a column of twos ten minutes from now."

One day, about half way through the course, I was told to report to battalion headquarters the next morning for an interview. All day long I wondered, "Did they decide to make use of my special talents after all?" Two field grade officers, one a major and the other a lieutenant colonel, were waiting for me. I had never been in a room alone with such brass and felt a bit flustered, but they did their best to make me feel at ease. They wanted to know about my German background. Where did I go to school, how old was I when I left, what happened to my family? Then they told me they were from the O.S.S. (Office of Strategic Services) and they were looking for volunteers to be dropped behind the German lines. What went through my mind just then was that many Germans knew how to tell Jews by their looks, and that young people were taught *Rassenkunde* ("racial science") in school, learning about the Jews' physical distinguishing marks. I recalled a particular conversation with an older boy in our street, just after he had seen my father come out of the house. I was surprised when he informed me that my father was born into a Jewish family in a rural area of Hessen, a province not far from Frankfurt. It was all true, and I asked him how he knew. He said there was something about the bone structure of my father's face which was characteristic of Jews in that area, and he had been taught to recognize it.

I told the two officers that it wouldn't take very long before someone would identify me as a Jew, and then my mission would be over. If there was any doubt, all the Germans had to do was make me drop my pants. The O.S.S. men seemed surprised, but said they understood. I went back to the rifle range.

Before the end of the course, I and a dozen other aliens undergoing basic training were naturalized as American citizens. As a rule, there was a five-year waiting period after arrival in the States, but in my case just over three years had gone by. The army speeded things up, so that no one would be sent overseas who was not a citizen. This was important in case we were taken prisoner; should the Germans find out we were not Americans they might shoot us as traitors. Whatever the reason, it was a festive day for me, and I wrote a glowing letter home about the oath I took as an American citizen before the federal judge of the Middle District of Georgia.

But an unpleasant surprise awaited me when the course was over. We were getting ready to be sent up north to embark for

England, where we would be assigned to infantry divisions in the force being built up by General Eisenhower for the invasion. Just at that time General MacArthur sent an urgent request for more troops to fight the Japanese in New Guinea, and our battalion was among those marked for shipment to the Far East. Our immediate destination now was Fort Ord, California, the staging area for the Pacific Theater of Operations (PTO), rather than Fort Meade, Maryland, where transports for the European Theater (ETO) were being staged. Fighting the Japanese was not what I had in mind, even though I understood how high this ranked on America's agenda after Pearl Harbor. But I had my own private agenda: being sent to Europe to look for my father.

We underwent a routine medical check before being shipped out, and as I stood in the line waiting for the doctor to listen to my heart, I thought of how Mutti would react if I wrote that I was being sent to the Far East. I felt my pulse racing. I remembered how, when I reported for the army medical in May, Mutti had hoped that I would be rejected because of the heart murmur our family doctor had detected a year earlier. Now the doctor dropped his stethoscope and glared at me: "Is something wrong with you, soldier? Why does your heart beat like that?" I told him about the murmur. "I'll send you to the hospital and have them take a good look at you," he decided. He looked for my name on the movement order and crossed it off.

I stayed in the post hospital for an entire week and was given all kinds of tests, from electro-cardiogram to basal metabolism. The food was good, the sheets starched white, and the nurses, first lieutenants all, gentle and competent. It was the first time I had been to a hospital since I was born, and I enjoyed the experience. In the end they found nothing wrong with me. When I came back to the barracks, it was empty. The battalion had left for California and points west. I found myself on the next shipment to Fort Meade, Maryland, with no one I knew. This time there were no Pullman cars and I sat up all day and all night, with my full field pack in the baggage net above. But I wasn't sorry. I was on my way to Europe.

Or so I thought.

Fort Meade

Soon after our group of freshly trained riflemen arrived at Fort Meade and was getting ready for shipment to England, another urgent message came from General MacArthur: he needed still more troops. The buildup for the invasion of France would have to wait while every available infantry replacement was being redirected to California. I was being put on embarkation alert and was not even allowed to leave the base for a last furlough in New York. Instead, I was told that my mother could visit and have Thanksgiving dinner with me in the company mess hall. So she took the train to Baltimore on that Thursday morning, and then a bus to Fort Meade, in the Maryland countryside. I could not keep the bad news from her; the tropical helmets and mosquito netting we had been issued earlier were laid out on everyone's bunk. She almost fainted with despair. I had a hard time consoling her, being quite unhappy myself.

Mutti's mood improved somewhat later in the day, when she was given a seat of honor at our table and, surrounded by respectful GIs, was served a turkey dinner "with all the trimmings." It reminded her of the evening on the s.s.Manhattan, when we had dinner together in the first class dining room. But when I accompanied her to the bus for the journey home, the tears started flowing again.

The next day, Friday, we were given leave after all; I made use of it to take the train to New York and bid farewell to my colleagues at Loew's-MGM. What happened next was another of those coincidences which shaped the course of my life. One of the people I came to say goodbye to was Jacob Weinstein, the lawyer whom I had befriended when I started out as an office boy in the Legal Department. He was also the only person I came across in the whole 15-story office building who seemed concerned about the fate of the Jews in Europe and took the initiative in talking with me about it.

Now Weinstein's ears perked up when he heard that I was at Fort Meade. It turned out that a friend of his from law school was a company commander there. After I let on somewhat mournfully that I was being shipped to the Far East, whereas I had hoped to look for my father in Europe, he called in his secretary: "Get me Captain Sharp at Fort Meade, Maryland." In another five minutes he was on the phone to his old friend and told him my story. "Does he know how to type?" I could hear the captain ask. "I can use a good company clerk." Weinstein assured him that I was a fast typist. "Send him to me," came the reply.

That same evening, back at the army base, I was once more taken off the list of those waiting to be shipped to California, this time by Captain Sharp. He had me reassigned to his own outfit as a member of the staff. After I turned in my tropical gear to the supply sergeant, I called Mutti. She was beside herself with joy and relief.

In the next few months, as Captain Sharp's right-hand man, I became familiar with the unit's tasks as laid down by army regulations, and how it functioned within the larger system of battalions and regiments on the base. Newly trained officers and enlisted men were constantly being attached to and reassigned from it as orders for movement overseas were prepared and transmitted up and down the chain of command. Every morning the precise complement of the unit was reported to regimental headquarters on a form called the Morning Report; there the information was consolidated and forwarded to division. I took my role in all this with the utmost seriousness, and my newly-found expertise in administration stood me in good stead later on.

By the time it was my turn to be sent overseas, in August 1944, Fort Meade had long since reverted to its accustomed role as a replacement depot for the armies in Europe. The specialty on my Form 20 was still 745 – Rifleman – but Captain Sharp had seen to it that some additional holes were punched on the card, which denoted my skills as a typist and company clerk.

Back to Europe

A few days after my 20th birthday I embarked in New York harbor for the long voyage to Scotland, after a last night at home. There were 15,000 infantry replacements on the *Ile de France*, converted from French luxury liner to American troopship. The crossing took twice as long as in peacetime, because the ship sailed a zigzag course to avoid German submarines We slept four bunks high, on E-deck under the waterline, knowing that if a torpedo hit we would not have a chance. We ate our meals at long tables standing up; the mess was open almost round the clock to serve each of the 15,000 GIs two meals a day.

I had been in the U.S. just over four years when I walked up the liner's gangplank, loaded down with full field pack and, though it was mid-August, a heavy wool overcoat. For one of the passengers the burden was too much: after we docked ten days later at a small port on Scotland's Firth of Clyde, the overweight soldier who had occupied the bunk below me dropped dead under the load as he tried to negotiate the narrow ladder off the ship. It was my first casualty of the war.

By the time the *Ile de France* arrived in Scotland, General Eisenhower's Battle for Europe had been underway for over two months. There were many casualties, and the 15,000 infantrymen the ship carried were needed to replace some of them. We travelled by train to a British army camp near Warminster, in the South of England, used by the U.S. forces as another

Replacement Depot. There we waited to be assigned to various units on the continent. In the meantime, we were issued more equipment to prepare us for our mission, such as M-1 rifles and steel helmets. The latter fitted on the plastic helmet liners we brought along and also served as a wash basin for our morning open-air toilet.

Then one day I received a movement order which once again separated me from the group I had been attached to. It looked very much like the dozens of orders with long lists of names I had myself typed up at Fort Meade, but this one applied only to myself. I was ordered to report the next day to a unit called the 30th MP CID, at still another American army camp, to which, the order read, I was now assigned. When I boarded the little train that puffed through the green and peaceful Wiltshire countryside, I had no idea that the initials stood for "Military Police Criminal Investigation Detachment." But when I reported to my new commanding officer, Lt. M., he welcomed me with a sigh of relief. He had been expecting me - or someone like me - for days, so that his unit could cross the channel and start working in France. Until my arrival, the Detachment had been complete with seven teams of two investigators each; waiting for number 15, the translator and clerk-typist (me) who was still missing. At the Replacement Depot (or Repple Depple in GI slang) thousands of Forms 20 were run through the hole-punch sorting device until the one with my name on it fell out. My days as a rifleman, having hardly begun, were now over.

My start with the new unit was not auspicious. Our orders were to proceed (in the army you always proceed, never just travel, or drive) with our jeeps to the port of Southampton. There we were to embark on an LST (Landing Ship Tanks) for Utah Beach, which was one of the two beachheads where the Normandy landings had taken place earlier that summer. Our destination was Le Havre, the headquarters of Channel Base Section, to which the 30th MP CID was attached.

The port at Southampton was about an hour's drive away from our camp. The lieutenant told me to get into jeep number eight and bring up the rear of the column.

It would have been too embarrassing for me to tell him that I didn't know how to drive. In America, every eighteen-year-old knew how to drive, just as every eight-year-old knew how to play baseball (which I also didn't know). Besides, I had seen some of the others get into their jeeps, turn the switch which started the engine and drive off. It looked easy. So I gave the lieutenant a smart salute to acknowledge that I understood the order. He got into his own vehicle, driven by a burly investigator - they were all sergeants - and was off. I got into my vehicle, confidently grasped the steering wheel and turned the switch. Nothing happened. Jeeps had no keys, and the engine should have started, but it didn't. I saw Lt. Miller's jeep disappear in a cloud of dust and became slightly panicky. But again, I was too embarrassed to ask for help. Instead, I fumbled around with the switch, looked on and under the dashboard for a starter button, got out of the jeep and lifted up the hood. I wondered whether the LST would wait or whether the other guys would drive their jeeps aboard without me.

Then there was another whirl of dust; and Lieutenant M. jumped out of his jeep. He had noticed that I wasn't following and had turned around to look for me. This time I admitted I couldn't drive. "Why didn't you tell me?" he grumbled. And then: "The first thing we do when we get to Le Havre is teach you how to drive."

And this is exactly what happened. The army headquarters was in a suburb of Le Havre called Ste. Adresse; the heart of the city having been completely leveled by American bombing raids after the Germans had used the port as a naval base. Among the rubble, devoid of traffic or any other sign of human activity, a lone U.S. army jeep was making U-turns and criss-crossing the ghostly streets. It was me, being taught how to drive.

I was already an experienced driver when I appeared in my jeep on September 28 at No.37, allée St. Cucufa in Vaucresson, the Parisian suburb where I had found refuge with the Reiss family five years earlier. When I walked into the Reiss' kitchen, David, the youngest of the four sons, recognized me. Bedlam broke loose. Somehow it seemed incredible to them that I had returned. Not just returned, but done so bathed in the glamour that went with all things American. I wrote home: "I doubt if ever royalty received a warmer and more heartfelt welcome than I did from these boys and their mother."

Willy Reiss, after being released from the French detention camp, was able to rejoin his family in the Pyrenees village where they had found refuge, only to be turned over to the Germans by the Vichy French gendarmerie. The records show that he was deported to Auschwitz – and the gas chamber – on transport No. 50 which left Drancy, outside of Paris, on March 3, 1943.

His wife and children had returned to their empty house in Vaucresson just days before my visit.

To describe the mission of the Criminal Investigation Division, I will quote from a pamphlet issued by the Orientation Branch, Information and Education Division, European Theater of Operations. On the inside front cover there is an inscription, "Passed by Censor for Mailing Home." I must have mailed the brochure home myself, since I discovered it decades later among my mother's papers. It says there:

In the wake of troops storming towards Germany there arose a horde of selfish opportunists who turned army supplies into ill-gotten gain. Petty scavengers pilfered and bartered, thus disintegrating Army lifelines.

Lawlessness spread, reaching alarming proportions. Armored columns spluttered to a gasless standstill as civilian cars drove unrestricted about Paris. (Presumably on gasoline stolen from U.S. army dumps - E.S.). *Cigarettes became scarce. In Parisian bars, a pack cost 150 to 200 francs.*

Then came a swift wedge which put fear into these treasonable racketeers. Beginning Nov. 8, 1944, picked criminal investigation agents, operating under the Theater Provost Marshal, placed the quarters and personnel of several Railway Operating Battalions under surveillance. Close watch was kept at Dreux, Valliers, Villeneuve, St. Georges, St. Cyr, Matelot Yards Versailles and the Batignolles Yards in Paris. Agents stoked locomotives, lived with the men, gathering evidence. Records of Army postal units were checked. The stage was set.

On Nov. 25, Military Police struck - CID agents, officers and men of the 709th and 787th MP Battalions. By nightfall the job was complete, the culprits apprehended.

Within approximately two months, eight officers and 235 enlisted men had netted nearly $200,000 through their traffic in essential Army goods. These merely were a few groups among many whom MP and CID agents constantly were breaking down.

The effect of the raid was immediately noticeable. Pilfering and profiteering on the French black market fell off. The weak, the susceptible, realized that MP's were ever alert.

CID Agents did more than operate in rear echelons. Suppression of crime was their interest in every locale. Though assigned to the various Armies and Headquarters, the central drive emanated from Lt. Col. James Edler, CID Chief in Paris, whose uncompromising and fixed determination to wipe out crime recognized no barriers. Rape, murder, assault, black market - Col. Edler and hundreds of trained agents hit them all, beating down crimes of violence.

A somewhat more sober picture emerges from a letter sent by General Eisenhower's headquarters to the Commanding Generals in the European Theater of Operations. It defines the

CID's mission as the "prevention, suppression and investigation of criminal acts affecting the army; recovery of lost, stolen or abandoned property, and apprehension of military personnel and civilians who have committed crimes and evaded arrest."

These documents might well give the impression that the U.S. army in Europe was so busy fighting crime within its ranks it's a wonder there was time and energy left to fight the Germans. This was obviously not the case. The vast majority of the soldiers were law-abiding and dedicated to their mission, just as they had been law-abiding citizens at home. But a few rotten apples could do a lot of damage, and the army had to have the tools to crack down on them. Further, the knowledge that there was an efficient military police, with its Criminal Investigation Division, did much to improve relations with the civilian population.

A glance at one of the reports of our detachment's activities, which I prepared twice a month for submission to the Provost Marshal (chief law enforcement officer) of Channel Base Section (of which I still have a copy in my file) shows that the majority of the investigations involved civilians as the victims. They included cases of rape, armed robbery, sale by an officer of penicillin (then still a rare drug unavailable on the civilian market), larceny of a vehicle and accidental shooting. Also housebreaking, assault and battery and illegal exchange of currency. My detailed report on the auto theft reads like a pulp detective story.

Three civilians, one of them an interpreter, came to the office with a receipt for a Packard (American-make luxury car) requisitioned in the name of General Bradley (the U.S. army commander of the European Theater of Operations). It was typed on the letterhead of the garage where it was parked: "I certify that the car is being requisitioned in the name of Gen. Omar Bradley. Signed – Richard Williams, Captain, CE (Corps of Engineers). One of our agents recalled that the man is wanted by a TPM (Theater Provost Marshal) circular for at least 100 armed robberies in France, together with M/Sgt. Mahoney (dangerous). Agent Higson went to the garage and learned from the owner that Williams' companion was to return for a jeep which had been left there when they got the car. MPs were posted at the garage and arrested Mahoney, alias Whaley. The owner of the Packard was a prominent Government official, Hayaut de Termicourt. Higson drew his pistol when Whaley entered the garage, then took him to the office for interrogation. He alleged he ignored whether Williams was real or phony, nor his whereabouts. Snotty and arrogant, he was a Chicago reform school alumnus. He was searched, and a captured German P38 pistol found on him. He confessed to some of the robberies after being shown the circular, including one at a Cherbourg priest's home, worth 200,000 francs. Mahoney gave us the address of his and Williams' apartment. We went there, and it turned out to be lavish, effeminate and luxurious; suitable for large parties. Surveillance was decided on, and four agents stayed in the apartment, with orders from the Provost Marshall to shoot if Williams resisted arrest. They covered both sides of the door with crossfire...

The bogus captain was eventually captured and incarcerated in the city jail, pending his trial. But he overpowered a guard and made his escape, until spotted by military police, who had been put on alert to be on the lookout for him. Inspector Maurice Bonheur, our liaison with the Brussels police, said he had never before come across such a resourceful and hardened criminal.

Being Jewish in the CID in Brussels in 1944 had two main consequences for me. First, it made me aware of the sub-surface anti-semitism that was present in the social stratum of which my detachment was a microcosm. And second, it exposed me to the plight of the Belgian Jewish community during the German occupation and put me into direct contact with some of the survivors.

As for the anti-semitism, I came to realize that this was not something connected with my behavior or over which I had any influence. It was simply there, and I had to come to terms with it, without letting it affect the relationship with my comrades, which was by and large friendly and even close. One day I walked into the office of the commanding officer, Lt. M., without knocking (something I shouldn't have done). I was surprised, and somewhat confused, to see that he had his Belgian girl friend on his lap, a woman he usually visited at her home in Antwerp. "What do you want, you little Jew boy?" he called out. I quickly withdrew and closed the door.

What should I have done? Shown the lieutenant that I was hurt or insulted? This might well have boomeranged, as he might have decided to get rid of me and have me reclassified as a rifleman to be sent as an infantry replacement to one of the divisions fighting not far away in the Ardennes forest. I was well aware of the privileged status I enjoyed being stationed in the Belgian capital and sleeping in a warm bed instead of in a foxhole. I bit my lips and decided to forgive him. After all, the officer was probably in a state of sexual excitement when I burst in on him. But the sound of that "little Jew boy" reverberated in my ears for a long time.

With one or two exceptions, the men in the unit all engaged in sexual peccadilloes and spoke freely about them. I was rather surprised that the married ones among them were not more discreet. The difference was that they tended to have more serious liaisons, usually with women of a somewhat higher social class. One of my colleagues, a senior police officer in a Boston suburb in civilian life, had moved into the apartment of the owner of a ladies' fashion store, both in the same building on the elegant Avenue Louise. He took me along to a party at her home one evening, and I told him I admired his judgment.

I do not want to give the impression that I was being puritanical, or holier-than-thou. But I was certainly less experienced. My initiation had come only weeks earlier, when the unit passed through Paris on the way from Le Havre to Brussels, our next base of operations. The French capital had not yet lost the festive, almost delirious mood brought on by its liberation a few weeks earlier, and the American uniform still cast its spell. I felt like roaming the streets by myself, since my buddies could not possibly share my excitement at being back in the city from which I had fled as a boy four years earlier. I walked from the Hotel de Paris, near the Opera, which had been requisitioned by the army, along the *Grands Boulevards*, until I sat down at one of the outdoor cafes to take in the scene.

It was after nine; the street was brightly lit, the café terrace crowded. Before long a young woman of about 21 or 22, dark haired and rather pretty, pointed to the empty chair next to me and asked in broken English if I minded if she joined me. I told her in fluent French that I did not. It turned out that she had been waiting for a Canadian officer but was giving up on him. He must have left town. It seemed that I made do as a substitute, perhaps because of my French. Her name was Lilo, and I soon knew her life story. She had fallen in love with a German captain in her hometown in Normandy, and when her parents disapproved, she left home and moved in with him. Then the Germans pulled back before the advancing Americans, and Lilo came to Paris to look for her lover. One day she spotted him in a long column of retreating *Wehrmacht* units and had barely time to wave goodbye. She remained in the capital, not daring to go home to her parents.

We talked some more, and then she asked me if I wanted to come with her. She took me to a small hotel in the nearby rue de Londres, where she had a room. She sensed it was the first time for me. I gave her ten dollars before I left in the morning, and we were both glad we had met.

Later in Brussels, another affair (in which I was involved only indirectly) ended unhappily. It left me feeling bad, both because a Jewish marriage broke up over it, and because I had been responsible for the introductions. Actually, the couple was only half-Jewish: the woman was a statuesque Flemish blonde called Annabelle, and I assumed that it was Henri's marriage to her which had helped him survive without being deported by the German occupiers, as were so many of his fellow Jews. I knew him ever since he had come up to me in the synagogue one Shabbat morning, and invited me home for lunch in his newly-furnished apartment. I could see he was proud of his wife and the way she prepared Jewish dishes. Before I left, they both urged me to come again and bring a friend. That is how I introduced them to H., another police officer in the unit for whom I had great respect. He had somewhat rough-hewn features, was nearly six feet tall and altogether handsome in appearance. I could see that he and Annabelle took a liking to each other, but still I was taken aback when he told me later that she had asked him to come back while her husband was away at work.

H. took up the offer, and stopped by the apartment several times a week when his duties allowed it. That was until the day Henri came home unexpectedly and found the two in bed together. Although usually a shy and considerate person, he acted resolutely in this case and threw his wife out of the house.

I spent a part of my spare time, and also some working hours, being of assistance in one way or another to Jews who had survived the Nazi occupation. Because of my contacts with the Belgian police, I was sometimes asked to intervene on behalf of Jews who were caught black-marketing or in illegal currency dealings. The intermediary was Charlie, a Jewish survivor whom we had taken on as an interpreter, as my other duties often kept me from going out on investigations. I managed to get some of the accused off the hook, and sometimes they

showed up at the office to thank me. My colleagues understood my involvement, and I never heard any criticism about
my extracurricular activities. Other Jews would ask me to help
locate relatives in the U.S., a task in which I enlisted the help of
my mother in New York. The V-mail (letters written on forms
which the army postal service microfilmed and then sent by
air) was fast and efficient at a time when civilian mail was
either non-existent or painfully slow. Often the American relatives sent packages through my APO (Army Post Office) address, which Charlie helped guide to their destination. Through
Charlie I learned many details of the fate of Brussels Jewry,
including the sad fact that some of them had been denounced
by a fellow Jew who drove with the Gestapo through the streets
and pointed out Jews so they could be arrested.

It's quite probable that in this Brussels period (which lasted
from September 44 to May 45) the psychological groundwork
was laid for my later professional involvement in the Jewish
community. I certainly derived more satisfaction from my af-
ter-hours activity on behalf of fellow Jews than I did in helping
to track down malefactors in the U.S. army.

As I said, my buddies saw nothing wrong with this and some
were even supportive. Lt. M., the commanding officer, let me
travel to Germany with one of the men assigned to a case, so I
could visit Frankfurt, my old home town. The city was eighty
per cent destroyed, and nearly empty of people. I felt strangely triumphant as I drove the U.S. army jeep through the once
proud streets now reduced to rubble and lined with ghost-like
ruins.

But the payoff for my policy of ignoring the lieutenant's offensive remark and maintaining good relations with him came
when the war in Europe ended on May 8, 1945 (VE Day),
and I saw an opportunity to look for my father in Holland. On
the map, Brussels was only a few hours' jeep ride away from
Utrecht, the Dutch city where we knew Dad had been in hiding

with a local couple. The last message Mutti had received from him through the International Red Cross (under a false name, but we recognized his handwriting) was dated October 1943, a year and a half earlier. We were not sure he was still alive. Now I asked the lieutenant for permission to look for him. He not only granted it readily, but assigned my buddy, Sgt. Herb Cannon, to drive up to Holland with me in his jeep. The lieutenant also gave me permission to draw all kinds of provisions from the mess, both for sustenance on the way and as gifts for my father.

It took us more than 24 hours to reach our destination. Bridges across rivers and canals on the way were destroyed, and we had to find alternate routes. In Utrecht people stared at us with some surprise, as we were the first U.S. personnel to be seen in an area assigned to the British and Canadian armies. I used my investigative skills to locate Dad's current abode, checking out the cover addresses he had used on his Red Cross letters to America. Then I spotted him sitting behind a ground floor window at Weerdsingel 63, watching Herb park the jeep. He saw me climbing out and staring at him. *"Kennst Du mich nicht?"* I called up to him (Don't you know me?) The GI helmet I wore must have confused him. *"Nein, ich kenn Dich nicht,"* came the reply from the window. (No, I don't know you.) Then me: *"Ich bin Dein Sohn, Ernst!"*

The next few minutes are blurred in my memory. Herb, my tall, strong, policeman-buddy later said he was wiping off tears himself.

Papa had to wait for more than a year longer, until the U.S. consular bureaucracy was back on track and ready to issue him an immigration visa in place of the one which had long since expired. He arrived in the U.S. in June 1946 and lived there for another thirty-three years. This is the letter he wrote to Mutti and Lotte (and to my grandfather, who stayed with them) describing our reunion: *(my translation from the German)*:

May 13, 1945

My dearest, dearest Julie, dear Lottchen, and all dear ones, especially Opa!

*It is a long time ago that Heinrich Hirsch [the murdered brother-in-law] said to me, "There are no **Nissim** (miracles)!" Oh how wrong he was! Today I lived through a miracle! Unexpected, sensational, dramatic! Like an appearance from another world an American soldier comes driving up (the first one I got to see in this war) and called out: "Don't you know me?" No, I didn't know him. And yet! It was he, my boy, one of the three human beings around whom my thoughts revolved in the daytime and my dreams by night; one of the three who lent me the strength and the energy to live through the past few years. But this must not turn into a letter of lament either for myself or the fate of millions of others. Joy, gratitude, happiness – let us now feel nothing else. Let us forget the past for a bit and look forward to the happier days that lie ahead of us. You want to ask a thousand questions, I know! There will be lovely hours together in which to schmuss and to tell. For today only the following:*

Ernst will confirm to you, that I've remained the same in every respect.

Healthy, not having been sick for even a day, well dressed and well nourished (not having suffered hunger), never lost my nerves, and in spite of many excitements only today had the first sleepless night! Talked and talked until two in the morning and then I couldn't sleep for joy. Then I read your wonderful letter for the nth time and many of your letters to Ernst. Oh, what an amazing person you are, what a proud mother, in love with your children. And I had to leave all the care, all the joys and all the happiness over the children to you alone, during all those terribly long years! How I envy you and how I feel sorry for you, because I know that my absence was like an open wound for you during those years. But now this wound will heal, and never shall any power on earth keep us apart for even a single day! As it's written in the Bible: seven (long, long) years did I serve for you. But the prize which awaited me was worth the endurance. I never longed for you as much as on this day, and never did a man love his wife as much as I do the mother of my wonderful children, my dear, dear Julchen

About a month after the dramatic encounter in Utrecht, my unit left Brussels for a transit camp in the south of France, "Camp Brooklyn," near Marseille. There we awaited trans-shipment to the Pacific as part of the planned invasion of Japan. This time I had no objection, since both the public and private missions which made me prefer Europe over the Far East as my personal "theater of operations" had been accomplished. The war against Hitler had been won, and I had found my father.

On August 6, 1945, my 21st birthday, the atomic bomb was dropped on Hiroshima and a few days later Japan surrendered. Our unit had been on alert to board the s.s. John Ericsson at Marseille for the long voyage East, but then the orders were changed: the ship sailed for New York.

The Ericsson was in mid-Atlantic when the calendar showed it was *Rosh Hashana*, the Jewish New Year, which fell unusually early that year. There were dozens of Jewish soldiers on board, but no rabbi to conduct the services. Much to our surprise, a Protestant chaplain turned up to deliver the sermon, after a knowledgeable Jewish GI had volunteered to lead the prayers in the small chapel that had been turned into a makeshift synagogue. The chaplain dwelled on our common Judeo-Christian heritage, citing copiously from the Hebrew Bible.

The army had come up with a rather complex point system to determine the order in which servicemen would be discharged; and much time on the ship was spent figuring out where we stood on the scale. Each month in the service was worth a point; the award of battle stars and other decorations was given due weight, and family status also played a part. Those with less than 50 points to their credit had to stay in longer. This included me and one or two others in the unit; after two weeks' home leave we had to report to the 4th CI Detachment at Fort Sam Houston, Texas, just outside of San Antonio. Our commanding officer being up for discharge, he was replaced by Capt. H. before the unit embarked from Marseille. H. was a dashing paratroop officer whom I remember mainly for his two passions: 1) shining his brown boots to a brilliant polish and 2) army nurses. He pulled every possible string to have himself assigned to a cabin close to a returning nurses' unit on the ship's deck reserved for officers.

"Nothing of Interest to Report"
On November 11, I wrote in a letter home from Texas that

There is absolutely nothing of interest to report from here… tomorrow we'll have to turn all our equipment in, and the unit will be deactivated in the next few days. I may have to write a unit history yet for the War Department files. Every outfit should keep one, but we never did. We are attached to an MP Battalion for rations, quarters and administration. They have been in the States all the time, and think we're quite the boys with our one battle star on the ETO (European Theater of Operations) ribbon.

Imagine that I got a big bundle of mail sent here from Marseille, among them a lot of letters from Belgium (apparently from some of the Brussels Jews I had befriended*). I had to forward the mail to all those who were discharged, and had quite a problem with the letters from the various girl friends in Europe of the boys who are married. Of course I can't send them straight to their house, the wife might open them. Some of the mail clerks in the other sections just tear 'em up, but I have too much pity with the poor gals over there who cry their* *hearts out over their lovers they never hear from again, to do that. Yes, it's quite a problem. My friend Higson's wife is divorcing him; she found out he had a baby in England, so he's re-enlisting in the army....*

Apart from getting to know another, picturesque part of the country, I also encountered a new type of anti-semitism in San Antonio, peculiar to the fundamentalist Deep South. Picking up my dress uniform from the cleaner's one day, I had a minor argument with the owner about the price. "Don't try to jew me out of my money," he said. One of the men from my old unit, who was with me in the store, tried to reassure me. "It doesn't mean anything," he said. "That's just the way he talks. He doesn't even know you are Jewish."

With the other men in the new unit, relations remained somewhat distant; I was now the only Jew in the outfit, and no one talked about it. But the issue did come up when I declined to join the group as they prepared to go to midnight mass on Christmas Eve. One of the men, John, asked me what religion I was. They all seemed a bit surprised when I said I was Jewish. John said, "You certainly don't have any Jewish features." Then he added, "Your name's Jewish, though." I said, "Not necessarily. There were sixty Stocks listed in the phone book in the town where I came from, and we were the only Jewish ones."

Another soldier whom everyone called the Mink looked at me and said, "So you're a German Jew. They're pretty smart people." Then he added, "Well, you're not a Coney Island Jew anyway."

I asked, "Is that good?" and he said, "Yes. They're pigs."

I must have gotten a little red in the face then and was trying to keep my voice from quivering when I said, "I've known a lot of goddam Irishmen too that were pigs." John intervened: "Cut it out fellows, this is supposed to be Christmas Eve!"

A few minutes later John said, "I guess the Jewish people get kicked around quite a bit in this country." He must have mulled the thing over in his mind, and still couldn't get over the idea that I was Jewish. "They get kicked around just about every place they go," I said. And then I added, "Just like any minority."

"Minority bullshit," the Mink said. "A lot of it is their fault, too."

John tried to mediate: "Well, it's just like everything else. They all have to suffer for the few that make themselves obnoxious." Then he began telling a story about a first sergeant in an outfit he had been in by the name of Rosenberg, and how he put two guys on KP duty once as a gig for something or other. One of the two, a six-foot two Irishman by name of Cobb, said to the other one, "Why that goddam Jew bastard!" So this other boy turned around – his name was Greenberg – and said, "I'm a Jew myself." John said, "That made old Cobb shut up." Then John went on about all the Jewish pals he used to have in school.

There was little investigative work to be done, and I had lots of spare time at Fort Sam Houston. Part of it I spent in the post library, eagerly following the daily accounts in the New York Times of the Nuremberg War Crimes trials of the Nazi leadership, which were just then getting underway. The gruesome details of the murders of millions of Jews were coming to light, and I was deeply shaken. But the story received little attention in the local paper, The San Antonio Light, and all around me on the army post none at all. It was as if I had to bear a terrible burden all by myself.

The U.S. government expressed the nation's gratitude to the men who had fought in the war by having Congress pass the GI Bill of Rights, which enabled ex-soldiers to attend college at government expense. The bill, which was passed into law at about this time, provided for one month's tuition and maintenance expense for each month in the service. I decided I would take advantage of this generous offer and go back to study full time, nearly eight years after leaving school in Germany.

One day I saw an announcement that the army was administering a test which the colleges and universities would recognize in considering applications by war veterans. The problem was that the location for taking the exam was Governors Island, an army post off the tip of Manhattan. My new C.O., Captain H., was sympathetic to the idea of my taking the test and helped me get a ride on an air force transport leaving Love Field, Dallas, for New York. By Texas standards, the field was not far away from our post; it took me eight hours' hitch-hiking to get there.

The plane was an ancient DC-3, making many stops on the way, but I arrived at my destination in time. The examination took an entire day. I don't remember the questions, but when I got the result, some time after my discharge in January, the score was very high. High enough to get me admitted to Princeton University as of the spring semester, 1946.

Chapter Fourteen

On the GI Bill at Princeton

Shortly before being discharged from the army on January 13, 1946, I received the letter of acceptance from Princeton. I had completed the equivalent of freshman year at the City College (Evening Session) in New York before being drafted. But with Mutti now earning her living selling life insurance, Lotte working as a secretary, and my father expected to arrive soon in the U.S., there was no need for me any longer to help support the family. I could afford the luxury of full-time study. Especially since the GI Bill of Rights recently passed by Congress called for the government to pay for tuition (plus living expenses) at the college of one's choice, so I saw no need to return to the tuition-free City College. In fairness I must admit that, in my last year as a civilian, I greatly enjoyed being a student at its evening session. The faculty was excellent; some of the subjects I studied, such as Psychology and English Literature, were entirely new to me, and the grades I earned boosted my self-esteem. I was especially proud of the "A" in English composition. There was even time for extra-curricular activity: I wrote for the student newspaper, *Main Events*, and joined the staff of a literary magazine, *Pulse,* which circulated in all four municipal colleges. In looking at an old copy recently, I was surprised to see myself listed as Associate Editor. In addition to short stories, my contributions included movie and theater reviews (the latter based on the free tickets I received from the MGM Drama Department).

The *Pulse* editorial board met on Sunday afternoons at the home of Ray Fuller, the editor, who showed a warm friendship for me. So did two of his associates, Beatrice Hopp and Ruth Popofsky; I later corresponded regularly with all three while I was in the army. I felt very much at home with these young Jewish intellectuals; I liked their seriousness when it came to the work at hand, and their light-hearted banter in other matters. One of the men asked me if I was interested in joining a discussion group he belonged to. To get there, I took the subway into deepest Brooklyn, on a BMT line I had never been on before. Soon I found myself in a room full of people arguing passionately about things that were way over my head. I realized I had much to learn to hold my own among this sort of group; later I suspected they might have been Marxists or Communists, but I couldn't be sure.

It was a world I left behind and exchanged for a far different and unfamiliar one when I became a soldier. Then, after discharge and a brief interval at home, I entered still another, unfamiliar world when I embarked on my sophomore year at Princeton. At the time I applied for admission, I was not really aware that this was not just another undergraduate college reputed for its academic excellence, but also a kind of high-level playground for the youth of the WASP (White Anglo-Saxon Protestant) elite. Jews were a small minority among those enrolled (140 out of 3,000) at the time I arrived on the campus, or about five percent. Negroes (as black Americans were called then) were absent altogether, except for three young men who were holdovers from a wartime Navy program on campus. Jewish faculty members could be counted on the fingers of one hand.

But I was lucky in my timing: in the postwar era, admissions at Princeton became more liberal and inclusive. The GI Bill of Rights prompted applications by army veterans who would not normally have applied (myself among them), and the new class entering in 1946 was more mature and variegated in its composition than its predecessors. Still, I was surprised to find that only 40 per cent of the student body were graduates of public high schools; the rest were products of "prep" (preparatory) schools, meaning private secondary, mostly boarding schools located on picturesque rural campuses with much emphasis on competitive sports. The high tuition fees pretty much limited the student bodies to the sons of the elite; with the benefit of small classes and excellent teaching staff they were much better prepared for the demands of the prestige colleges than your average high school graduate.

In spite of the changes wrought by the war, this group still set the style and spirit of life on the campus. Its main characteristic, as I recall it, was a great deal of self-assurance, such as one rarely encounters in people so young. It was entirely different from my experience at City College, where the students tended to be full of uncertainty, about themselves, about society and their place in it, and about politics at home and abroad. In the army too, uncertainty was almost built in. The individual could never be sure what the next day would bring; "orders" issued somewhere along the chain of command could determine his fate or that of his unit.

Part of the self-confidence I felt around me at Princeton may have derived from the very fact of having been accepted into that exclusive community; but another part was no doubt due to belonging to an elite, and to awareness of wealth in the family which obviated any worries about the future. There was no pressure or urgency about grades: a "Gentleman's C" in a course was quite adequate, leaving time for sports and other extracurricular activities. It also made for a relaxed atmosphere in the classroom, and for an easygoing relationship with most teachers. Most courses consisted of lectures and "preceptorials," in which small groups of students met once or twice a week with a "preceptor" (junior faculty member) to discuss the assigned reading in an informal manner. There was no faculty presence at exams: instead, there was the honor system. To his answers, the student added and signed this statement: "I pledge my honor as a gentleman that, during this examination, I have neither given nor received assistance." The system appeared to work – there were very few reports of violations. Anyone found cheating was suspended immediately. I was permitted to use my portable typewriter and typed away all by myself in an empty classroom

Students who studied hard for superior grades were known, disparagingly, as "grinds." It appeared that a disproportionate number of the Jewish students were in this category.

Princeton was essentially a liberal arts college; the "University" in the name merely indicated that there was also a graduate school granting M.A. and Ph.D. degrees. The same faculty taught both graduate and undergraduate courses. There were no professional schools such as law, medicine or business, except for engineering and architecture. The idea was to produce a well-rounded, educated individual, leaving specialized training for later. Students could choose from a broad range of courses in the humanities, the exact sciences and social sciences; as upperclassmen (junior and senior years), they were expected to concentrate on a particular area, such as economics or romance languages, but not to the exclusion of other subjects. Every student had to submit a senior thesis in his major area of interest; an unusual requirement for the B.A. degree which provided valuable experience in library research, and often in field research as well.

Once again, I managed to fit into this new and unaccustomed environment with remarkable ease. I took courses in subjects that were entirely new to me, such as American Colonial History and 18th Century English Literature, Northern Renaissance Art and Classical Greek Drama, and in others that built on and expanded some of the basic knowledge I had acquired years earlier at the *Philanthropin*. Among these were French and German literature, taught by Professors Ira Wade and Bernard

Ulmer respectively, both of them outstanding authorities and fine teachers. I found that German lyric poetry, some of which I had learned by heart as a boy, still had a power to move me which neither the English nor the French poets I now studied could match. Prof. Ulmer tried to get me to consider teaching German literature as a career, but I had to tell him that in light of the recent past I couldn't see immersing myself in German culture. He understood.

Professor Robert Friend, the soft-spoken scholar who taught a course on Northern Renaissance art, made us understand how the philosophical and religious ideas of the age influenced its plastic artists. The reading in the course included such texts as Thomas Aquinas and Thomas à Kempis' *Imitation of Christ*, as background to the paintings. An essay I wrote on "Peace and Consciousness" (reflected in the works of art) earned me an A for the course.

Another subject that intrigued me was Linguistics, taught by Professor Harold Bender. This was before the theories of Noam Chomski began to dominate the field, and we spent a good part of the course on the Indo-European origins of modern European languages. I felt in my element, and thought for a while of choosing this field for my concentration. But then something happened that dissuaded me. A student in the class, Irish by origin and already an expert in Gaelic, produced a term paper whose subject was Yiddish words that had penetrated American-English vernacular. He had found about 200 of them. It was so thorough a piece of work that Professor Bender decided to read parts of it in class. It also made me realize that this young Irishman was far more talented a linguistic scholar than I would ever be, and that it would be irrational to specialize in a field in which I was not even the best student in the class. Altogether, the Princeton experience provided a healthy antidote to the temptation of intellectual arrogance; I came to realize that there were quite a few people around who were much smarter than I was.

Sex after Six

Princeton was an all-male campus at the time (it has long since followed the mainstream and gone co-educational) which had both its pluses and minuses. On the plus side, there was more time for study and other serious (or less serious) pursuits; the emotional investment in relationships with the opposite sex could find other outlets. The minus side is quite obvious: such relationships are a normal part of adolescent development, and their enforced absence is frustrating. The university tried to partially offset this by opening the campus to female visitors during one weekend in May. The result (for me at least) was a frantic search for the right girl to invite; arranging for accommodations, and for feeding and entertaining. Members of the eating clubs were able to invite their guests for "houseparty weekend" at their club, featuring dining, drinking, dancing and merry-making. There was no relaxation of the rule against female visitors in the dormitories after 6 p.m., which prompted the *Daily Princetonian* to engage in a vigorous but unsuccessful campaign on behalf of what it called "Sex after Six."

I must admit that I was not very lucky during my student days when it came to women. I first met C. at a party in New York shortly before enrolling at Princeton, and I promptly fell in love with her. She was petite, dark-haired, with an expressive face and an impish sense of humor, and she seemed to take a liking to me. After our first date, she invited me to her house. Her parents were not at home; she sat down at the piano and played the Moonlight Sonata for me. I'm not very musical, but her playing made me giddy. We parted with a chaste kiss, and I went home with my head in the clouds. She was about to return to her campus in the Midwest, where she was in her senior year, and we agreed to correspond. In my first letter I confessed how I felt about her, but her reply, when it finally came, was far from ardent. She told me all about a visit to Maxwell Street, the Jewish section of Chicago; very little about herself, or about the two of us. To my next letter there was no reply. Every additional day without mail deepened my despair. I began making inquiries about flights from Newark to Chicago, to drop in on her unannounced. Only my heavy reading list and course schedule kept me from going through with these travel plans. Slowly, the pain subsided.

In June, I attended my sister Lotte's graduation from George Washington High School. The ceremony took place in the open, and I spotted C. sitting with her parents two rows ahead of us. Her sister was in the same graduating class. I went up to C. after it was over and, in a somewhat shaky voice, asked her what happened. While we were walking to the exit, a few steps ahead of our two families, she told me the story. All her friends were becoming engaged in their senior year, and this put a great deal of pressure on her to do likewise. She said she had no way of knowing if I was really serious, and so she accepted the proposal of one of the men in her class. They were to be married in the fall.

There was a postscript: A few years later, while enrolled at Columbia University, I attended a lecture at the Jewish Students' Club. C. was in the audience. I went up to her to say hello, and she told me she was divorced. For old time's sake, I took her to lunch the next day, but the magic was gone.

Meanwhile, back at Princeton, there was the question of whom to invite for house party weekend. In the summer of '46 I had walked into the office of the American Committee of OSE *(Œuvre de Secours aux Enfants)*, the French Jewish child care agency which had been the home base of Mme. Andrée Salomon who had been so helpful to Lotte and me at our arrival in France. Andrée had written to me, asking me to meet with Dr. Leon Wollman, the director of OSE's New York office, to see if, on the basis of my first-hand experience with the OSE's work, I could be of help in their fundraising. On my visit to his office I met A., who as Dr. Wollman's secretary, sat in on the meeting. She had a fluent command of French, which I found remarkable considering that she had never been to France but had learned it all at Brooklyn College. She in turn was fascinated by my European background, and on the basis of our mutual admiration a friendship developed. Aside from our common love of French, we also shared a secret. The OSE's main source of support in the U.S. was among Yiddish-speaking immigrants from Eastern Europe, where the organization had once been active and popular. Dr. Wollman made fund-raising speeches in Yiddish to their organizations (*Landsmannschaften)* and also employed an experienced journalist, V., to write articles for the Yiddish press. He was a short, rotund man in his fifties, with a perpetual twinkle in his eyes and an inexhaustible fund of Yiddish stories. One day he failed to show up for work, and the next morning Dr. Wollman was shocked to see his obituary in the Yiddish daily, the *Forward.* Later that day A., who was friendly with V's wife, drew me aside and made me promise not to tell the secret to anyone: our journalist had paid a visit after work to a lady who lived on Central Park; he took a bath in her apartment before going home and succumbed to a heart attack in the bathtub.

I invited A. to house party weekend at my club. She proved smart and sophisticated enough to justify my decision, but I realized that her Jewish looks and ever-so-slight Brooklyn accent made her stand out a bit among the bevy of Smith, Vassar and Wellesley girls who were guests at the club that weekend. Perhaps A. was conscious of this as well; at any rate, I felt a certain coolness when I took her to my room for a rest (before six). But the real reason for the distance that seemed to have come between us was elsewhere. She phoned me later in the week to tell me that she had become engaged.

This time the pain was less than it had been a year earlier. It was more like resentment, or hurt pride. Also a relief of sorts: not having a girl friend cleared my mind for my studies. I did a vast amount of reading in the mere two and a half years I spent at Princeton; if it weren't for the fact that I still possess brief summaries of some forty major works I ingested, I would find it hard to credit the sheer quantity. In addition, I devoted several evenings a week to my duties as co-managing editor of the *Princetonian,* with frequent late-night sessions at the press, putting the paper to bed. When the lone linotype operator was too busy with other duties, I would sit down at the machine myself to make the needed corrections in the columns of leaden type.

My work on the *Prince* gave me a certain status on campus, and it steered me in the direction of journalism as a choice of career. It also helped me get accepted by Prospect, one of the eating clubs where upperclassmen (juniors and seniors) took their meals in a convivial atmosphere. Prospect was different from the dozen or so other clubs in that it was run on a cooperative basis, with the members taking turns waiting on tables and washing dishes in the place of hired help (which substantially reduced the membership fee). Prospect also practiced a more liberal admissions policy (meaning it did not discriminate against Jews, as did most of the other clubs). Still, my club took part in the notorious "bicker" process, in which applicants for membership were subject to thorough scrutiny and often turned down as unsuitable. The most humiliating scenario was when a hapless candidate waited all evening in his room for the bicker committee to show up, but it never came.

Jewish Affairs

I became involved in Jewish affairs on the campus not long after my arrival. The University obliged all the undergraduates to attend chapel services twice a month; probably a holdover from Princeton's early days as a theological seminary. The service was "non-denominational," but nonetheless unmistakably Christian. Jewish students had the alternative of attending the town's only synagogue, where the service was orthodox and, to most of the young men, all but unintelligible. I went there one Sabbath morning and came away unimpressed. The chapel service, with its hymn singing and choir, at least offered the Jewish students an esthetic, if not a religious experience. But I decided to explore the possibility of holding Jewish services on the campus, which would earn chapel credit. When I approached the Associate Dean of the Chapel with the idea, he was enthusiastic and offered his support and encouragement. The first step was to organize a group that would sponsor the services. Together with three or four Jewish fellow students we founded SHA, the Student Hebrew Association, and I was later asked to serve as its chairman. The name was chosen as a counterpart to SCA, the Student Christian Association, and as such it implied conformity with campus norms and traditions. We received official university recognition as a religious group, and were assigned a spacious room in Murray-Dodge Hall, the student center, in which to conduct services.

But there was opposition on the part of quite a few of the Jewish students. They simply did not want to have a Jewish group officially representing them on the campus. Apparently they thought it was better to downplay their Jewishness; to cope with it as individuals if necessary, rather than as members of an organized body. It seemed that about a third of the 140 or so students who were registered as Jews (whose names were supplied to the SHA by the university) made up this group; they included some of those prominent in sports and other extracurricular activities. There were also quite a few Jews who had written "no religion" on their application forms, and these did not even bother to protest the initiative.

There remained the question of who would conduct the services. I was familiar with the work of the B'nai B'rith Hillel Foundations among Jewish students on campuses, and I contacted their New York headquarters to see if they were willing to help. It turned out that at Hillel they were not only willing but positively eager to gain a foothold on the prestigious Princeton campus. They offered to send us one of their senior staff on Friday evenings, both to conduct services and to engage the students in discussions. The two associate national Hillel directors, Rabbi Arthur Lelyveld and Dr. Judah Shapiro, who made the trip from New York on alternate Fridays, were both well suited for the assignment. Lelyveld was a young reform rabbi, earnest and eloquent, and well versed in the liturgy. Dr. Shapiro was a sociologist by training, scholarly yet passionate about his Jewishness. Their presence made the weekly services attractive even to students who showed up mainly to earn their chapel credits.

These informal but highly satisfying arrangements came to an end after Rabbi Lelyveld was appointed the National Hillel Director, to succeed Dr. Abram Sachar when the latter became president of Brandeis University, and Dr. Judah Shapiro left his Hillel post soon afterward.

On alternate Fridays, I invited outside personalities to meet with the Jewish students. One of them was Ludwig Lewisohn, then a popular Jewish writer (now all but forgotten) whose novels dealt with problems of Jewish identity in post-World War I America. Another was Rabbi Stephen Wise, a foremost Zionist leader and a fiery orator. At the time the "Palestine problem" was before the United Nations, and he agreed to address a campus-wide audience that eventually filled one of the largest lecture halls to overflowing. Although his wife was gravely ill at the time, he kept his date at Princeton because, he told his listeners, he "had been waiting for this invitation for 2,000 years."

But the biggest star of all lived just off the campus, at 112 Mercer Street. Albert Einstein accepted my invitation to join us on a Friday night, on condition that it was an informal meeting, without prior publicity. When I came to pick him up, he was wearing slippers and an old threadbare sweater, and I was ready to keep the car waiting while he changed. But no, he left the house with me just the way he was dressed. In the encounter with the students he was as informal as his attire; and they responded in the same vein. Informality was the keynote; not even a slight sense of awe at being in the presence of one of the world's towering personalities. I remember that a student asked him whether he believed in God, and he replied that he believed in the logical simplicity of the universe. He responded to all the questions good-naturedly, but when I took him back to his house, I began to feel that the students had overdone the informality and failed to show him the called-for respect. I wrote him a thank-you letter (in German) in which I apologized for their behavior, and he promptly wrote back (my translation):

Dear Mr. Stock:

I was very glad to receive your letter, as I had the feeling that I expressed myself repeatedly too harshly. It also seemed to me that these young people are on the whole spoiled and too self-satisfied, and not tending to serious reflection. Your letter leaves the hope that this impression was too pessimistic. In any case, I was pleased by your letter and thank you cordially for it.

The Palestine problem impinged on my university experience in more ways than one. At the School of Public and International Affairs (SPIA), which I chose as my "major" for the two upperclass years, I took part in a semester-long seminar which dealt with the problem and hammered out possible solutions. Students were assigned specific sub-topics on which they wrote papers for discussion in the plenary session. One of the faculty members in charge of the seminar was Professor Philip Hitti, then head of the Near Eastern Studies Department. Syrian by origin and the author of a standard work on Arab history, Hitti was an outspoken critic of the Zionist project. He once told the seminar that every Jew in Brooklyn supported the creation of a Jewish state because he would like to become American ambassador there. The smiles and snickering around the seminar table showed that the professor's sense of humor was being appreciated.

I used my position on the *Prince* to take up the cudgels editorially for the Jewish side, but the general mood was against me. When the U.N. General Assembly passed the Partition Resolution on November 29, 1947, I felt great joy and enthusiasm, but I found little understanding on the campus of the historic importance of the event, not even among the Jewish students.

A significant incident in the Jewish context occurred at the end of my first semester. Since I didn't know anyone when I first arrived on the campus, I left the choice of a roommate to chance. I was assigned to share a small suite (living room and two bedrooms) with a sophomore from New Jersey, also an army veteran. E. was a WASP, but we got along quite well together. At least so I thought, until he told me one day, with a bit of embarrassment, that he would be moving out at the end of the term. He said he liked me well enough, but his father would not permit him to room with a Jew. I was stunned.

I shared my perplexity with a Jewish senior who lived on the floor below in my dormitory, with whom I had become acquainted. He shrugged, as if to say, "that's the way things are around here, there's nothing you can do." It was he who suggested I apply to join his club, Prospect, and recommended me for membership.

Taking meals at the club brought me into daily contact with a much wider range of fellow students than previously. Some of my new friends were deeply serious about their Christian faith and were planning to become Protestant ministers; conversations we had about religion sometimes brought out their feelings about Jews. They felt they could discuss these with me quite freely; perhaps because I didn't accuse them of being prejudiced but responded calmly and dispassionately. The questions were mostly of the kind: Why don't Jews like to drink (get drunk)? why are they so clannish? why are they such "grinds"? I realized that one shouldn't blame an individual for such views and feelings, but that these stemmed from the milieu he grew up in. It became apparent to me that the amalgam of negative opinions and emotions about Jews was deeply rooted in the society, even at its apex.

It was perhaps naïve of me to expect that the friendships I formed at the club would carry over into "life after campus," or off the campus while I was a student. But no. Never once did anyone suggest that I visit him at his home (some lived relatively close by), or that I join them when they went to New York on a weekend to meet some girls or take in a show.

It was probably then that I made up my mind to become part of a society (if there was such a one) where I would be truly at home, where I would not have to apologize for what I was and where no doors would be closed to me because I was a Jew.

Having learned my lesson, I moved in with a Jewish roommate in my junior year. Our interests were not the same; M. was an engineering student. He was a pleasant enough person to room with, except for one problem: he kept the radio going while he was studying. He said he couldn't concentrate without music (and it wasn't classical, either). I had no choice but to move my desk into my tiny bedroom and close the door. I now realize that M. represented an early version of the type seen everywhere nowadays, earphones on their head or digital sound device glued to one ear. This relationship, too, came to an abrupt end: M. got failing grades in three of his courses at the end of the spring semester and had to resign from the university.

My next roommate was not only Jewish, but German-Jewish like myself. Stefan was a chemistry major, which meant that again our interests differed. But we roomed together in harmony until graduation, and even corresponded for some years after that.

For my senior thesis I chose a subject which was of no topical relevance but had considerable attraction for me: "The German Traveler and the America of the Twenties." In addition to reading dozens of travelogues and journalistic accounts, I researched letters and reports by German exchange students at the Institute for International Education in New York. Perhaps subconsciously, I looked at their impressions of the New World for parallels to my own experience in America. My thesis adviser, Prof. Elmer Beller, with whom I was taking a course in German History, gave the work a high mark, which enabled me to graduate *magna cum laude*.

I understand that the situation on campus has radically changed since those days. There are far more Jewish students than ever before; there is a Center for Jewish Life, with kosher dining facilities and a vast array of cultural activities. A program of Jewish studies is listed in the official catalogue. Altogether, it's a much more pluralistic campus than it was in my time: women are in the majority; Blacks, Hispanics and other minorities abound.

Chapter Fifteen

Coincidences

The Princeton period was a hard act to follow, and indeed the academic year, 1948-49, spent at the Columbia School of Journalism, was a letdown. The positive experience at the *Daily Princetonian* steered me in the direction of journalism as a profession, but I had been warned that there was really no need for formal study to enter it. If I nevertheless applied to Columbia, it was because I had sufficient credit left on my G.I. Bill account for an additional year of study, and it seemed a pity to let it go to waste. Not surprisingly, I was accepted. The fact that the main classroom resembled a newsroom, with each of the 50 students assigned a desk for his typewriter, made it clear that this was a professional school, not an academic exercise. The instructors and guest lecturers were former or practicing newspapermen; the students eager to emulate them and join their ranks. I realized that I missed my chance when, as a member of the editorial board of the "Prince," I was invited to have lunch with our counterpart of the New York Times in their executive dining room, and could have easily used my connection to get a start as copy boy on the paper after graduation. Now I was being taught the essentials of copy editing (which I already knew) by a middle-level Times editor. It soon became clear to me that I would not be one of the three most promising students from each year's graduating class whom the paper invited to join its staff. I found that daily journalism required the kind of speed and aggressiveness which were not in my nature; the top students in the class possessed these qualities to a far greater degree than

I did. My own kind of talent was appreciated when I spent a week of internship on a daily paper in Kingston, New York, a somewhat sleepy provincial town two hours by train from the city. I struck up a friendship with the editor, who liked the feature articles I wrote and offered me a job on the paper after graduation. I thanked him but remained non-committal, hoping for something more exciting to come up by the end of the academic year.

And something did.

The class put out a weekly newspaper, with the students covering events in the city. Because of my interest in Israel, I was assigned to report on a fund-raising speech at the Plaza Hotel by Gershon Agronsky (later Agron), the editor of the *Palestine Post* (later *Jerusalem Post*). I was deeply impressed by the man and by what he had to say. A leading figure in Mapai, the ruling socialist party, Agronsky told the audience, made up mainly of wealthy donors to Israel's cultural institutions, that in his country "decency forbids" the amassing of private wealth. At the end of the meeting, I went up to the *Post* editor and asked him about a job on his paper. He said he couldn't promise me anything, but that I should look him up if I got to Israel.

That was enough encouragement for me, except that I didn't have money for the trip. Then another one of those coincidences which seem to govern my life came to the rescue. Just before graduation time, the university was visited by a chain letter craze known as the Pyramid Club. In return for putting one dollar into the kitty, your name was added to a list. With each passing day, your name moved closer to the head of the chain. After eight days you were either at the top and received all the money (for that day), or else the chain had run out of names and you were left with nothing. Guess what happened? On the eighth day people kept ringing the doorbell of my parents' apartment from morning to night, bringing money. Each of them dumped eight dollar bills on the bed, turned around and walked out. By the time the last one was gone there was a big heap of dollar bills on that bed. My father was dumbfounded; he had never seen anything like it. I let him count the money: it came to $240, a bit more than it took to fly by charter to Europe, but not enough to get me to Israel. I obtained a letter from a Jewish Agency official in New York, Gideon Rafael, to the Jewish Agency in Marseille, suggesting they let me work my way to Haifa on one of their immigrant ships. And this actually worked out. I was taken on as assistant purser on the *Atzma'ut* (Independence), an old freighter converted to carrying 1,500 passengers on bunks in the cargo holds. My job was to act as liaison with the passengers. A thousand Moroccan immigrants boarded the ship at Marseille, and my French came in handy in assigning them to their accommodations. This was another coincidence: these immigrants had been awaiting embarkation, after arriving from Morocco, in a camp outside Marseille called Grands Arènas. It was now being run by the Jewish Agency as a transit station. Just four years earlier it had been an American army camp, and I had been stationed there with my unit awaiting embarkation for the Far East, after the war in Europe was over. Then, just as we were about to board the ship in August 1945, the atom bomb was dropped on Hiroshima and the troopship was diverted to the U.S.

The *Atzma'ut* then made a stop at the port of Bari, near the heel of the Italian boot on the Adriatic, to take on 500 more immigrants who had arrived there by rail from Hungary. It was the middle of the night; my job was to assign them to bunks, reassuring them that the ship would look more seaworthy in the daytime, and that the air would be better on deck in the open sea. I was able to talk with them in either English or German. Sure enough, the next morning after the ship sailed I found many of the younger ones among the Hungarians sunbathing among the lifeboats, and wherever else they could find some empty deck space. Some of the girls wore bikinis, which had just come into fashion. It was then that I got my first taste of the potential for tension that lay in the ethnic mix. The sight of the bikini-clad girls scandalized the rabbis who were the spiritual leaders of the Moroccan Jews, and they sent a delegation to the captain to protest. I was told to make an announcement that the wearing of two-part bathing suits on deck was forbidden. One of the Hungarian young women asked me innocently, "Which part shall I take off?"

When I phoned Agronsky at the *Palestine Post* in Jerusalem for an appointment, I was told that he had taken a leave from the paper to serve as head of the government's information services, at the *Kirya* (government compound) in Tel Aviv. I called on him there, and to my consternation, he didn't remember either me or our meeting in New York. But he gave me the benefit of the doubt. "If you say so, I believe you," he said, and handed me a sealed note to his deputy and acting editor, Ted Lurie. In Jerusalem, Lurie glanced at me wearily after he read the note and asked, "What kind of bill of goods did you sell him?" But he also dictated a memo to his secretary that I would join the staff as foreign news editor at a salary of 60 Israeli pounds (then about $250) a month.

The year I spent in Israel, working on the Post and freelancing for the United Press and for an American trade paper syndicate, made a powerful impact on me, causing me to resolve to return. (For more details, see Part III, "Israel: Conversations with My Son.") Meanwhile, there were other tugs that drew me back to the U.S., chief among them the conscience of the dutiful son who was not prepared to leave his family behind on the new continent. I arrived back in New York in July, 1950, ten years after I had first landed there.

My stay in Israel had a negative influence on the way I looked upon journalism as a choice of a profession. Even though I enjoyed my work at the *Post*, I felt that a career in English-language journalism in Israel would mean opting for permanent outsider status. In the U.S., the field had also lost its fascination for me, and in my search for a job I did not make use of the glowing recommendations I brought back with me. Instead, I decided to look for work in the Jewish community, preferably in the area of relations with Israel.

Hillel, Marriage, and Israel Again

I paid a courtesy call on Rabbi Arthur Lelyveld, the National Director of the Hillel Foundations, with whom I had maintained contact since our cooperation at Princeton. He asked me whether I would like to become his assistant. He made it sound attractive to me by stressing that the work involved liaison with the press and producing public relations material for the Foundations. I accepted, and began work in September. Again, I was entering a new world: that of Jewish organizational life. The national Hillel office provided services to the Foundations on more than a hundred campuses all over the country. Their directors, most of them rabbis, were appointed - and paid - from New York, where a relatively small staff was in charge of complex budgeting and personnel procedures. Hillel was then a project of the nationwide B'nai B'rith fraternal order, which supplied much of the funding and was given due credit for its contribution. Hillel, however, had its own Board of Governors which met from time to time to hear reports and set policy. There were seminars and conferences to be arranged on Jewish topics, which brought me into contact with directors and students on the various campuses. The national office also published program materials for use by the Foundations, in the production of which I collaborated. But I missed the connection with Israel... until one October day, a young Israeli woman with a mane of chestnut hair walked into the office, and into my life.

Bracha had arrived in New York from Tel Aviv some weeks earlier to visit relatives and inquire about opportunities for

studying journalism. Someone told her that Hillel offered schol-
arships to foreign students. But the official she was referred to,
Rabbi Ben Lowell, had to disappoint her: financial support was
available only to Holocaust survivors. As a consolation prize,
Rabbi Lowell turned her over to me: "I'll introduce you to
someone here who studied journalism and who recently came
back from Israel; he might have an idea for you." My idea was
a brilliant one: she should give me private Hebrew lessons, as
a way of earning some money. It took only three months from
that first meeting until we stood under the wedding canopy at
my father's synagogue, Beth Israel of Washington Heights.
Conducting the ceremony was Dr. Irving Levey, the Hillel rabbi at Princeton whom I had introduced to the campus community in the months before graduation.

An excursion to the Princeton campus had been a highlight
of our whirlwind courtship. The occasion I chose was the
Princeton-Dartmouth football game. It was the last match of
the Ivy League season, played in Palmer Stadium on a particularly nasty Saturday in late November. A driving cold rain
lashed at the car I had borrowed from my father, and when the
gale reached near-hurricane force, Bracha was certain that the
game would be called off. But no, it went on as scheduled; the
large stadium was filled, even though the players were fighting
the elements and the mud on the field more than their adversar-
ies. If I had tried to impress Bracha, I succeeded, but she also
began to doubt the Americans' sanity. Soaked to the skin, we
went to a post-game party at my former club afterwards, where
I met old friends. Bracha was introduced. The prescient girl-
friend of one of my classmates took me aside and whispered in
my ear, "You may not know it yet, but you're going to marry
that girl!"

The two of us were saddened by the resignation, later in the
year, of Rabbi Ben Lowell, the jovial administrator at national
Hillel who had introduced us. We were both fond of him, and

considered him a good friend. His sudden departure came as a shock, and the murky circumstances, of which I had been unaware, emerged only gradually from the whisperings of the other staff and Lelyveld's own laconic comments. They reminded me of a research seminar I had participated in as an undergraduate at Princeton's School of Public and International Affairs three years earlier. The subject was the Committee on Un-American Activities of the U.S. House of Representatives, which engaged in a relentless hunt for Communists in public life, long before the notorious Senator McCarthy did the same in the Senate. Lowell had been rabbi of a Reform temple in Alabama, whose members were displeased with his activities on behalf of the black community. Someone claimed that he had been a Communist at an earlier stage, and his congregation did not renew his contract. In other words, he was fired. His wife was related to Rabbi Stephen Wise, who headed the Reform rabbinical seminary where both Lowell and Lelyveld had been ordained. It was through this connection that he obtained the post with Hillel. But then a Jewish Commie-hunter, Rabbi Benjamin Schultz, operating as the head of the American Jewish League Against Communism, called on the Hillel Foundations to get rid of Lowell before he would corrupt Jewish youth on college campuses. The leadership of B'nai B'rith joined in the pressure. The Hillel Board of Governors convened and concluded that Lowell had lied to them when he declared that he had never been a Communist. It called on him to resign, which he did.

Hillel before long forged its own close relationship with Israel, and I had a part in it. The Board of Governors decided to open a Hillel House at the Hebrew University, which was then housed in temporary buildings all over Jewish Jerusalem (after its campus on Mount Scopus had become inaccessible in the conflict.) An experienced and charismatic Hillel director, Rabbi Maurice Pekarsky of the University of Chicago, was chosen to be in charge. He soon arrived in Israel with his family. Rabbi Pekarski was obliged to invite students to his apartment while looking for a suitable location; his reports to New York reflected his mounting frustration as his search yielded no results. There was no suitable building, he reported, to be found for rent or for sale.

Then one evening, while at my parents' house for dinner, I picked up the *Aufbau,* the German-language weekly to which almost every German-Jewish family in New York subscribed. A small advertisement caught my eye. It offered the Swiss Consulate building in Jerusalem for sale for $60,000. The amount was reasonable, the location perfect: at number 4 Balfour Street, just opposite Terra Sancta College, where the Hebrew University made its temporary headquarters. A cable went out to Rabbi Pekarsky (whose apartment was within earshot) and he was overjoyed. The new Hillel Foundation in Jerusalem had found a home.

When Bracha and were I married in February 1951, we agreed that we would one day return to live in Israel. It was like an unwritten clause in our *ketubah*, the marriage contract which the rabbi read aloud at the ceremony. But neither of us could have predicted then that less than two years later we would already find ourselves back in Tel Aviv

One day in the spring of 1952, I came across another advertisement, this time not in the *Aufbau* but in the *New York Times.* The Ford Foundation, recently launched by the heirs of the auto maker, invited applications for a program of Near East Area Training Fellowships, which included a stipend for travel and living expenses in the area. I decided to apply for one of the grants, submitting a project for research into the America-Israel relationship in all its aspects. The method proposed consisted of both interviews and newspaper content analysis; the research was to be conducted within the framework of the Israel Institute of Social Research, headed by Professor Louis Guttman.

A few months later, I received notice that I was one of four applicants chosen for a research grant in Israel. We began to prepare for a November departure. Rabbi Lelyveld, as an ardent Zionist, gave his blessing to my project. Although we had developed a smooth working relationship, we both understood that, since I was not a rabbi or Jewish scholar or communal worker, my future did not lie with Hillel.

I spent my last few months at Hillel assisting in the search for my successor. An ad in the Help Wanted section of the Times brought in more than 80 replies, which were sifted through carefully. About 15 applicants were invited for personal interviews. There emerged four or five finalists, who were asked to come in for a second interview. In the end, Rabbi Lelyveld himself chose the candidate he found most suitable to replace me. But then I learned that he resigned after just over a year on the job, and the search had to start all over again.

We sailed on the Queen Elizabeth for Cherbourg on November 9, 1952, Cabin Class, courtesy of the Ford Foundation. Passing through Paris on the way to Marseille, I bought a Morris Minor car which, though used and very small, made the 20 months we were about to spend in Israel a good deal more comfortable. A "private," as a personal vehicle was called in Hebrew at the time, was still a rarity, and as the owners of one, we were besieged by requests for "tramps" (rides) from friends and acquaintances. To cope with them, we maintained a waiting list for the two vacant seats on weekend trips to the beach. Eventually, the slow, then sudden increase in the number of cars on the road became a measuring rod for the country's economic progress; two or three decades later I felt left behind. I was still driving a modest compact vehicle, while the same friends who had once vied for a seat in my Morris Minor were now riding around in Volvos and BMWs.

In my research on the economic side of America-Israel relations, I spent a good deal of time interviewing experts of the

U.S. "Point Four" program, which was the Truman Administration's economic assistance program for underdeveloped countries. Under the aegis of a country director attached to the Embassy, a dozen or more experts in various fields, from tourism to cotton growing, were teaching their skills to Israeli counterparts, helping to lay the foundations for a sophisticated modern economy. Through their experienced eyes I learned to evaluate progress in the various fields, which enabled the country to provide housing and employment for the hundreds of thousands of newcomers who swelled its population in the first years of statehood. These experts' positive reports helped convince the U.S. government that the amounts allocated to Israel in the annual budget for foreign aid were well spent. Within little more than a decade, Israel would itself become a valued source of technical and agricultural assistance to developing economies in the third world.

Except for the Labor Attaché, Milton Fried, there were no Jews on the Embassy staff in the early 'fifties; for the State Department it was axiomatic then that Jewish diplomats should not be assigned to Israel. The reasons seemed obvious. But like so many other axioms in diplomacy, in later years this one too went by the board. Eventually American Jews even served as ambassadors.

The embassy put me on the mailing list for its daily bulletin of translations from the Hebrew press, which saved me endless hours of laboring through the originals for my content analysis. Most of the papers were sponsored by the political parties, which made for a wide range of opinion expressed on every subject. It was the height of the Cold War, and I was struck by the vehement anti-Americanism displayed in the party press on the left. The labor majority, led by Ben-Gurion as the prime minister, was firmly on America's side, as could be expected of a major beneficiary of U.S. economic and political assistance.

Supplementing the newspaper content analysis, I interviewed some fifty "opinion makers," such as writers, Knesset members and party functionaries, to elicit their ideas on the Israel-American Jewish relationship. The Ford Foundation reference was a door opener, and some of the contacts I made then remained valuable resources at later stages. A frequently encountered opinion, somewhat to my surprise, was the downgrading of the financial aspect, which for the American side was all-important.

I will quote from one interview to demonstrate this. My interlocutor was Avraham Ofer, who was then (June 12, 1953) Secretary of the Tel Aviv branch of the Labor Party. This was an influential position, and Ofer was considered an up-and-coming figure on the political chessboard. In fact, he had become Minister of Housing in Ben-Gurion's cabinet by the time I left Israel a year or so later. Still another year after that, I was shocked to read that he had committed suicide, apparently unable to bear the rumors of financial irregularities that were swirling around his person.

Mr. Ofer, a heavy-set, burly individual in his early thirties who could well be an American trade union organizer, spoke up readily, even eagerly, when I explained the purpose of my visit to him. He started out by explaining that his views do not represent those of the rank-and-file membership of Mapai, most of whom are older than himself, more recent immigrants (he came here as a child), life-long workers some of whom have lately become government clerks or officials, and who find it hard to express themselves freely on any subject without "declaiming."

"They will always think – perhaps subconsciously – 'what am I expected to say, what's best for me, or the party?' and unless you are lucky enough to come close to them in a really private conversation, you won't be able to get at what they really think. Especially on a subject as touchy as that of America and American Jewry, where even Ben-Gurion doesn't speak his mind any more."

Therefore, he went on, what he had to say should not be taken as typical of the party; if it's typical at all, then of the views of the younger generation, or rather – he corrected himself – of the "in-between generation" which is just now making its way into some of the more important offices in the party and government apparatus, and which will undoubtedly control the most responsible posts ten and twenty years from now as the generation ahead is eliminated by the biological process. (Here he interpolated that he had been serving in his present post for only a year and still didn't know why he had been chosen for it.)

Ofer resents the State's financial dependence on American Jewry and would like to see it emancipated from that dependence as quickly as possible. He sees it leading to no constructive relationship, but instead corroding on both sides. It diverts every incipient relationship into financial channels; American Jewry feels that that is their only task – Israel that this is all that is to be expected from them.

He relates that he was, until a year ago, in charge of a youth village which received a part of its support from a certain American organization. Every time some members of the organization visited Israel they spent some time there, acted as though the village were their property, coddled the children and made sure that every building had the plaque of the donor(s) on it. The children hated it, and so did the staff, but nothing could be done about it. So Ofer decided to renounce the American support and manage to make the village self-supporting by increasing agricultural production and other measures. The organization came and begged him to accept their money for a library, but he refused.

Ofer does not mean that the State should refuse the proffered gifts of American Jewry, but he would like to see a change in its attitude. In other words, stop soliciting funds. "It seems to me that here is a case of the cow wanting to be suckled just as badly as the calf wants to feed," he said. American Jewry feels itself tied to Israel; Israel adds content to their lives, they want to have a stake in the country, so why shouldn't they want to give spontaneously, just as that organization came forward on its own with the library? Furthermore, there are vested interests, organizations which subsist by collecting charity, and they probably wouldn't give up so easily.

However, Ofer believes it would be much better if, instead of contributing gifts, American Jewry were to invest in enterprises, such as Alliance Tires, built with the capital of 500 American Jewish investors. "Everyone of them is now personally interested in what goes on here, in what happens to his money," Ofer says.

He is against sending emissaries to the States to help fund drives, or to encourage aliyah, for that matter. To be an emissary is good for learning English, or to broaden one's view of the world, but not for other purposes. The will to give, or to emigrate, has to grow spontaneously, and be nourished by Americans.

He does not believe that emigration can be stimulated artificially; it has to either grow out of an inner yearning or out of external circumstances, such as persecution. Lecturing to Americans that they are wrong not to emigrate is foolish and will bring no results. Ofer thinks that if Americans Jews feel themselves at ease, spiritually and materially, in their country, that is fine.

He is not one to "preach socialism for socialism's sake; if the American worker is well off, so much the better for him, then he doesn't need socialism." The same goes for the Jews. Nevertheless, he knows from experience that there are some American Jews who feel impelled to come to Israel, and these he welcomes. He believes that to the extent that the State becomes more attractive and red tape and interference with individual freedom disappears, more will come.

Ofer also finds that young American Jews and young Israelis hit it off remarkably well together; they have a certain outlook in common. He believes that, once the present generation of Israeli leaders will have disappeared, together with the generation of American *askanim* (functionaries) who purport to represent American Jewry but really don't, the new generation of Israelis and their American counterparts will get along quite well together. He says he has a definite feeling that the organized Zionists do not really represent the character and feelings of American Jews. All these organizations, he feels, are staffed by "middlemen" who make a living out of the relations between American Jewry and Israel. Their corresponding numbers are to be found on the Israeli side as well. He thinks that in due time direct contact between the respective populations will supplant this kind of artificial contact. With capital investment here and relatives in the Land, members of American Jewish families will come to visit more and more frequently, strengthen personal ties, and now and then one of them will decide to settle here.

By and large, experiencing Israel on the Ford Foundation fellowship reinforced my intention to return there. However, it was somewhat shaken by the so-called Qibya incident in October 1953. To counter a series of incursions from across the border with Jordan in which several Israelis died, the army trained a special unit to retaliate against Arab population centers. Its commander was a young officer much favored by Prime Minister Ben-Gurion (who was also Minister of Defense), Ariel Sharon. In a particularly bloody retaliation raid on October 16, Sharon's men killed 63 villagers - men, women and children - who had no share in the incident that provoked the massacre. In the face of universal condemnation – even America's loyal Hadassah Women lodged a protest – Ben-Gurion made up a story about outraged Israeli farmers seeking revenge. While it may have influenced world opinion, it did little to assuage my own feeling of outrage. In the doctoral thesis I submitted to Columbia University some years later, which is based to an extent on my research as a Ford fellow, I trace the outbreak of the 1956 Sinai Campaign to the sequence of Arab border raids ("infiltration") and Israeli retaliation. (The thesis was published by Cornell University Press in 1967 under the title, *Israel on the Road to Sinai*).

I used the remaining period of our stay to write up the results of my interviews and newspaper content analysis in a book-length study of America-Israel relations, which I entitled "God's Country and Promised Land." An academic publisher, Praeger, expressed an interest in putting out the book but asked for a $2,000 subsidy, which seemed like an exorbitant sum to me at the time. While the manuscript remained unpublished, it earned me a reward of a different kind. I sent the part which dealt with the Jewish aspect of the relationship to Philip Bernstein, the executive director of the Council of Jewish Federations and Welfare Funds, for his comments. In response, he offered me a job with the Council. I conditioned my acceptance on being allowed to study part-time for my Ph.D. at Columbia, to which Phil agreed.

We returned to New York in September 1954, via Italy and France.

Chapter Sixteen

Inside the American Jewish Community

The Council's office, to which I reported soon after the return to New York, was located in the same building as the B'nai B'rith Hillel Foundations, where I had worked before leaving. The elevator operators remembered me and greeted me like an old friend. The Council occupied the 11th floor; Hillel had been on the 10th. I say "had been," because the Hillel office had moved out in the meantime, and I never got to meet Rabbi Lelyveld in the elevator. They had relocated to Washington, D.C., into the office building of B'nai B'rith, the sponsoring body, which had decreed the move for reasons of economy. Rabbi Lelyveld had opposed it; his wife, Toby, who was the Hillel Director at Hunter College in Manhattan, was unwilling to leave New York. But to no avail. He chose to resign his post, and accepted a position as executive director of the America-Israel Cultural Foundation (based in New York).

But the match didn't last. His son Joseph (later executive editor of the New York Times) relates in his memoir: "my dad... proved to be unsuited to the task of buffing the egos of wealthy donors."[4]

The person who welcomed me when I reported to the Council was S.P. ("Pete") Goldberg, whose title was Director of Budget Research. I was to be a member of his department, and we discussed the *modus operandi*. After a few minutes of pleasantries, Pete shot a piercing glance at me and asked, "Have you ever been a Communist?" He must have tried to catch me

---

4. Joseph Lelyveld, *Omaha Blues: A Memory Loop* (New York, 2006) p. 164

off balance and reveal a dark corner of my past. But I kept my composure. "No," I said simply. "Why do you ask?"

Evidently satisfied that I spoke the truth, Pete took me into his confidence. It turned out that my predecessor, Dr. Harold Glasser, had been recommended to the Council as an economist by his superior in the U.S. Treasury Department, Harry Dexter White, who later was revealed to be a key figure in a Soviet spy ring in Washington. When Glasser's name also came up in congressional hearings in connection with the same conspiracy, he resigned his post.[5] Pete Goldberg now wanted to make sure that there was nothing in my record that might cause further embarrassment to the Council.

Whereas Dr. Glasser had been the head of an autonomous Department of Overseas Studies, I was taken on as a Consultant in Goldberg's Budget Research Department. This would entail less than full time work, which fitted in well with my plans for graduate study at Columbia. My main task was to prepare a monthly "Israel Report" covering an aspect of Israel's economic and social welfare scene as it affected American-Jewish support. Although not as ambitious as the role assigned to Dr. Glasser, my work would still contribute to the Council's reputation for objective follow-up on the use of community funds. There was a professionalism to the Council's reports and publications which fitted in well with my own outlook and temperament. My new colleagues I found both serious and congenial; with one or two of them I formed lasting friendships. I returned from Israel with some definite views on the Israel-American Jewish relationship; my work with the CJF enabled me to test their validity. Above all, I found myself in a position where I could use my knowledge of Israel and channel it to the "consumer."

---

5. See David Rees, *Harry Dexter White: A Study in Paradox* (New York, 1973) pp.83 ff

Since the Council concerned itself with the whole gamut of Jewish voluntary activity supported by its member federations, I was enabled, in the six years on its staff, to learn much about the community's structure and functioning. Taking part in the annual General Assembly, which was rotated among the larger cities, and frequent field visits for lectures or seminars, helped round out my education.

I learned that, beneath the cover of Jewish unity and harmony, there were deep divisions and differences. Among the countrywide, or national organizations there had always been rivalries and disputes over turf and finances; then the rise of Israel and its developing relationship with the Diaspora introduced new controversies and exacerbated old ones. In what follows, I will enumerate some of the main issues and actors involved. But I want to make it clear that the time frame is the 1950's, and that a great deal has changed since then on the American Jewish scene.

Finances

Money is such an important factor in the Jewish community – as in the country generally - I sometimes imagined that, if the flow were to suddenly stop, everything would come to a halt. Jewish life is identified with organizations run by professionals who are paid a salary. Without them, many of the structures would simply collapse. This was not always so, of course. For centuries, the basic unit in the community had been the *minyan*, the group of ten adult males assembled for prayer. One of them led the service; no money changed hands. Then, as populations grew larger, synagogues were built and rabbis employed at a salary. At the same time, structures grew up to serve the secular needs of the communities: education, welfare, hospitals, care for the aged, all of them employing salaried personnel.

In the financing of their secular institutions, American Jews emulated their non-Jewish neighbors by setting up community chests, or united funds, which conduct a single annual campaign in each locality. The proceeds were then allocated to the participating organizations on condition that they refrain from raising funds on their own. In the Jewish communities these structures were known as either welfare funds or federations. They soon became synonymous with the community itself; and the largest contributors to the campaigns were, *ipso facto,* also its most influential members. The synagogues remained outside this framework, responsible for their own finances, based on their membership.

The United Jewish Appeal

The next step was for the agencies active overseas to be included in the federation campaigns. The major ones among these, the United Palestine Appeal and the American Joint Distribution Committee, joined forces shortly before World War II to form the United Jewish Appeal (UJA). Except for the smaller communities where there was no federation, the UJA negotiated with each local community for its share in the proceeds of the local campaign. The division of the UJA share among the two partners at first favored the JDC, but when the gates of Israel were opened to mass immigration in 1948, the ratio was reversed.

Representing the needs of both European Jewry under the threat of the Nazi juggernaut, and of the Jews of Palestine/Israel at a crucial turning point, the UJA had a strong claim on the proceeds of the campaigns. Since the local agencies and services also depended on these funds, the federations' allocations committees often faced a daunting task in deciding on their division.

While the campaigns were organized and conducted locally, the national UJA office in New York supplied material and speakers, among them charismatic personages from Israel. After 1948, the emphasis was on the burden the country faced in absorbing the masses of immigrants, and the role of UJA funds in footing the bill. This remained the major theme of the campaigns for years to come. The perception thus took hold that Israel was a poverty-stricken place, barely kept afloat through the generosity of American Jewry. My monthly publications at the Council, circulated among the member federations, presented a more balanced point of view, with emphasis on Israel's achievements in the economic and social spheres despite the challenges posed by mass immigration. That there was a tension between the two approaches, that of the UJA and the CJF, could not be denied, with the latter seen in Israel as representing the interests of the local communities. The Council took the position that there were enough potential resources to serve the needs of both sides, and that these could be tapped by improved campaign techniques, such as upgrading gifts and enlisting more contributors.

However, after reaching a peak in 1948 when the emotional impact of the founding of the state loosened the purse strings, by 1950 campaign income and the UJA's share were on the decline. To offset the loss, the Israel government decided to sell Treasury-backed securities to Jews in the Diaspora, with the proceeds to be used for capital investments through the government budget. The Israel Bond Drive, with offices in all the major cities, circumvented the federations with a structure of its own. The timing of the two campaigns was coordinated between them, but there was a good deal of bickering about which was of more benefit to Israel. The argument was settled when Ben Gurion declared that both were of equal importance.

The Internal Revenue Code

Nevertheless, the federation campaign continued to constitute the central event each year in the life of the community. Its success was measured by the amount of money it raised; the causes for which it was destined and the techniques employed by professionals and volunteers were part of the discourse. For better or for worse, the largest contributors were in most cases also the community's leading figures. This contributed to the image of the Jewish community as money-driven, an image further enhanced by the custom of holding the annual meetings of national organizations in first-class hotels at locations throughout the country. The considerable expense involved was usually borne by the delegates themselves. The cost of travel to these conventions was tax-deductible as a charitable contribution under paragraph 522 (c) of the internal revenue code, so that those sufficiently well off to benefit from this provision could enjoy a vacation at reduced expense. The Council, too, followed this custom in its annual General Assemblies. As a staff member, I had my expenses paid and got to know interesting parts of the continent, from Toronto to New Orleans and San Francisco.

The section of the income tax code which provided for charitable deductions was thus an important factor in the financing of the Jewish community. Almost all the organizations were dependent on it for their income, and the federations had to ensure that the beneficiaries complied with its provisions. The "big givers," whose donations brought in 80 per cent of the funds collected, calibrated the size of their contributions with the tax code in mind; it was axiomatic that a man who gave $100,000 to the federation campaign was likely to pay only 25 per cent of it out-of-pocket.

There was thus a great deal of consternation among the professionals when, ca. 1959, the status of the largest beneficiary (the Jewish Agency, through the UJA) was called into question. In a ruling which applied to a British university raising funds in the United States but, by implication, also to the Jewish Agency, The Internal Revenue Service made it clear that tax exempt funds must be destined to American organizations, not to foreign ones. By these criteria, the Jewish Agency was ineligible to be the recipient of community funding. It was an emergency reminiscent of 1948, when the IRS briefly suspended the UJA's tax exemption after discovering that funds had been used to purchase weapons for Haganah, the pre-state military organization. Then, only a firm pledge to the Treasury that there would be no recurrence saved the situation. This time, a solution was devised by the Jewish Agency's legal counsel in New York, Maurice Boukstein. His proposal was ingenious, yet simple. The UJA would remit the funds destined for Israel to a newly empowered body to be called the Jewish Agency for Israel, Inc. Twenty of its 21 officers and directors were to be Americans; the twenty-first was the chairman of the Jerusalem Executive, *ex officio*. This body of 21 would adopt a budget of expenditures and appoint the Jewish Agency in Jerusalem as its agent to administer it.

There was some dissatisfaction at first about the similarity in the names of both agent and principal, but Boukstein probably intended this so as to make the plan more palatable to his clients in Jerusalem. He must have persuaded them that little would change in the Agency's status, except for the formal, legal structure. With the nomenclature so similar, who would make the distinction between agent and principal, or care about it? The main thing was that the Internal Revenue Service approved the new arrangement, which it did. The Jewish Agency's tax-exempt status was safe.

World Zionist Organization and Jewish Agency

But some things did change. On paper at least, the Jewish Agency was to be separated from the World Zionist Organization, and UJA funds would no longer be used for the financing of the latter. Some of its programs were classed as political, which made the WZO ineligible for tax exemption. Its activities in the U.S. were henceforth to be financed by the American Zionist organizations directly, without the input of community funds. This was welcomed by the federations, who had recently been surprised – and annoyed – that the WZO was making grants to Hebrew schools in certain cities which were direct beneficiaries of the campaigns. In other words, funds intended for use in Israel were channeled back to local communities, without their knowledge or consent, via the WZO.

Actually, there had been an earlier separation of the two bodies, back in 1929. The League of Nations Mandate for Palestine called for a "Jewish agency" to represent the interests of the Jewish community vis-à-vis the mandatory power (Great Britain), and also provided that the World Zionist Organization should act as that agency. But it turned out that leading Jews the world over, while supportive of the Jewish National Home in Palestine, were reluctant to identify themselves as Zionists. They called for the establishment of a separate "Jewish agency." After protracted negotiations, the WZO President, Dr. Chaim Weizmann, agreed that the time had come for such a body. In 1929 the Jewish Agency for Palestine, including both Zionists and non-Zionists among its members but separated from the WZO, was called into being at a festive ceremony in Zurich. But the timing turned out to be inauspicious. The stock market crash came just weeks later, and with the worldwide depression following on its heels, the expected financial benefits for the Jewish Agency never materialized.

Following the outbreak of World War II, the American non-Zionist members could no longer attend meetings in Europe, and the WZO once again became synonymous with the Jewish Agency. And there was no thought of renewing the partnership after the war, as the struggle for statehood claimed everyone's attention. Thus it came about that, though it raised record sums for the cause through the UJA-Federation campaigns, American Jewry no longer had any say about how the funds were spent.

The CJF stood for transparency in the use of communal funds, and the reports it issued analyzed the programs and budgets of the beneficiaries. But the Jewish Agency saw itself as a full-fledged partner, through UJA, in the local campaigns rather than as another "beneficiary," and for some time it resisted the Council's pressure for more information. When I met with the Jewish Agency Treasurer, Dr. Giora Josephtal, in New York in 1955, he promised to send us the Agency's audited financial reports, but he also warned that an excess of information among the contributors could be harmful. I was somewhat disturbed by this remark and its implications, but had no qualms about disseminating my analyses of the Jewish Agency's finances.

Behind the Agency's reluctance to cooperate with the Council and mistrust of its motives was the suspicion that it sought a greater role for itself in the allocation of the funds raised by - or through – its member federations. There was a historical basis for this suspicion, as I was to learn later on. A decade earlier the Council had in fact proposed a plan for "National Budgeting" which would have a central body make recommendations on how the proceeds of the local campaigns should be divided ("allocated") among the beneficiaries. The plan ran into violent opposition, and the Council eventually withdrew it. Instead of the proposed budgeting machinery, it set up an advisory body called the Large Cities Budgeting Conference (LCBC), with strictly limited functions. But the suspicion of its motives lingered on, not only by the Jewish Agency but by other bodies who would be affected.

The fact that quite a few of the Council's own member federations opposed "national budgeting" sheds light on an interesting aspect of the way the community functioned. Its center of gravity was on the local level, and the local organizations (in this case, the federations), were reluctant to delegate power to a national body, even if they themselves created it. This reflected the distrust of centralized power among Americans generally, lest it be abused. It is a distrust permanently embedded in the constitution, and in its system of checks and balances, not only among branches of the federal government, but also between the states and the central authority.

Reinforcing the weight of the local element was the absence of a nationwide body which could claim to speak for American Jewry as a whole. The attempt to set up a representative "American Jewish Congress" during World War II never got off the ground; the body by that name that still existed was one of several "community relations" agencies representing only its own membership (Rabbi Lelyveld served for a time as its president). True, there were any number of nationwide organizations, but their competence was limited to their special field of activity. They operated through local branches, such as Hadassah, the Women's Zionist Organization, or Women's American ORT, which supported a network of vocational schools in Israel. Others were "roof organizations" constituted by local bodies to provide them with services, such as the American Association for Jewish Education.

Dr. Nachum Goldmann, a veteran European Zionist leader who had come to live and be active in the U.S. during the war, was appalled by what he called the "organized chaos" in the Jewish community. In particular, he was unhappy about the absence of a national body allowing America's Jews "to speak with one voice" in matters concerning Israel, and he set out to do something about it.

Goldmann had earlier demonstrated his talent as an organizer: in 1936 he had founded the World Jewish Congress to give a voice to world Jewry at the height of the Nazi threat. Then, in 1952, having successfully conducted negotiations with the German government over payment of reparations to Israel, he founded the Conference on Jewish Material Claims Against Germany in which Jewish groups from two dozen countries participated. Now, in America, he managed to persuade the heads of 23 organizations to join a "Presidents' Club" to deal with Israel-related issues. It was to function only by consensus, not by majority vote, and was not endowed with any powers other than making announcements. A major weakness was the absence from its ranks of the American Jewish Committee, which continued to be opposed to the idea of a single body speaking for the entire community. The AJC still represented old-fashioned non-Zionism, as it was embodied in the so-called Ben Gurion-Blaustein agreement of 1950, in which AJC president Jacob Blaustein had wrested an agreement from Israel's Prime Minister not to interfere in the affairs of American Jewry. Then the Committee had confronted Israel on its own, and was planning to continue to do so.

But the AJC did join up eventually, after the informal Presidents' Club had constituted itself more formally into the Conference of Presidents of Major Jewish Organizations. While its competence had not been expanded, it had managed to build up its prestige, in part by providing a platform to visiting Israeli dignitaries. Above all, it had remained non-political, with the entire range of religious and ideological trends in the Jewish community reflected in its membership. The American Jewish Committee, in turn, gradually abandoned its historic non-Zionist stance and espoused a mainstream pro-Israel policy. And It joined the Presidents' Conference.

Dr. Goldmann, the outsider, had thus achieved considerable success in his quest to impose a degree of order on what he perceived as a chaotic situation. But if he believed that his creation could evolve into a Diaspora power base which might serve as a counterweight to Israel on certain issues, he was mistaken. Goldmann himself was an outspoken critic of Israeli policies in the conflict with the Arabs. But he found it difficult to integrate into Israel's political system, and by preferring to live in the Diaspora, he remained ineffectual. Since the Presidents' Conference took action only by consensus, it rarely adopted an official position of its own. Nor was it a breeding ground for leadership. While the chairmanship rotated every two years, the professional executive director remained in his post and developed close relations with the Israel government. As a result, the Conference tended to serve as a channel for conveying Israeli positions to American Jewry, rather than the other way around, as Dr. Goldmann had intended.

Lawyer Boukstein's 1960 scheme for a corporate reorganization was meant to meet the criteria of the income tax authorities, while leaving the reality on the ground more or less undisturbed. But it set in motion a process which would eventually lead to much greater Diaspora involvement in the Agency's budgeting and decision making.

It also provided the impetus for my own return to Israel.

A part of Boukstein's proposal was the presence in Israel of a representative of the (American) Jewish Agency Inc. to make recommendations for the budget, and then observe how the Jerusalem Agency implemented its provisions. To impress the IRS with the seriousness of the plan, this was to be a person with a solid reputation, preferably an economist, who was willing to take up residence in Israel. The search turned up a man who met the first two requirements, but would not commit himself to the third. He was Dr. Isidore Lubin, a leading member of President Roosevelt's "brains trust" which was responsible for much of the New Deal's economic and social legislation. FDR later appointed him head of his administration's Bureau of Labor Statistics.

Lubin made acceptance of the assignment conditional on having a deputy who would take up residence in Jerusalem, while he himself would only pay periodic visits. The choice for this assignment fell on me. I was overjoyed. By June 1961 Bracha and I were again on our way to Israel, this time accompanied by our one-year-old son.

PART THREE

Israel: Conversations with my Son

Conversations with my Son

In 1961 the Stock family, consisting of myself, my wife Bracha and our son migrated to Israel. The boy was then one year old. More than twenty years later, in 1982, he began to probe into my motives for making the move. By then he had become a full-blown Israeli, having graduated from high school, with his army service behind him and studying graphic design at the Bezalel Art Academy in Jerusalem. His persistent questioning, which began with my views on the local political scene and soon drifted into related topics such as religion and anti-semitism, gave me an opportunity to examine and formulate my own ideas. I took extensive notes on our conversations and now find that they have not lost their relevance.

Chapter Seventeen

Are You Sorry You Came to Israel?

"I've meant to ask you this for quite a while," my son began his questioning. "Are you sorry you came to Israel, or do you think you would have been better off staying in America?"

"No, I've never been sorry I decided to live in Israel," I told him. "and I'm not sorry now, in spite of everything that's been happening." It was a short time after the massacre at Sabra and Shatilla, and he had accompanied me to the mass rally in Tel Aviv which the Peace Now movement had called to protest the failure of the Israeli army in Lebanon to prevent the slaughter. I could see that the demonstration had made a deep impression on him, and I sought to reassure him. "For me, and for others in my generation, the creation of a Jewish state was such an overwhelming experience that I felt I would have missed out on a unique opportunity if I had not taken part in it. To observe the Jews regain control of their own destiny, after suffering the worst kind of persecution a people could experience, makes even everyday living in Israel more meaningful for me than it would be elsewhere."

But this evidently did not satisfy him.

Son: And what happens when things go wrong, as they did just now?

Then I certainly don't ask myself, "Why did I ever get mixed up in this mess?" My reaction is more like, "So we Jews are not so smart after all! Given the opportunity, we make mistakes like everybody else. I find it fascinating to see our people here defy and contradict some of the notions that the world has held about us, and instead come up with patterns of behavior that are not typically Jewish at all."

Son: When you said before, "my generation", did you mean those of you who came from Europe and went through the Nazi period there?

It's true that being born in Germany and experiencing the Hitler regime leaves you with a special sensitivity that you can't really expect of everybody, certainly not of Jews who were born and raised in America.

But I would say there were objective as well as subjective reasons in my case for coming to Israel. The objective reasons are historical and sociological—abstractions if you will. But if these abstractions then become an integral part of one's life experience, that makes the motivation so much more powerful.

Son: Would you say that anti-semitism is part of it?

Yes, I think anti-semitism is a good example of an objective condition that becomes subjective. The historical phenomenon of anti-semitism (perhaps Jew hatred is a better term for it) as it was perceived by Herzl and other Zionist thinkers, was certainly a basic rationale for wanting to establish a Jewish state, or rather a state of Jews, which is a better translation of the title of Herzl's pamphlet, *Der Judenstaat.* You will find in it as good an analysis of Jew hatred as anywhere, and one that is still valid today. But if you've also had a direct and personal experience of it, then I think you'll be so much more amenable to implementing the idea yourself.

Son: Could you tell me what some of your own experiences were?

Yes, but before I go into that, I' like to mention another subjective element in the motivation for *aliyah* to Israel. You may have heard about the "push-and-pull" paradigm: first there has to be a push from the outside, such as anti-semitism, then you must also feel the pull from within Israel. You might say that the push is a composite of many elements, each one of which runs on its own continuum from a minus to a plus zone. They include age (the older you are, the more difficult it is to make a change, uproot your family if there is one, get readjusted in the new environment); status (if you've attained some status in your profession or socially, you may not want to give it up); professional satisfaction and outlook (obviously, if you're happy in your job and hope for advancement, you are less likely to make the move); ties with parents and siblings (these could be a real obstacle to leaving), and uprooting school-age children can also be a risk factor; finances (a major move of this kind takes money) and of course ideology: where there's strong ideological motivation, it can make up for some minus factors in other areas. Here I would include the element of Jewishness: how comfortable one feels as a Jew in the Diaspora.

I doubt whether many people actually sit down and draw up a balance sheet along these lines. But if they're smart, they will take all these factors into account.

And then things have to be attractive enough within Israel to make them want to come here and not somewhere else. That's the pull.

Son: How would you define the pull?

It's usually expressed in terms of physical conditions: standard of living, the quality of life, cultural and employment opportunities. Actually, the pull is difficult to quantify because it's often not based on solid information but on hearsay and an imagined reality. The testimony of the Israeli *shlichim* (emissaries) is not always reliable, because it's their job to bring in *olim*. Even the impressions that are formed in a personal visit can be deceiving, especially if the visit is brief. But in my own case, as you know, my first visit lasted almost a year. What I felt to be most important was the more intangible aspect of one's existence here; call it the sense of belonging.

Son: Don't you think there might come a point when you'll find yourself so out of step with the majority political outlook (which some call the national consensus), that you'll feel just as much of an outsider as you did elsewhere?

Yes, that's a possibility. But in the meantime, it felt good to be among so many like-minded people, and to see that there are still a couple of hundred thousand around who take the trouble to come to this kind of a demonstration.

Chapter Eighteen

The Two Models of Jewish Existence

<u>Son:</u> Do you think that the kind of motivation that brought you here could also apply to people like myself, who were either born here or came as young children?

The assumption of those who came here for ideological reasons has been that the next generation would naturally grow up with that same sense of belonging, of rightness, of being in tune with their environment, that would make them want to live their lives here. I think among the majority of the young generation this has been the case. But for young people like yourself to really become convinced that this is your place, you may have to go abroad for a while and experience the difference yourself. When you were 14 going on 15, you spent six months with us in London, and I remember your saying to me once, "I wouldn't want to be a Jew outside Israel!" You obviously already felt then the ambiguity, and perhaps the marginality of the Jewish position in the Diaspora. And I recall that you added, "I want to be a part of the majority." So you actually put the case for living in Israel very succinctly, and very convincingly. The question is whether you'll still have the same convictions as an adult. Perhaps you will have to test them out again to make up your mind. But of course the basic assumption behind Zionism is that the Jewish problem will be solved by moving to the Jewish state. Meaning that for the second generation the problem should no longer exist. They will be Israelis, and the notion of reverting to Jewish existence in the Diaspora would not even be seriously considered by them.

Giving serious thought to *Yerida*, to emigrating from Israel, really means negating the very basic premise of Zionism.

For us ideological immigrants, there were two models of Jewish existence in the world: 1) the communal model, whereby the Jews constitute a religious, or quasi-religious community, under non-Jewish sovereignty; and 2) the model of Jewish sovereignty with its emphasis on Israeli nationality, rather than on the Jewish religious element.

As Zionists, we deliberately chose the second model over the first. If you native, or near-native, Israelis decide to leave again and return to the Diaspora, I assume it's not because you prefer the communal model over the national one.

<u>Son</u>: That's correct. Young people don't emigrate because they want to be Jews elsewhere. In fact, I've heard that many of them abandon their Jewish affiliation altogether when they live abroad. They form some kind of an Israeli colony, and often don't bother to become part of the local Jewish community.

True. We've observed this also on university campuses, where Israeli students have kept aloof from the Jewish student body. You might say that there are three categories of Israelis who leave, of *Yordim*:

1) The ideological Zionists who are dissatisfied or disillusioned with the way the Zionist idea is being implemented in Israel.

2) People who immigrated here for non-ideological reasons (such as many Russian Jews), and who hope to find better economic or social conditions elsewhere.

3) Native-born Israelis who are indifferent to Zionist ideology, and whose sense of adventure or restlessness causes them to seek their luck elsewhere.

Getting back to your original question of whether I've regretted the move: I never had any doubts for myself, but I've occasionally had qualms about whether I was justified in making the decision on your behalf -- after all, you were a one-year old baby when we brought you here. We were taking you, without asking your permission, out of your native land and into an entirely different environment.

I more or less knew what I was giving up myself. But I couldn't be sure that you might not have had a better opportunity for developing your own talents and personality--or whether America might not have been a better environment for you. I felt especially torn when it was time for you to go into the army, even though you were lucky enough not to have to serve during a war. But it meant that you had to give three years of your life to military routine, at a time when young people your age in the U.S. are studying, preparing for a career, or just enjoying a carefree period in their lives. I hope that the benefits of growing up in Israel will have compensated for whatever it is you lost.

When we came here to live in 1961, I was sure that the Arab conflict would have been settled by then. Had I foreseen that there still would be young people killed decades later, I probably would not have made the move.

Chapter Nineteen

Religion, Myth and Politics

<u>Son:</u> Isn't it true that what you call the pull consists of much more than your subjective feeling of "rightness," of being at home in the society? Shouldn't there also be the religious, or at least the historical dimension, depending on whether or not you are a religious Jew, that draws you back to the land of your fathers, the place where Jewish history began, the Land of the Bible?

Yes, there is that, undoubtedly. And you're right to distinguish between the secular and the religious Jew, in whom the connection with the locale is so much stronger because it's instilled in him from childhood, through the prayers and the holidays, and constantly reinforced in the ritual that is part of his daily life. In a secular person, that motive is much weaker, although it does exist to some extent. You can't be a Jew without absorbing, in the process of growing up, at least some of the lore of our forefathers —the biblical stories, the festivals, Purim, Chanukkah, Pesach - all of the many references to places, starting with Jerusalem.

If this collective memory isn't part of your faith, then it's a part of the myth by which people live. And there is a considerable attraction, even for a secular Jew, in returning to the place where the myth first originated. But there is also a point of diminishing returns here: the attraction is part of the original pull, but it wears off. After a while, it no longer plays much of a role in daily living. Take the *Kotel*, the Wailing Wall, as an example. When you first encounter it, you have this feeling of awe, an overpowering emotion. But in the course of the years, indifference sets in. I myself don't feel drawn to visit the Wall any more, except as an escort to tourists. On the contrary, one becomes worried about the political implications of the exaggerated worship of places and stones. You develop a distaste for the new type of politicized religion that has been springing up around these places, and this also tends to affect your attachment to the myths connected with the sites.

Let me put it another way: in one's childhood and formative years, the myths have a powerful hold on your imagination. But when, as an adult, you actually live in their proximity, then the political and social realities become far more important for you than the myths. I suspect that among truly religious persons the geographical element also plays a secondary role. The most intensely religious people, those that you see in Mea Shearim and in B'nai Brak, seem to be the least concerned about the Wall and the other so-called holy places. They are even forbidden to visit the Temple Mount! Nor do you see them take up residence in Shiloh on the West Bank because the Holy Ark was kept there at one time. The extremely religious group, the *Eda Haredit*, does not take part in the political game at all, as you know. And the most orthodox among the political parties, the Agudat Israel, for many years had no territorial ambitions. One of their leading rabbis was quoted as saying that Jewish lives are more important than territory. They also realize that the spiritual messages in the story of the Ark of the Covenant and the events at Shiloh are much more meaningful than the physical contact with the place, and that even if there is a desire for physical contact, as there often is in pilgrimages in almost every religion, this need not result in a claim for sovereignty over the place. Orthodox Jews visited the Wailing Wall for decades, even hundreds of years, without any thought of whether its location was under Jewish sovereignty.

But on another level, the myth does retain some of its power. The whole story of the revival of the Jewish people as a sovereign nation after two thousand years certainly has a powerful appeal. It's a kind of fantasy, a romantic notion that you're part of that ancient tribe that's coming back to its homeland. Now this part of the motivation for coming here does retain some of its potency even after years of living in the country. It adds a kind of odd metaphysical dimension to daily life, the living out of this great myth of ours, as though we were adding, each of us, a chapter to our millenia-old history. Whoever comes on Aliyah becomes a participant in that history.

America, too, has its myth; some people used to call it "the American dream," but it's a rather vague and largely materialist one; much of it is based on individual success rather than on a common adventure as a people. Again, I don't mind telling you that my hope was that this sense of historical continuity would communicate itself to your generation as well. If it didn't, then something very important went wrong. Because it is essentially this myth which supplies the cement that binds us together as a nation here, with all our differences. I've already mentioned two distinct groups, the religious and the secular. Then we have all the ethnic divisions. There's long been tension between the Sefardim and the Ashkenazim, and now there is a growing gap between rich and poor. There are sharp political differences over the Palestinian issue and the occupied territories as well as historic party political rivalries. So it really takes a very powerful cement to keep people pulling together in spite of all these differences. Especially if the Arab hostility diminishes. From the start, the feeling that we were being constantly threatened and endangered by our neighbors has made for a very effective binding force.

Son: When you keep mentioning myths, aren't you talking about something anachronistic, which is no longer very relevant to our own time and society?

In a way, yes. One has to be careful when one is managing a state to recognize where the myth is useful as a constructive element, and where it can become counterproductive by getting in the way of political arrangements and pragmatic considerations in dealing with other states. I think there's a real danger here of people being totally captivated by either the myth in its secular form, transforming it into a modern ideology, or else with its religious side, through the sacred writings. It's the job of the government to carry on the business of the state according to the norms of the political arena, and in the light of the changing political constellation in the area and the world at large.

To do that consistently, even if it means sometimes acting contrary to the myth, requires a good deal of maturity. I'm afraid that Israel as a state has not yet reached that point of maturity. States need to grow up too; one can't always expect relatively new states to act like older, more experienced ones.

Son: Could you be a bit more specific on that?

Well, I think that it's something to keep in mind when we talk about Israel's place in the Middle East and its relationship to the Palestinians and the Arab states. Let me just say that one of the things that set a statesman apart from a mere politician is that the former is able to distinguish between myth and reality, and shape policy accordingly. But you don't always have that kind of people available. Too often a country is led by politicians rather than statesmen. Politicians sometimes know the difference but exploit the myth skilfully for their purposes. Then we run into the danger of demagoguery, of whipping up popular hysteria.

Politics, as you must know, is the art of the possible; and it is practiced by compromise. This applies both to internal and external affairs. Internally, there are the various parties, and if you have a coalition government, then you must compromise on your own principles to satisfy at least some of the demands of your partners. You won't be able to attain all your aims. In the international arena, you have other states whose interests you must take into account, because if you don't you will simply perpetuate conflicts. A good example is the withdrawal from Sinai after 1967. There are some people who maintained that the revelation at Mount Sinai, the cradle of our spiritual history, gave us a claim to the area. But Begin realized that peace with Egypt was worth more than any historical or religious claim, and he agreed to give back the territory.

Son: Since we're on the subject of Sinai, do you think it was necessary to give up Yamit and the Rafiah settlements, as part of giving back the Sinai peninsula to Egypt?

I think it was necessary to give them up because they should not have been there in the first place. The huge investments in resources, and in human toil and hopes and idealism were wasted because of the basic misapprehension that it is possible to treat another country's territory as though it were your own. No one in Israel ever disputed that the entire Sinai peninsula (including the Yamit area) was sovereign Egyptian territory. To establish permanent settlements on it without Egypt's consent was *de facto* annexation. In fact, President Sadat said that Israel's decision to build Yamit was for him the signal to prepare for the Yom Kippur War, because it meant that Israel would never give back the territory voluntarily. The reasoning behind the government's decision at the time must have been that Israel would always be in a position to dictate terms of peace to Egypt, and these terms would include retention of the Rafiah salient with Yamit as the centerpiece. We know now that this assumption was proved wrong by the Yom Kippur War. It was the Labor government, incidentally, which made the cost-ly mistake, led on by Moshe Dayan. Perhaps the name of the town of Yamit should have been "Dayan's folly."

This is the kind of decision which I would ascribe to immaturity, to lack of experience in the ways of sovereignty; in dealing on a level of equality with other sovereign states, respecting their interests and imposing voluntary restraints on one's own ambitions. Begin acted maturely when he decided to give it all back, on the assumption that a satisfied power to the south would be a better neighbor than one which harbored resentment over lost territory. History is full of instances where retention of disputed territory, even if signed away by the rightful owner but under duress, has led to new wars. It's part of maturity for states to be aware of such lessons in history, and to learn from them.

Son: Shouldn't it be the job of professors to teach the politicians some of these lessons?

Yes, it would be nice if the politicians were willing to listen. But most of the time they think they know better themselves.

Chapter Twenty

The Holocaust (1)

<u>Son:</u> Why don't we get back to anti-semitism, or Jew hatred, as you seem to prefer. We have shied away from it all this time.

It's not a very pleasant subject. But it's basic--both to my own motivation in coming here, and to the whole *raison d'être* of Israel as a state. You may have noticed that whenever eminent foreign visitors arrive here, the first stop on their schedule tends to be the Holocaust Memorial, *Yad Vashem*. That says something about the importance we attach to having outsiders understand the impact of the Holocaust, not only on our national psyche, but also on the policy-making process. And the Holocaust, of course, was the ultimate expression of Jew hatred.

<u>Son:</u> But after you experienced Jew hatred in Nazi Germany, you went to America. Does that mean you came to Israel as a result of American anti-semitism?

That would be an oversimplification. I came to look upon anti-semitism as a kind of natural phenomenon that occurs in the interaction between Jews and non-Jews in a society. The nature of the society, its culture in the wider sense, including its history and ethos, produce different varieties of the phenomenon, but there are few societies in which Jews live that are totally exempt from it.

The German variety was the most virulent one, and it was distinguished by the fact that anti-semitism became government policy - the policy of annihilating the Jews was eventually pursued by the Nazi government with ferocious intensity. Fortunately, I was able to leave Germany before the final solution was implemented. What's more, even after Hitler came to power in 1933, until I left Germany at the end of 1938, I had a fairly normal childhood. The really traumatic episode came only at the end, with the so-called *Kristallnacht* and the pogroms that accompanied it. Then I saw the synagogues in my city on fire, saw the Nazi gangs hunt down my father at home and haul him off to a concentration camp, my mother humiliated, and the Jewish school that I went to shut down.

But until that time I had felt rather secure as part of a tight-knit Jewish community which managed to lead an intensive cultural, religious and social life even under the increasingly oppressive anti-Jewish laws and policies of the government. I remember being active in sports and taking part in all kinds of competitions among Jewish clubs in neighboring cities. In the little volume on my school, *The Philanthropin in Frankfurt*, which we have at home, you can find me in the picture of the soccer team.

The community maintained the local branch of the *Kulturbund*, the (Jewish) Culture Foundation, which sponsored lectures, plays, concerts and even operas. I went to hear a concert performance of Beethoven's *Fidelio*, by and for Jews. The authorities kept an eye on these events to make sure they had no political content, but on the whole the officials in charge of Jewish affairs displayed a benevolent attitude.

I suppose it was pretty much like Jewish existence as an oppressed but tolerated minority in the Europe of the Middle Ages. Then, too, the Jews accepted their inferior status as a given, but it did not prevent a flourishing and creative communal life. So when I look back on my childhood in Germany, I find that the strongest memories relate much more to school, friendships, little love affairs, holidays and family than to the rise of Nazism or the impact of anti-semitism.

Still, I had wanted to leave Germany already in 1936, when I was 12, and I made inquiries then about joining relatives in America, or going to boarding school in England, two years before my parents finally made up their minds to emigrate. I think that I wanted to leave not only because I saw no point in staying on as a Jew, but also because I really disliked German culture. I'm not talking about the literature and the poetry which I studied until the last day in the Jewish school, but the kind of sub-culture of the streets which I came across all the time. There was an obscenity and a brutality which were covered by only a very thin veneer of manners. And the craving after uniforms, which had half the population decked out in shades of brown and black, turned me off completely.

It was on this pervasive sub-culture that Hitler was able to draw in recruiting his Storm Troopers and his elite guards, the S.S., as well as the Gestapo (Secret Police) who carried out the carefully planned crimes against the Jewish population.

Son: And would you say this sub-culture was peculiar to Germany?

What was peculiar to Germany is probably not the underlying hatred of the Jew, which exists in other societies as well, but the fact that the government of the state adopted this hatred as official policy and gave expression to it in acts of unparalleled cruelty up to and including mass murder. And in that process, it sought out and promoted people to whom bestiality was second nature.

I also suspect that there is -- or was --an especially wide stratum of this type in German society. In spite of the attainments of German culture in music, poetry, philosophy and science, the influence of those cultural achievements did not really penetrate very deeply, and was probably confined to a fairly narrow elite. The urban proletariat and the mass of the rural population were very little touched by the attainments of high culture. Unlike the French population of these same classes, for example. And that wide lower stratum was especially open to hatred of the Jew. Just why this was the case I don't think has been adequately explained, and may not be subject to rational explanation. There have been attempts to analyze the German national character, or the French, or the Polish for that matter, and answers were sought in the religious background of these peoples, and the residues of barbarism in their cultures, and also in the role and status of the Jews themselves. That we were forced to become moneylenders, and that we segregated ourselves, that our religion forbade intermarriage and the laws of *kashrut* kept us from eating with non-Jews. But all of this would seem scarcely adequate to provoke the kind of response we've been subjected to.

Our universities have chairs for the study of anti-semitism, and we may one day see objective, scholarly research dealing with this phenomenon. But until we have the results, it's enough for us to know that the Jewish presence causes a negative reaction in the host society. In some places more intense; in others less. Also that this reaction can be extremely dangerous for us Jews, and that the one effective response we've found to it (as recommended by Herzl) was to establish our own state and live in it.

It's one of the advantages of being sovereign and independent to be able to explore such subjects dispassionately and objectively. I remember a number of years ago how stunned I was when an acquaintance of mine, a German Jew who had escaped to America, said to me, "I've always had a feeling that we Jews were somehow guilty, that there was something in ourselves that brought on these horrors." On second thought, what he probably meant to say was, "What is it that made us so repugnant to the Germans? What did they find so hateful in us that they would not stop short of killing us like animals?"

As you probably know, it's widely accepted that anti-semitism in Christian Europe owes much to the Church's tradition that the Jews killed Christ. This would seem to be supported by the history of the Crusades, when the Crusaders on their way to the Holy Land massacred the Jews in the cities they passed through, and other such episodes of Church-related persecution. But there is also evidence that anti-semitism predates Christianity. In the Diaspora Museum in Tel-Aviv, I once saw a diorama depicting an encounter between a Jew and a Gentile in ancient Alexandria. In the sound track that went with the exhibit there was a concise statement on the origins of anti-semitism. The Gentile asks the Jew: Why can't you be like the rest of us? And the Jew somewhat disdainfully explains the difference between his own monotheistic belief and the idolatry of the rest. And the Greek replies: "That's just what we don't like about you. You think yourselves superior." Here we have the basic ingredients already at work between Jew and Greek in ancient Alexandria.

Chapter Twenty-One
The Experience in America

<u>Son:</u> What was your experience in America? Was it anything like what happened to you in Germany?

God forbid. America is a humane, democratic society, with a great deal of tolerance for ethnic and religious differences, where the type of sub-culture that I described makes up a much smaller segment of the population. And therefore the obscene expressions of Jew hatred that I recall from Germany are much less likely to occur there. Nevertheless, it was my bad luck to be confronted by some very virulent strains when I served in the American army. And perhaps the shock of finding it there such a short time after I left Europe had a greater impact on me than some of the things I experienced in Germany itself.

<u>Son:</u> Did you have any experiences of that kind in civilian life afterwards?

I've already described life at the university. I was lucky enough to be admitted to Princeton for my sophomore year, where I found myself among the sons (no daughters at that time) of the country's social and economic elite. And I mentioned the incident with my roommate whose father did not permit him to room with a Jew. It was probably then that I made up my mind to become part of a society (if there was such a one) where I would be truly at home, where I would not have to apologize for what I was, and where no doors would be closed to me because I was a Jew.

Later on I was admitted to one of the eating clubs – Princeton's version of the college fraternity – and I met some terrific guys. Most of the clubs discriminated against Jewish students; mine was an exception. What helped me get in, I surmise, was that I was managing editor of the *Daily Princetonian*, which made me somewhat of a campus personality.

Some of my friends at the club were devout Protestants and were even planning to enter the ministry; they would discuss their negative feelings about Jews with me quite openly. I didn't accuse them of being prejudiced but responded calmly and dispassionately to their questions. I realized that one couldn't blame them as individuals for the views and feelings they absorbed in the milieu they grew up in. It became clear to me that the amalgam of opinions and emotions that we call anti-semitism was deeply rooted in the society. In that context, I wouldn't equate anti-semitism with actual hatred of Jews, but rather with a greater or lesser degree of antipathy toward them.

Son: What about the other Jewish students?

I'm sure that many had experiences similar to mine, even though they may not have been as sensitized as I was by my past history. The Holocaust was very real to me; I was constantly aware that I had barely escaped it. As a soldier in Europe, I had seen the pitiful remnants of the Jewish people after the mass slaughter, and the idea of a Jewish homeland was to me an historical necessity. So that it was both intellectual persuasion and emotional identification that brought me to the Zionist cause. But in public, when the Palestine problem (as it was then called) was discussed, no one ever mentioned the psychological hurts of young Jews in free, democratic countries like the U.S. The whole case for a Jewish state hinged on the plight of homeless Jews, survivors of the Holocaust, who needed a homeland. It's only when we get back to the sources, to the analysis by Herzl and others of the existential conditions of the Jewish people among the nations long before the extermination camps (even though Herzl in his prophetic moments extrapolated something like Auschwitz from what he observed at the Dreyfus trial) that we realize the original case was based not merely on physical but also on psychological needs.

But those were different times. To Herzl and the early Zionist movement, the acquisition of a piece of territory for a homeless people was a distinct possibility. Palestine itself was a part of the Ottoman Empire, which he believed its rulers might be persuaded to give up even without consulting the local population. The slogan, "A land without a people to the people without a land" is attributed to Herzl. But by 1947 there were half a dozen Arab states and a Palestinian Arab delegation representing the Arab cause at the UN General Assembly, and the Partition Resolution would never have gotten the required two-thirds majority if it had not been for the impact of the Holocaust.

By the way, there was quite a bit of opposition to the Zionist cause on my campus. Princeton had a strong Near Eastern Studies Department, whose Arabic scholars--and students-- were vocal about asserting the Arabs' rights. I found myself pretty isolated as a spokesman for the Jewish side, with only very few students and maybe one or two faculty members on my side.

Son: What were some of the arguments you used?

At the time, the idea of Partition appeared to be the least unjust solution: dividing the land among the two peoples, with each getting the part where it had the largest concentration of population. It was a good proposal, but the Arabs turned it down. The UN vote was a tremendous victory for the Jews; it gave international approval to the establishment of a Jewish state within those boundaries.

<u>Son:</u> Then what happened?

As I said, the Palestine Arabs and the neighboring states fought the idea of partition; they went to war over it and lost, and the UN Partition borders gave way to the 1949 armistice lines. Then there were more wars, and more Arab defeats. I still believe the basic idea of partition—the two-state solution-- is the right one.

But you are touching on something important: namely, the failure of the vision of Israel to make an impact on the vast majority of young Jews in the Diaspora, an impact strong enough to make them want to become part of it. It's true that the act of migration, of picking oneself up, leaving one's family and friends and going through the sometimes very painful process of settling down elsewhere, is a big deterrent. People are naturally inert. Just think of my own family history. It was only in 1938 that my father decided we would leave Germany. To say that the handwriting was on the wall long before then would be an understatement. At the end of that year, my sister and I managed to get out -- you know the story. But Grandpa himself was thrown into a concentration camp and got away by the skin of his teeth just before the war started. Grandma had to wait until April 1940 to get a visa and leave for America. So you can see what inertia can do even when physical destruction is threatened. I suppose it takes that to persuade people in the end -- the threat of physical destruction. That's also what triggered off the great Jewish migration from Russia: the pogroms in 1881.

In America there has never been such a threat, and Princeton is a very special place in America. The stakes are very high for those who graduate there. They have a good chance of going on from the top school into the top layers of the professions, of the universities, of the business world, and of partaking of the American dream in its most attractive and seductive version.

So why should they leave all that for an uncertain future, in a dangerous part of the world?

And the pangs of absorption in Israel, to use a cliché, can be very painful, even for an immigrant from the West like myself. I didn't have to put up with real hardships, like living in a transit camp as so many other immigrants did. But even today, after so many years, I'm not as fluent in Hebrew as in English. I do read the Hebrew paper, but I don't read books for pleasure. Whatever creativity I do have is expressed in English. This is a handicap: you don't feel a part of the creative and influential layer in the society if you express yourself in English. That's no longer true for you, of course.

Chapter Twenty-Two
Reactions to anti-Semitism

<u>Son:</u> But didn't you just tell me that you felt you couldn't become part of the elite in America, and that was one of the reasons you decided to come here?

I see you won't let me get away with anything. You certainly *can* take a crack at it, and perhaps even succeed in carving out a place for yourself. I know several such cases among the Jewish boys in my class. But there is a price to be paid for that kind of success, and to me that price seemed very high. No doubt there are exceptions - people who make it without paying the price. It depends on your own psychological make-up and background. As I said before, I was particularly sensitized. There are others who are thick-skinned enough that they are willing to pay the price without blinking an eye. Take Henry Kissinger: he had a background very similar to mine--came out of Germany as a 14-year-old, started working in a low-level job and went to high school at night like myself so he could support his parents; joined the army and worked in counter-intelligence. Then he went to Harvard and decided to become a professor. (I also thought of becoming a professor, but then I became fascinated with the newspaper world through my work at the Daily Princetonian.) You know, of course, about Kissinger's brilliant career in the government, and he himself referred to his Jewishness when he was sworn in as Secretary of State. But in his political memoirs, I think it's in the second volume, *Years of Upheaval,* he describes Nixon's anti-semitic needling, and how the President seemed to take a mischievous pleasure in berating the Jews in front of Henry.

On one such occasion, Henry comes back, rather lamely, "But Mr. President, there are Jews and Jews." That's all he had to say. So you can see the price Kissinger had to pay in order to get where he was and to stay there. Obviously, he felt it was worth it, and you can't blame him for that.

I became aware that something was amiss among my Jewish fellow students when I took the initiative in bringing a Hillel Foundation to Princeton. All the students at that time had to attend religious services at least twice a month, and because there was no Jewish service on campus, quite a few Jews went to the Protestant services in the chapel to get their "chapel credit." The alternative was a small synagogue in the town which was too Orthodox for most of the Jewish Princetonians.

So I made an arrangement with the national office of the Hillel Foundations to have a rabbi come to campus on Friday nights to conduct services for us, and this was the beginning of a regular Hillel Foundation at Princeton. But I ran into opposition on the part of some of the Jewish students who simply did not want to have an official Jewish presence on the campus. Apparently, they thought it was better to downplay their Jewishness; to cope with it as individuals when necessary, but not as members of an organized group.

Chapter Twenty-Three

A Psychic Freedom

This was a classic Jewish reaction to anti-semitism. Jews develop antennae that make them alert to the mood around them, and rather than confront the issue by owning up to their Jewishness, they take the path of least resistance by showing a low profile. I doubt whether I was familiar enough then with the historical and psychological background to fit my fellow students' behavior into this pattern. Today, we know enough and are also detached enough to recognize that as Jews in that kind of setting we are trapped in a vicious circle: the social attitudes towards us make us adopt certain evasive tactics; they put us on the defensive. And these defense mechanisms result in types of behavior and attitudes which non-Jews find disturbing and objectionable. Then if we prefer the company of other Jews so as to escape these pressures, they call us clannish. If we study hard in order to compensate for real or imaginary obstacles in our way, we are overly ambitious. At Princeton they called this type of student a "grind," and there was a high percentage of Jews among them, who wanted to be sure to get into a good law school or medical school through superior grades. These pressures work subtly and almost continuously, and even if the Jew isn't always conscious of them, they do affect his behaviour patterns and also his personality. And so these characteristics, induced by an unfriendly environment, in turn reinforce anti-semitism. One of the main aims of Zionism is to let us escape from this Catch-22 situation, so we can develop freely, as human beings, without the constant pressure.

Son: How were you personally affected by this? You told
me about some of the things that happened to you physically,
but did you find yourself also affected psychologically? Did it
make you hate yourself as a Jew?

I see you're wise to the jargon that has sprung up around this
problem. I personally object to the term "self-hatred," because it
implies an active hatred on the part of the individual, whereas his
reactions are really reflexes to the conditions to which he's exposed. But I did observe a disturbing phenomenon in myself. At
Princeton I was enrolled in a seminar in comparative literature,
given by the then well-known poet and critic, Richard Blackmur. It was part of a creative writing course he taught to selected students, of which I was one. One semester we discussed
Joyce's *Ulysses*. In my meetings with Blackmur to discuss the
work I had submitted for his critique, he would, with a kind of
enigmatic smile, address me as Leopold Bloom, which was the
name of the Jewish hero (or anti-hero) of the novel. Bloom is
actually a rather sympathetic figure, and perhaps I should have
felt flattered by the comparison. But instead I was embarrassed
by it. When Mr. Blackmur talked in the seminar about Bloom's
character and his peregrinations through Dublin, and especially
when he referred to Bloom's Jewishness, I found myself blushing and was sure that everybody in the room was looking at
me. We discussed *Ulysses* for an entire semester, and I actually
dreaded those weekly seminars. I fidgeted in my chair, waiting
for Blackmur to make some remark about Bloom or his Jewish
background, or about Jewish history, or the Jews in general, and
I wished I were somewhere else. The remarks were really innoc-
uous most of the time; quite in keeping with the general tenor of
the discussion; yet I was blushing to the roots of my hair, hoping
only that people wouldn't look at me and take notice.
There was obviously some psychological damage here; a
feeling of guilt, of being exposed, which I couldn't analyze at

the time, but which I recognized as something quite unhealthy. And the damage was probably more hurtful, or deeper than that caused by vulgar anti-semitism. Of that there was none at all here; I remember the atmosphere as being easy-going and urbane. There were other Jews in the seminar, by the way, including prominent faculty. I recall that the famous atomic physicist, J. Robert Oppenheimer, sat in regularly with his wife.

Son: Wouldn't you say that your special background made you so sensitive, or do you think yours was a normal reaction?

What I'm saying is that the position of the Jew in Gentile society is not normal, and it induces abnormal reactions. This is definitely one of the basic strains in Zionism -- this quest for normalcy, and I think what it means is we should stop living our lives in an abnormal situation. That includes not only the effect on the personality, as I've just described it, but also the fact that Jewishness itself becomes an embarrassment and a burden. And that's a very bad thing, when your heritage and your history become a source of embarrassment, rather than of strength and inspiration.

I still want to react to the implication in your question, that I was a bit overwrought about all this, had perhaps become somewhat of a neurotic as a result of my earlier experiences, and was altogether taking the whole thing much too seriously. I'd like to read to you a few quotations from books that I've read these past months. It so happens that they were all in French, which is simply because I've been doing most of my reading in French recently. Mind you, these are not books that deal especially with the Jewish problem.

These quotes are from books of much more general interest, where the Jewish problem shows up only incidentally. One of the authors is Elias Canetti, who received the Nobel Prize for Literature in 1981. He writes in his memoirs, *Histoire d'une*

Jeunesse, about the Latin teacher at the high school he attended in Zurich shortly after the end of World War One, who reproached him for raising his hand too quickly to respond to questions in class. Elias was puzzled, because he had been taught at home that being quick-witted was a virtue to be cultivated. One day the teacher simply ignored the boy's raised hand and instead encouraged another, slower student to reply. "Take your time, Ernie," he said to him. "I'm sure you will find the answer. You are not going to let a Viennese Jew get the better of you." Canetti was touched to the quick. When anti-semitic remarks by students almost drove a Jewish boy in another class to suicide, a group of Jewish students got together to draw up a petition to the principal. Weeks later, Canetti, as the ringleader, was called to the Assistant Principal's office. "Don't raise your hand too much in class," was all the man told him. Then he tore up the petition. Canetti writes about the impact of all this: "The beginnings of a new ideology began to take shape in me. (President) Wilson had undertaken to save humanity. I couldn't ignore these problems, which remained the principal topic of conversation. But inwardly -- since there was no one I could discuss this with -- my thoughts turned to the destiny of the Jews."

Then there was Albert Cohen, a well-known French novelist who died not long ago. He was born on the Greek island of Corfu, but after a pogrom there around the turn of the century his family fled to Marseille. There the young Cohen developed a fervent admiration for the French and their language. But when he was twelve, someone told him at school, "You are a Jew, go back to Jerusalem, we don't want you here." Albert closed himself up in his room and refused to come out for weeks. (It's interesting that toward the end of his life he again did not come out of his room). His Jewishness is a constantly recurrent theme in his autobiographical sketches and novels, and one gets the impression of a man who has spent his entire life trying to work out the childhood injury. He did it in solitary fashion, avoiding the life of the community. A stranger in his native Corfu, a stranger in France, he then went to live in Switzerland, the land of strangers.

My third example is Raymond Aron, quite a well known philosopher, journalist and political scientist. He published a book of conversations about his life and views, and there he talks about how in London, on General de Gaulle's staff during the war, he took somewhat of a back-seat position. His interviewer asked him why, and he said, "Because I am Jewish." In other words, he was reticent to come forward because of his Jewishness. This man, who was outwardly so unconcerned with the Jewish fate, seemed to be inwardly deeply marked by his Jewishness.

Son: You seem to be all alike--yourself, Raymond Aron, Canetti and Albert Cohen.

Possibly. That's one way of describing the effect of the *Golah* on the individual Jew: It influences the personality in ways that are sometimes positive, sometimes negative. You might say of some of the great Jewish geniuses, Einstein, Freud, Marx, Proust, that the breeding ground for their genius was the ambition to excel, so as to overcome the handicap of being Jewish. That's part of the neurosis -- the creativity. The other part is the crippling of some aspect of the personality. Try to think back to our stay in England in 1975, and the effect on yourself. You remember how hard you worked in school. You came home once and said, "I've got to show them that I'm better, because I'm a Jew" or something like that. You felt you had to prove something because they were beginning to make little anti-semitic remarks about you--isn't that right? Now, if you'd stayed on in that school, or gone to America, instead of coming back to Israel with us, you probably would have developed into a very serious student, instead of being just an average one at the *Gymnasia* in Jerusalem. You would have gone to college, and maybe to graduate school, and become a scholar, a professor of literature, or of music, or of French (which were your strong subjects in London) instead of going to the army and to Bezalel Art School to become a graphic designer.

Son: Which do you think would have been better?

Who knows? My own view is that it's better to develop your personality freely, without those pressures and constraints, even if it means not attaining the maximum of which you are capable. There is also an optimum, which takes into account other factors. You don't always have to strive for the maximum.

Son: Do you think Israel brings out the optimum in a person?

I really don't know. That was the theory. In your case, we noticed for instance that, when you were abroad as a boy, you tended to be much more polite, more considerate of others, and in general more pleasant to be with. In Israel, you were more abrupt, tougher, less easy-going. I suppose that's a tendency to conform to the environment. After all, Israel is a pretty tough place, and politeness is not one of its dominant values.

I don't think we really know for sure what happens to the individual in Israel. We know what happens in the *Golah*, because we've had so much time to observe it. In Israel everything is still tentative. But we can speculate, and we can also generalize from our personal experience. There's no doubt that living in Israel gives you a psychic freedom that is hard to come by in the *Golah*. Some people say this simply means freedom from being Jewish, a kind of escape from your Jewishness. But I think that is oversimplifying. Being rid of the constraints of living in a non-Jewish society, your Jewishness becomes a positive component of your total personality. Part of your freedom is that you choose for yourself how large a role your Jewishness will play in your daily life, in your intellectual and leisure time pursuits. You have the entire gamut open to you, from a totally secular existence to the ultra-Orthodox. It's true that the same gamut is also available in the Diaspora. But here there is no stigma attached to rejection if that's what you choose, no accusation of self-hatred, or deserting your heritage. Because even if you reject the religious side of Judaism, you are still a Jew by virtue of being an Israeli. No inner conflict need arise. The individual doesn't face the dilemma of what Jewishness is -- a religion, or a nationality, or a people, or an ethnic group; questions which we debated at great length when I was a student, and which still cause confusion in the minds of young people in the Diaspora. That's because we attempt to put something which is much older than these concepts and really transcends them into limiting, modern categories. The phenomenon of Jewishness as a total national experience, in which religion plays a part but doesn't dominate, just doesn't fit in with the standard models that are current in modern Western society. That again is one of the aspects of the "abnormality" of the Jews on the collective level.

Chapter Twenty-Four

More on Religion - and Politics

<u>Son:</u> It seems to me that most of the immigrants from the West right now are religious Jews.

True. Here we are talking about a different push-pull phenomenon. I don't think that a Jew who practices his religion to the extent that he is totally absorbed in it is subject to the same psychological pressures from the outside as one to whom religion is marginal. But at the same time, the restrictions that their religious practice imposes on them, make for a specially wide gulf between them and the non-Jewish population. It makes them highly visible and, again, is likely to cause feelings of resentment, the kind of "dislike of the unlike" which is one of the classic components of anti-semitism.

One might say then that these people come to Israel both to escape the effects of anti-semitism, and to find complete freedom to practice their religion as they please. I happen to think that the total immersion in religion is also a neurotic response to the constraints of the environment, and that existence under conditions of Jewish sovereignty attenuates the religious features of the life-style. But you also have the phenomenon of Mea Shearim where you see ultra-Orthodox Jews pursuing the way of life that their fathers brought with them from Eastern Europe a hundred or more years ago. Some of them, completely rejecting the national experience, try to remain an enclave which takes no part in secular life. They also reject the State itself as premature and counter to their expectations of the Messiah. But they are entirely outside the mainstream.

Son: What would you say is the mainstream?

The religious mainstream, I think, runs in the direction of the Yeshivot which combine orthodoxy with a militant nationalism to form a new type of religious Jew. We haven't had this combination in our history since the Bar Kochba revolt--and I don't even know whether those militants against the Romans were religious in our sense of the word. You might say that this type of Jew is an original creation of the Israeli environment, just as the type of the *Halutz*, the agricultural pioneer, was an original creation of the pre-State period. Even though their numerical importance isn't that great, the militant religious type has in a short time become a dominant figure on the Israeli scene. The religious Jew in the Diaspora had been a relatively passive figure in public life, first because of the self-segregation we spoke about, and second, because he was so busy with his religious practice that he had no time left to become involved in secular controversies. Now what we have here is a religious Jew who is often hyperactive politically.

The faith that motivates this group, when translated into politics, is volatile stuff. When people are absolutely sure that they represent God's will, it keeps them from compromising. How can they back down, say, in negotiations over territory? They function on the one hand in the real world of facts, and on the other, in the abstract world of faith. And when they bring the norms of the one into the other, the consequences can be unpredictable.

Son: Aren't you saying then that the effect of the Jewish religion on our political system can be quite dangerous?

In a way, yes. When you take two separate elements, each of which has its own dynamics, and mix them together, you are getting, just like in chemistry, a third element with different characteristics which may be difficult to deal with. Moreover, we know from the field of social psychology, and in particular from the studies of an American law professor and sociologist, the late Harold Lasswell, that politics has its own pathology, and indeed often attracts pathological individuals. If this type of person is also subject to religious fanaticism, then he can represent a real danger to the environment.

Chapter Twenty-Five

Is Judaism Racist?

Son: According to your thinking, anti-semitism should have more or less disappeared since there is a State. And yet we keep hearing about anti-semitic and even terrorist acts in Europe. You yourself were in Paris when the bomb went off at the Rue Copernic synagogue.

I think we have to distinguish very carefully between different phenomena. It's too bad that these are being tossed about indiscriminately, and in the end everything is labelled as anti-semitism. Actually, we are also dealing with anti-Zionism, and anti-Israel attitudes. Ever since Zionism became a force in the world, it has had its detractors, and, of course, the State of Israel has also generated some strong opposition, especially among the Arabs. So we are no longer talking simply about the classical hatred of Jews, but of opposition to the concept of a Jewish State or to the policies of the State of Israel. Sometimes these three attitudes, or at least two of them, become intertwined, and this leads to confusion. The Israelis have not done very much to clear up that confusion. I suspect that quite a few people here think it's in Israel's interest to perpetuate it, for two reasons. Once is that when there is strong opposition to Israel's actions, or policies, it's quite convenient to be able to say, well there you are, it's anti-semitism.

Son: You mean to say when an Arab country comes out against Israel…

Yes, you've heard the accusation that the Arabs are anti-semitic, and therefore everything they say or do relating to Israel is influenced by anti-semitism. But we know that things are much more complex than that.

Son: What's the second factor?

The second factor is that Israel does not like to see a rift between the State and the Jewish people over this terminology. For instance, the Arabs often plead that they are not anti-Semites, only anti-Zionist, or anti-Israel. If we were to accept that differentiation, then the Jews outside of Israel might well say, "Okay, we don't want to be held responsible for what Israel does. We'll go our own way, have our relations with Saudi Arabia, Syria, and so forth," and the results might well be a gradual turning away from Israel. And that, of course, would be very undesirable from the Israeli point of view. So it makes sense to have these categories blurred and intertwined.

Son: And you are not in favor of that? Why do you think that's bad?

First, let's have some clarity in our own minds about these concepts. Anti-semitism we've talked about before. What Herzl had in mind was that sooner or later all the Jews in the Diaspora would want to come to the Jewish state (he of course didn't know it was going to be called Israel), or else merge into their host societies and even convert. Then, in the absence of Jews, anti-semitism would also disappear. This turned out to be a fallacy, on all counts. He could not have foreseen that these notions were so strongly rooted in the popular mind that even in a country like Poland, where there were only a few thousand Jews left out of the three million who lived there before the war, anti-semitism was still a fac-

tor in the postwar period. Part of it was due to political ex-
ploitation, with the government finding it expedient to blame
Jews who were in high positions for some of the problems the
country was facing.

Anti-Zionism, I would say, is a response to the idea of a Jewish homeland, which can be felt and expressed by both Jews
and non-Jews. I think it's an anachronistic concept today, but
it's being kept alive by confusion over what Zionism is. When
the UN decided that Zionism was racist, then it made sense to
be anti-Zionist. As long as the Begin government encouraged
the notion that Zionism meant settlement in the occupied territories, then people who opposed such settlement were justified
in calling themselves anti-Zionist.

Son: And how do you feel about this?

I think it's just the opposite of Zionism, because Zionism
means concentrating the Jews in a country of their own, so they
can live among their own people, whereas settlement in the territories means going out among strangers again, the Arabs this
time, and deliberately leaving your own people behind.

Son: How would you answer the racism accusation?

I'd say it's simply irrelevant. Zionism deals with the fate of
the Jewish people, not with any other. It's like saying that the
Corsican Nationalist movement is racist, because it cares only
about the Corsicans, and not about the blacks in South Africa.
Parochial, yes, but not racist. You can argue that Judaism is
racist, or that Israel pursues racist policies, but to say Zionism
is racist simply doesn't make sense.

Son: And is Judaism racist?

Look, Judaism is a very old category, and "racist" is of recent vintage, so to apply the one to the other is first of all an anachronism. You can call Judaism exclusionist, if you will, or exclusivist. Its roots go back millenia, when peoples and religions were closed corporations. You belonged to one and didn't ordinarily cross over from one to the other. But there were exceptions, and we've always accepted converts, even though it's never been easy to become a Jew. On the other hand, the convert has had an honored position in our history; as you know, Ruth, the ancestress of King David, started out as a Moabite. From her sprang not only our most revered royal line; even the Messiah himself, through David, will eventually be her descendant *(ha-Mashiach ben-David.)* If racism means that some races (or one) are considered superior and others inferior, then it's a notion that's completely foreign to Judaism as expressed in its key sources: the Bible, the Mishna, the prayers and the medieval philosophers. Our ancestors were probably dark-skinned anyway; certainly the ravishing beauty in the Song of Songs is almost black.

When I lived in America, I had trouble relating seriously to the notion that skin color was in any way related to intelligence or other attributes, on which much of racial discrimination was based. Part of this may have been a reaction to the insane German racial theories to which I had been exposed, but a major part was simply my Jewish upbringing.

Son: Then what about the State of Israel?

I take it you have in mind attitudes and policies toward the Arab population. That's a very complex subject; I've written a book about it, and I can't give a one-sentence answer. It has to do with the way Israel views itself as a Jewish state, which on the face of it would exclude non-Jews from participating in the common experience. But this has nothing to do with race.

I have publicly stated my own view that a multi-cultural population is preferable to a mono-cultural one, because the presence of "the other" acts as a foil against which to hold up the values and actions of your own group.

Now let's get back to--where were we, anyway?

Son: You were about to tell me what Zionism means.

Oh yes. It means simply concentrating the Jewish people in a state of their own, and establishing that state in Zion. Sometimes this idea is called political Zionism, as distinct from the cultural Zionism of Ahad ha-Am (who thought of Zion as a cultural center for Jews the world over, without necessarily concentrating them here). But when we refer to Zionism today, we really mean political Zionism. Basically, it's the realization of Herzl's idea of the Jewish state; thus, a Zionist is someone who supports that idea, possibly to the extent of wanting to implement it in his own person. But since the State is an established fact, Zionism is more of a historic concept than one of current relevance. It was Ben Gurion who maintained that once there was a State there were no more Zionists, only Israelis and Jews. He also said that if people who spend their lives in the Diaspora call themselves Zionists, then he himself was not a Zionist. He thought the term Jew was sufficient to designate those people who remain outside of Israel. I tend to agree that these two concepts, Jew and Israeli, can cause enough semantic and intellectual problems, and we needn't complicate things further by retaining the term Zionist. Once a person has come on *aliyah*, he becomes an Israeli, and no longer has to emphasize that he is a Zionist. Calling Israel a Zionist state is a redundancy.

That leaves anti-Israelism. This attitude is, to my mind, a normal feature of world politics, just as there is an anti-British attitude which doesn't necessarily deal with the British national character, or the British in general, but with British policy. Just as anti-Americanism may relate to a particular aspect of American foreign policy.

Once you have a state, you must be prepared to have your policies criticized and opposed by others. Let's acknowledge that our actions are apt to provoke hostile responses among other states, or individuals; responses that have nothing to do with anti-semitism. I think we should try to eliminate that word from our political vocabulary. Let's recall that anti-semitism is a phenomenon that pertains to the Diaspora, whereas we founded our own State to escape its influence.

Son: But isn't it true that when Israel proclaims itself a Jewish state, people tend to identify Israel with Jews everywhere? And if they are opposed to Israeli policies, they will also take it out on the Jews outside of Israel?

Yes, there is some truth to that. There is a fallout of anti-Israel feeling which covers Diaspora Jews, and it may have serious consequences. The fact that the latter, who are vulnerable, are thus exposed to danger because of Israeli policies would seem to impose a restraint on the Israeli policymakers; it's something they should think about. In the past, Israel has taken it for granted that the existence of these Jewish communities in other countries has been to her advantage: the money they contributed and the political influence they exerted on their governments have added to Israel's strength. But they may also become a liability, and then it's up to Israel to demonstrate that she really has a responsibility for Jews everywhere; and that this isn't just empty talk.

Chapter Twenty-Six

Let's talk about the Arabs

Son: Can we get away from the Jews for a while and talk about the Arabs? After all, they make up a fifth of the population. And I remember that, when I was a little boy, you spent a lot of your spare time with Arabs.

You remember correctly, and you also had a right to be annoyed at them, because I didn't spend the time playing with you. Besides, you were afraid of Arabs when you were of kindergarten age, and even beyond. I recall how you once yelled at me: "Abba, don't bring any Arabs into the house!" You picked that up in our neighborhood, obviously. But why do you think I devoted so much time to these relationships? For one thing, I was very much aware of where I came from. As a Jew in Germany I had been discriminated against; as a Jew in America, I claimed equality. So I couldn't abide seeing Arabs as second-class citizens after the Jews got their own state.

Son: But didn't you take account of the fact that the Arabs have twenty or more states of their own, whereas Israel is the world's only Jewish state? And that they fought a war which was supposed to keep a Jewish state from coming into being?

I'm surprised to hear you repeat such a cliché as the business of the twenty states. We're concerned with what happens here, not in Saudi Arabia or Libya. Once the Arabs are admitted to citizenship, they're entitled to equal treatment. As for Israel being a Jewish state, I see a problem with that. Theodor Herzl's pamphlet, *The Jewish State,* is actually called *Der Judenstaat* in the original German, which means the State of the Jews. Herzl was enough of a political scientist to know that a state is not Jewish, only people are Jewish. If there are enough Jews in a state (such as Herzl foresaw in his *Judenstaat)* then Jews will feel at home in it and will practice their religion and culture freely. But it doesn't mean that the Jewishness has to be anchored in the constitution, or the law, any more than Christianity is anchored in the law of the United States, or of France. I should think keeping the Sabbath as the weekly day of rest and permitting every Jew to enter the country freely makes Israel Jewish enough without making its Arab citizens feel uncomfortable.

In recent years, the problem has often been posed in the form of the question, "Should Israel be a Jewish state or a state of all its citizens?" My own view is that any state must be a state of all its citizens.

It's true that there is this legacy of the War of Independence, but the Palestinian Arabs who fought against Israel are not the same ones who stayed behind. Even if they did, by becoming citizens of Israel, they made a new start. Up to1967, there were very few instances of Israeli Arabs becoming enemy agents, or acting disloyally in the major wars. But there's no doubt that since then their position has become more ambivalent. They were reunited with their brothers across the Green Line, refugees and others, and they were no longer dependent on Israel alone for their status, cultural and political. Some of us Jews were somewhat disappointed that Israeli Arabs didn't play more of a role in bringing about peace, or at least better understanding, but I suppose the continued occupation of the territories prevented that. Israel continued to be the enemy, and her Arabs did not want to appear as collaborators. So there was little attempt at mediation on their part. The Arab Knesset members (of whom there are about ten) also play a somewhat ambivalent role. One of them, Dr. Ahmed Tibi, served for a while as adviser to Yasser Arafat, and the question of his loyalty came up from time to time. It reminded me of how, in the old days, some people in America accused Jews of dual loyalty when they became too involved in Zionist affairs.

Son: I see that you are still influenced by your American experience. But weren't you a bit naive to think that you could have much of an impact on the Arab issue?

The years I spent in America certainly had a profound influence on me. I may have been naive, but I also accomplished a few things, sometimes together with other people. In 1966 I did the research for the little book, *From Conflict to Understanding: Relations between Jews and Arabs in Israel since 1948,* which was published by the American Jewish Committee and drew attention to the problem in a concise and, I think, objective fashion. I recently looked over the book and found that quite a bit of it if is still relevant. I think you might want to read the introduction at least. The American Jewish Committee also helped out with the founding of the Israel Association for Civil Rights, which I brought into being, along with a couple of other people, in the early seventies. The model was the American Civil Liberties Union, with which I was familiar. My co-founders of the Israel body were Dr. Bernard Resnikoff, then the director of the AJC Israel office who paid for a part-time secretary in the initial period: my friend Nissim Rejwan, whom you know; Professor Menachem Amir, a Hebrew University criminologist; Professor Leslie Sebba of the Faculty of Law and the late Bill Weisgal, an American lawyer with the Ministry of Justice. We worked out of the offices of the AJC on Ethiopia Street, which was also the address of the Jerusalem branch of Brandeis University, of which I was then the director. Our method of operation was to receive complaints, investigate them as best we could and suggest a solution.

Since then, the Association has become far more profession-al and influential; I served on its board of directors in later years but have since been just a dues-paying member.

Son: Some day you'll have to tell me about some of those American Jewish organizations you were associated with. They all sound the same to me.

I'll gladly do that. In the meantime, we're still with the Is-raeli Arabs. In a talk I gave at the Hebrew University Hillel when I was in Jerusalem on the Ford Foundation grant in 1953, I said I would rather live in a multi-cultural society than in a mono-cultural one; because the presence of "the other" in our midst could be enriching and also was a challenge to our own ethical standards and behavior. That's still my view.

Early in the sixties, I helped a woman called Nina DiNur (who was married to the author who wrote books about the Ho-locaust under the name of *Ka-tzetnik*) to organize a discussion group among young Jewish and Arab intellectuals. We met once a week in private homes in Tel Aviv, and I recall that there was a feeling of openness and mutual respect at those meetings which was quite different from the atmosphere in the country at large. Later in the decade, I placed the American students in the Brandeis program with Arab families in Nazareth for a long weekend. Most of the students hit it off well with their hosts. As one of the Arab host ladies said to me, "If only the Jews here were like these Americans!" But that was, of course, simplistic. Our students were outsiders, faced with a different existential situation. Still, the experience made them aware, in a concrete way, that Israel was not only the land of the Jews, but of the Arabs as well.

You may be right that I was a bit naive in all this: most Israeli Jews were suspicious of the Arabs, and they were also suspi-cious of someone who was too chummy with Arabs. When I did the research for my book, I was asked repeatedly in one form or another: "Why are you so concerned about the Arabs? Isn't there enough to write about the Jews?" And I was given to understand that Nina diNur's social evenings were not considered quite *kosher* in some quarters. One of Mommy's former classmates was married to a *Shabak* agent, and he found a way to let her know that I was under investigation. I sent word back that I would like to talk to them. But *they* don't want to talk to *you*, came the reply. Later on, I sometimes had the feeling that I had a black mark somewhere in a secret file that interfered with my career. Even you may have been affected by it. Remember when you applied to serve in the army Intelligence branch while you were still in high school, and you were turned down when other boys in your class were accepted? It's quite likely that your Dad's extracurricular activities had something to do with it.

Son: Isn't this more or less what they called McCarthyism in America?

Not exactly. The Israelis had more reason to be worried about Arabs than the Americans about Communists. And Israeli politicians didn't try to build themselves up through an Arab scare the way McCarthy did through his Commie-scare. I still remember the time when every university professor in America had to take a loyalty oath. And there was McCarthyism also in some of the Jewish organizations I was working for.

Son: And do you think it's all right for these American Jewish groups to become so involved in the Arab issue?

From my point of view, they were a resource I could turn to. I told the American Jewish Committee more or less: Look, you're advocating racial and religious equality in the United

States, so how can you not stand for the same principles in Israel? As long as you maintain an office there, you've got to speak out. And they bought that. It's true that ultimately the Israelis themselves have to decide on the kind of society they want, but American Jews can do a bit of prodding, especially if it's in an area where they have a major interest. The Association for Civil Rights in Israel has also been getting much of its support from American Jewry, through an annual fund-raising appeal called the New Israel Fund. The money they raise through membership dues here makes up only a fraction of their annual budget; most of it comes from contributions of American Jews. And quite a few of these give to the New Israel Fund rather than to the United Jewish Appeal, most of the money from which goes to the Jewish Agency. But here we're getting into the field of Israel-Diaspora relations, which is a separate chapter.

Son: And a major one in your own life, so I understand.

Yes, I spent a good part of my professional life in it. But we didn't exhaust the subject of the Arabs, did we?

Chapter Twenty-Seven
The Arab Refugees

<u>Son:</u> I've really wanted to ask you how you feel about the Arab refugee problem.

The way I feel about them is terribly sad... sad that as a result of the rise of Israel, so many thousands -- hundreds of thousands -- of people lost their homes and had to live through years of deprivation and misery. I know that we have found all kinds of rationales to avoid facing the problem, and until 1967 it was simple enough, because the refugees were across the border. So it was easy to say they left of their own accord, and that it was up to the Arab states to resettle them. Or that there was an exchange of populations: Jews from the Arab countries came here and took the place of the Arabs who left. Both left their property behind. But after the Six Day war some of the camps were right at our doorstep, in Gaza and the West Bank, and it was hard not to be aware of them and sympathize with the refugees. But we somehow managed it.

Ninety-nine and more percent of the population never set foot in one of the camps or showed any curiosity about them. Officially, they were the responsibility of the U.N., through UNRWA, the United Nations Relief and Works Administration (for Palestine Refugees), and Israel contributed to its annual budget through its membership in the U.N. As for paying compensation for the property the refugees left behind, that would be part of an eventual peace settlement. But one also can understand that most people were apprehensive about how they would be received in those camps. After all, we were the enemy, who kept them from going back to their homes. The indifference may well have been the most human reaction to the situation.

It so happened that I was in a favored position to study the situation, first as an academic, and then as an American. In my academic capacity, as the director of the Brandeis University program here, and as the author of a book on the Arabs in Israel which had just been published, I was invited to be part of a team of three faculty members of the Hebrew University School of Social Work, who were asked by the Ministry of Defense to submit recommendations from a social welfare perspective. The four of us drove down to Gaza almost every Shabbat morning – you were eight or nine at the time, and you were probably angry about the whole thing because it was quality time I should have spent with you. The UNRWA director in Gaza, a Mr. Geany, was an American. He delegated one of his assistants to work with us, a Palestinian social worker called Majdalawi. M. interpreted for us and showed us around the camps and the UNRWA institutions, such as food distribution points, clinics and schools. We developed a rather warm relationship with him, and also invited him to Jerusalem. The head of our team, Prof. Yona Rosenfeld, wrote a little essay about the friendship which he called "Colleagues and Enemies."

Part of the friendly reception we received in the camps and elsewhere in Gaza probably had to do with the fact that the Palestinians were still waiting for some kind of gesture from Israel which would change their lives for the better, and they welcomed our project as a step in that direction.

Son: And did anything come of it?

Not that I know of. After six months, we submitted a report which recommended a series of steps that were designed to ease the lot of the worst welfare cases at moderate cost, but the army apparently got cold feet and shelved the report. It was marked Confidential at the time, but by now I suppose I'm not giving away any secrets. I must tell you that for me visiting those camps was a sobering experience. Sometimes I woke up in the middle of the night wondering whether it was morally justified to build up our prospering state and society at the cost of so much misery and suffering on the part of so many people. I realized that there was very little one could do as an individual, and even projects such as the ones we proposed in our report could only be palliatives. But as a government we had a responsibility to help bring about a solution, instead of waiting for the problem to go away by itself.

In our case, I was convinced that this was not pure altruism; there was also a good deal of self-interest involved. I saw the alleys in the refugee camps teeming with thousands of children, and I said to myself that if something is not done soon those kids will grow up to hate us and to fight against us. Sure enough, twenty years later there came the Intifada, which started in Gaza.

<u>Son:</u> Meaning nothing was done to solve the refugee problem.

Nothing worth mentioning. I made one attempt to use a contact I had in high places. I sent a letter to Simha Dinitz, who was an adviser to Prime Minister Golda Meir (she later appointed him ambassador to the United States). Simha was our neighbor in Jerusalem, and a friend. I wrote him about my impressions, and that I saw in the Gaza refugee camps seedbeds of future conflict. And I suggested a formula for liquidating those camps: let Israel take back a third of the inhabitants, the Arab countries one-third, and the rest of the world the remaining third. Simha wrote back that the refugee problem would be part of the agenda of a permanent peace settlement between Israel and the Palestinians.

To me it's clear that, by the time a permanent peace settlement is reached, the older generation of the refugees will have died off, without having benefited from any compensation for the property they left behind. This is painful to contemplate, in light of our own experience. Not that there is any basis for comparing the German crimes against the Jews with the Arab-Israel situation, but the rights of the refugees need to be acknowledged on an absolute basis, without any such comparison. The property they left behind, especially the real estate, has certainly contributed to Israel's economic progress and prosperity. After the annexation of East Jerusalem, Israel made an offer to compensate Arab residents who had owned property in formerly Arab parts of today's West Jerusalem, such as Katamon and Talbieh. But the offer was based on the value of the property in 1948, rather than the current value, and the Arabs refused to accept this. So in the end nothing came of that initiative.

I took advantage of the connection with the UNRWA people to arrange for visits to the camps for my Brandeis groups. I think ours were the only American students studying in Israel who were offered that experience as part of their course.

Apart from Gaza, we also visited the camp at Kalandia, north of Jerusalem, where I developed a special relationship with the UNRWA director, an Armenian called Tony Bakerjian who lived with his family in the Old City. He invited me to his home, and he showed me around the Armenian Quarter. Our friendship lasted for some years, until I left Jerusalem for Paris in 1979. There was never any trouble when we visited Kalandia with the students, but in later years there was often rioting and stone throwing at Israeli soldiers in the camp. I was impressed by the way most of the refugee families kept their small and crowded homes spotlessly clean, how they managed to live civilized lives without sanitary facilities and running water, and in general keep up their dignity and humanity without giving in to despair. In the classrooms we visited in the UNRWA schools, the children were neatly dressed, disciplined and polite, eager to show off their knowledge and skills to visitors.

<u>Son:</u> Wouldn't you say that at least part of your empathy for the Arab refugees derives from your background, first as a German Jew and then as an American? Whereas the rest of us tend to see the problem as above all a political one. In other words, what's our national interest?

Chapter Twenty-Eight

A New Type of Jew

You may have a point there. The Jew as Israeli is no longer the same type as the Jews in the Diaspora; he underwent a more or less thorough transformation. The Arabs here are aware of this; they find it much easier to deal with American Jews than with Israelis. I already told you about Nazareth. I also remember a visit I paid to Bir Zeit University, near Ramallah, soon after the Six-Day-War. I went there with a couple of friends who were on the Hebrew University faculty, to call on the President of Bir Zeit, Dr.Yusuf Nasr. His son, Hanna Nasr, who later succeeded him as president, was also in the room. "It's too bad you Jews chose to go into politics," the old man reproached us. "You should have stuck to religion, which everybody knows is your strongest side."

Politicization is part of the problem, but by no means the whole; much of it occurs on the level of the individual personality. The Israeli as a citizen of the state knows instinctively that adopting a humanitarian attitude on the refugee question will have political consequences, and he's not eager to see his government take on financial or moral obligations, except perhaps as part of an overall bargaining situation. This is essentially what Simha Dinitz wrote to me: wait until a peace settlement.

As an American Jew, I'm still programmed to see first the human, or humanitarian side of the question. The more so since I was working in the organized Jewish community, where welfare was a topmost concern, apart from religion. Even the money contributed to Israel was destined for welfare programs, which included immigrant absorption. When Israel entered

Lebanon in 1982, there was a timid attempt by the Joint Distribution Committee, the American partner in the UJA, to develop some kind of program on behalf of Palestinian refugees there, which didn't get very far.

Son: But didn't you study political science at university, and also teach it? So I'd expect you to come up with a more political approach to these problems.

You're right. But there's a difference between analyzing situations from a political perspective and being yourself caught up in a given situation. Besides, my main motivation for studying politics, and more specifically, international relations, was to have a better understanding of how we Jews would conduct our state, what having our state would do to us, and how that state would fit into the international arena.

Son: That really sounds like the assignment of a lifetime. And have you come up with the answers yet?

Only partial ones. But I'm still learning every day. Actually, the time that's elapsed since 1948 isn't really long enough for reaching conclusive answers. I think the generations that have lived through what I would call the Modern Jewish Experience, which includes of course the Holocaust, have to disappear before the true results can emerge. It's somewhat like the generation of the desert in the Book of Exodus, which had to pass on before the Children of Israel were ready to enter the Promised Land. Do you remember that from your Bible lessons?

Son: Vaguely. I'll have to read up on it some time. In what way do you think the Holocaust has left such an impact on the later generations?

First, let me explain why I think my generation has to make way before the true Israeli type, both as an individual and as a collective, something like national character, can emerge. The Diaspora fosters, and even calls for, a type of existence that's fundamentally different from that in a sovereign state. As you yourself put it so succinctly when we spent a few months in London in 1975, "I wouldn't want to live as a Jew in the Diaspora; I wouldn't want to be part of a minority." You were being exposed to anti-semitic ribbing in school, and at 15 you only saw the downside of being a Jew. You also sensed that Diaspora Jewishness was likely to breed a victim psychology, and you wanted no part of that.

Chapter Twenty-Nine

The Holocaust (2) and Legitimacy

As for the Holocaust, I don't think you can generalize about its impact, except in one respect: it's legitimized the rise of Israel in the sense that it's made Jews and others aware of the vulnerability of the Jewish people without a state. But the main impact has been on the individual survivor, and on the descendants of both survivors and victims. And there the effect has varied from one individual to another. In Israel, you constantly encounter people with concentration camp numbers branded on their arms who lead perfectly normal lives; and then there are others who were so completely broken by the horrors they endured that they've spent fifty or more years in psychiatric wards. I don't think anybody who's not actually been through it himself can claim to be a survivor. In my case, you'll never hear me say that I've survived the Holocaust; rather, that I've escaped it, that I got out in time.

No one questions, of course, that family and descendants are entitled to the property of the victims, or that the Germans must make restitution for what they stole and pay reparations for their crimes, or that Israel as a state is the proper address for the collective reparations that Germany has paid to the Jewish people. In that sense, Israel is the Jewish state as well as the state of the Jews.

Son: Are you implying that in areas other than Jewish property Israel should not be considered a successor state to the Holocaust victims?

Well, as long as survivors, or descendants of victims, are still counted among its population, I believe it's legitimate for Israel to assume the role of a successor state. That's also part of what I called the "generation of the desert" syndrome. Most of that role does consist of dealing with property, such as representing the claims of victims and their heirs on international committees, etc., together with worldwide Jewish organizations. Also, there is a grey area, where the Israel government may feel it's entitled to a certain moral advantage as the successor state. You may have noted that almost every important visitor is taken to *Yad vaShem* during his official visit. That makes a statement, of course. Insofar as it states that Israel is the custodian of the memory of the six million, that's legitimate. But if it goes beyond that to say: "in your dealings with us, remember the suffering we went through as a people," I don't think that's justified. The suffering was inflicted by the Germans, and not by the world as a whole, and those who suffered were the victims and the survivors, not the Israeli people as a whole.

I have a theory, for which there is no empirical evidence, that the Holocaust has some connection with the attitude towards death in Israel. I find that there is a certain stoicism among the population when it comes to accepting loss of lives as a result of military action or other disasters. That attitude seems to say that, if six million can be wiped out, then an individual life is not worth a great deal.

Son: I would have thought that, after such a tremendous loss, every single life would be precious.

You may be right. As I said, I have no proof for my theory.

There was a time, in the first decade of the state, when Israelis were much less concerned with the Holocaust. The *sabras* (native-born Israelis) in particular saw it as a somehow shameful episode, in which Jews let themselves be led to slaughter without putting up resistance. As if to say, those who chose to stay in the Diaspora when they could have come to Palestine had only themselves to blame. And the survivors among the immigrants sensed that there was not much interest in hearing about their suffering, so they kept quiet about it. Many didn't even talk about their experience with their own children.

When you were very young, Mommy and I debated whether to tell you about the Holocaust altogether. We were afraid you might get upset, and that it would shake your faith in humanity when you learned about the atrocious things that were done to the Jews. And that in the end you might ask yourself: Why be a Jew if such a thing could happen again? Similar thoughts may have motivated other Israeli parents in those days.

The turning point was the Eichmann Trial. For the survivors, it became a kind of catharsis, and for the population as a whole a lesson in history which made the Holocaust an indelible part of the national ethos. You might say it was one of Ben-Gurion's master strokes. The part about Eichmann's capture in Argentina and his abduction to Israel made the whole thing even more dramatic.

Son: Getting back to Israel's international relations, You seem to be fond of the word "legitimate" Don't you think that world politics is basically a power game, where everybody grabs what he can get? The Holocaust background has been an asset for Israel, and you can't blame the leadership for putting it to use. Begin tried to wreck the reparations agreement with Germany as a matter of principle, but Ben Gurion and his pragmatism won out.

I see you know quite a bit of Israel's early history. That was in 1952, before you were born.

It's true that the word "legitimate" has a prominent place in my political vocabulary. Maybe it's because much of the story of Zionism – and of Israel's early history, for that matter – is about legitimacy, which basically means recognition. Herzl sought recognition of the Jewish claim for a territory, and he wasn't around any more when the British granted it in the Balfour Declaration. The Peel Commission in 1937 gave legitimacy to the concept of a Jewish state in a partitioned Palestine, though on minimum territory. Then the U.N. Partition Resolution of 1947 took it a step further: it legitimized the declaration of Israel's sovereignty, even without the counterpart Arab state which the resolution called for. Then the Armistice Agreements, which were signed in 1949 by all the Arab countries that fought Israel (except for Iraq) lent a form of legitimacy to the Israeli state, which they subsequently proceeded to deny. So Israel had to fight hard for legitimacy, and should know to appreciate it.

To my mind it's the U.N. resolution which partitioned Palestine into a Jewish and an Arab state that gave legitimacy to the concept of a Jewish state, rather than merely a state of Jews, as Herzl had envisioned. And it's interesting that Ben Gurion decided to call that state Israel, rather than Judea. After all, the biblical state of Israel, with its ten tribes, disappeared without a trace. It's the two tribes which made up the state of Judea who survived as the Jewish people. By choosing the name Israel, so it seems to me, B-G meant to emphasize that the state, while related to the Jews of the Diaspora, was not synonymous with them. But that is strictly my own theory, you may take it or leave it. It jibes with that other doctrine of mine – that the state as such is not Jewish, but that Israel is the place where the Jews have their state. To rephrase what I just said, Israel was labelled as the Jewish state because the U.N. divided Palestine into a Jewish and an Arab state. Ultimately, because most of its population was Jewish, not because the state as such had any particular Jewish attributes.

I know you are going to ask, "What about Muslim states?" States where Islamic law is the law of the land have a right to call themselves Muslim states, but in Israel Jewish law is not the law of the land. Whoever wishes to adhere to it in his personal life, in addition to Knesset-legislated law, is welcome to do so.

Son: It seems to me that, the way you present it, Israel may eventually find itself closer to the Arabs than to the Diaspora. Am I right?

That's putting it a bit crassly, but there may be some truth in it. The way things started out, in 1948 when the state was born, the Arabs were unalterably opposed, made war, imposed a boycott, and showed their hostility in every way possible. The Diaspora Jews were the closest allies, lent support politically and materially, and were also the source of manpower, through immigration. There was a kind of reciprocal relationship between Arab hostility and Jewish closeness. The natural hinterland, the Arab world, was not accessible, so the Diaspora served as a substitute. There was a climactic moment at the time of the 1967 War when Israel felt isolated and the Jewish world revealed itself as a faithful partner. But that moment did not last. After the Yom Kippur War and the peace with Egypt, then Oslo, there came a gradual rapprochement with parts of the Arab world, and a corresponding decline in the strategic importance of Jewish support. Rabin even expressed annoyance with what he felt was too much Jewish involvement in Israel's relationship with the American administration.

Also, with Israel's growing prosperity, the role of Jewish financial aid became less crucial. When I first came to Israel, income from UJA and other such campaigns came to more than half as much as the total of all annual exports, and the dollars these campaigns brought in were desperately needed. There were no foreign currency reserves. Now we're in a different universe. Once there will be genuine interaction on the economic and cultural levels with our neighbors, the Palestinians, and with other Arab countries, the Diaspora may lose even more of its hinterland status. Our natural hinterland will be the Arab world and the Mediterranean.

Eventually, Israel's interest in the Diaspora may diminish not just in the political and economic spheres, but also people-to-people. The Jews as such are simply not that fascinating to the younger generation of Israelis, for whom the common origin in Eastern Europe (among the Ashkenazim) no longer plays a significant role. Have you ever heard of young people, after the army, going back-packing across the U.S. to discover Jewish communities there, unless the trip is sponsored by the establishment?

They go to India and South America. And this has worked both ways. In the first decades, Diaspora Jews derived a tremendous pride in Israel's accomplishments, and identified with its problems. Through the fund-raising campaigns, they were given a sense of participation in the nation-building process, primarily through financing the immigration. Then came the Six-Day War and brought about this powerful feeling of solidarity with Israel. The Yom Kippur War again raised emotions, mainly anxiety, to a fever pitch. But these dramatic events only delayed the drifting apart. It's true that a visit to Israel is still an inspiring experience for young Diaspora Jews. But Israeli high school students travel on subsidized trips to Poland, where they visit Auschwitz and other extermination camps. The idea is to strengthen their Jewish identity by a deeper knowledge of the Holocaust.

Chapter Thirty

Israel in 1949 - First Impressions

<u>Son:</u> What was your impression of the country in 1949?

I thought I already made it clear that I was in a state of euphoria. Everything seemed so right. That goes both for my personal status and for the surroundings. There was an upbeat mood everywhere, in spite of the economic hardship which forced a regime of *tzena*, which means austerity. The Jewish population was still well under a million; with a genuine sense of community. The political party system, which was taken over from the pre-state *Yishuv* (Jewish community under the British mandate) seemed functional enough, and its leaders were mostly people of real stature who inspired confidence. Ben-Gurion's leadership was unchallenged. Jerusalem was small and divided, but it had that special aura about it which made you feel privileged to live there. For me, the nightly walk home by moonlight to my rented room on Abyssinia Street after putting the paper to bed at 1 a.m. was an almost mystical experience. The paper itself, all four pages of it (eight on Fridays) -- the shortage of foreign currency caused a shortage of newsprint -- seemed to me the equal of the New York Times.

The Post editorial staff, mostly Americans, were a close-knit bunch; with some of them I remained friends for life. The young American immigrants who came at that time were a select group; the idealism that brought them here lent them an ennobling quality, and they were looked up to with admiration. Imagine, giving up the fleshpots of America for our austerity! I was pleased to be counted among them, even though I was not quite an immigrant. Nor, for that matter, quite an American.

But there was another part of my identity which got quite a boost in Jerusalem.

Son: Let's see, what could that be? Being a German Jew?

Exactly. How did you guess?

Son: There are not that many alternatives.

The fact is, I found myself attracted to the *Yekke* (German Jewish) community, and became acquainted with some of the academics and intellectuals among them. They were mostly people who had been Zionists in Europe; some of them, such as Ernst Simon and Hugo Bergmann, even before Hitler.

These names probably don't mean anything to you, but they were among the leading lights at the Hebrew University at the time. On the whole, the *Yekkes* I met in Jerusalem were an entirely different breed from the lower middle class types who inhabited Washington Heights. I felt not only drawn to them, but considered myself a part of them. With my Princeton B.A., I had suddenly become an academic, a *Yekke* and a Jerusalemite, in addition to being an American, and a journalist on a respected paper.

Son: That's quite a mix. I'm beginning to think that part of your Zionism is simply nostalgia for that first year in Jerusalem. Was it Robert Browning or Elizabeth who wrote about that "first, fine carefree rapture that you never can recapture?"

Careless rapture. There may be something to that. Actually, I haven't told you half the things I was able to cram into that one year. I worked as a part-time correspondent for the United Press of America, and on the basis of the stories I wrote, their bureau chief in Tel Aviv, Eliav Simon, gave me a glowing letter of recommendation to the home office in New York when I went back. One of those stories was about the Magic Carpet airlift of 50,000 Yemenite Jews from Aden to Tel Aviv in the spring of 1950. Aden, which is now part of Yemen, was still a British Crown Colony then, and the "Joint," the American Jewish Joint Distribution Committee, maintained a transit camp just outside the city. After a long trek through the desert, the *olim* were given a warm welcome there, including medical attention, and were readied for the flight to Israel. I flew back to Tel Aviv with a group of them; the flight on the ancient DC-4 took eight hours, but for the passengers it was like a leap over centuries. The Yemenites are a folk of rather small build, and the JDC people were able to squeeze over 100 of them into a plane meant for 50. There were wrenching scenes when the passengers were told they had to leave their heavy Torah scrolls behind (to be shipped separately) because of the weight limit of the aircraft. Once in Israel, the Yemenites adapted quickly to the twentieth century environment and became valuable citizens.

Son: But if you had such a great time, why did you go back to the States?

I went back in June 1950 mainly because I didn't want to run out on my parents. My dad had arrived in the U.S. just four years earlier, after spending the war hiding in Holland. My mother was still the main breadwinner, with her insurance agency. They were proud of me, relied on me, and it would have been a terrific blow to them if I had stayed away. A decade later, when I moved to Israel permanently, I still had qualms about leaving them.

Son: You said they were the main reason you went back in 1950. Were there others?

Yes, there were others. One was called Ruthie. She was one of the reasons I went to Israel in the first place, and also for coming back. She was a beautiful girl, the only daughter of a Hungarian immigrant couple. I was in love with her – what else is there to say? But she was a bit on the young side (I won't tell you her age), and I didn't seem to make much of an impression on her. She was an ardent Zionist, and belonged to the *Hashomer Hatzair* youth movement, which prepared its members for life on a kibbutz. She constantly told me about her *gar'in*, the nucleus of a future kibbutz to which she belonged, and the impressive young people who were part of it and would be going together on *aliyah* to Israel. She looked on me as an outsider to this aspect of her life, and altogether hopelessly bourgeois, what with my Princeton education. Moreover, she was a talented illustrator, about to graduate from the High School of Music and Arts, and was part of a circle of young bohemians which was closed to me. I probably thought my going to Israel before she got there herself would make a big impression on her. I said I'd be waiting for her when she got there with her *gar'in*.

Son: So what happened?

She didn't get there. As I said, the thought of her helped bring me back to the U.S.

Son: And what did you find?

That she had another boy friend, an Armenian fellow, also quite a bit older than she. The *gar'in* left for Israel and Kibbutz Sassa in the Galilee without her.

Son: Weren't you angry at her for giving up her ideals just like that?

Not really. My friend Lee Caligor used to be a *madrikh* (counselor) in the *Shomer ha-Tzair* youth movement, and when he later looked back on that period from the vantage point of his calling as a psychoanalyst, he thought the movement offered an adolescent philosophy, and that those who stuck with it remained emotional adolescents. Ruthie later did spend some time in Israel – after I had left – even though she had quit the movement. We remained friends, and she and Mommy also got along well. Then both her parents died within one week, and the two of us supported her in her distress. Her father was struck down by a heart attack; then her mother, still young and very handsome, put her head in the kitchen gas stove. Ruthie herself later married a Jewish journalist, and they had two lovely daughters. The couple worked together as free-lancers on magazine articles, with her doing the illustrations. Then one day she fell off a boat in Long Island Sound and drowned. Her husband later visited us in Jerusalem, but I don't think you met him.

Chapter Thirty-One

Aliyah de Luxe

<u>Son:</u> Did you marry Mommy because she was an Israeli?

I don't think that's enough of a reason to marry somebody. But there was definitely something about the Israeli type she represented that I was attracted to. Besides, I was planning to go back to Israel sooner or later, and marrying an Israeli would make the move easier (so I must have thought). Actually, Mommy adjusted easily to the States and was in no great rush to go back. Her personality went over well with Americans, and her natural charm helped her make friends quickly. She fitted in easily in all kinds of *milieux*, whether it was at a Princeton football game or a group of Jewish intellectuals. And also among my family. In fact, even to this day, Mommy sometimes mentions that she finds it easier to talk to Americans than to Israelis. But she agreed with me that Israel was a better place in which to develop one's true personality, without having to adapt it to the demands of the current environment. And above all, to bring up children.

<u>Son:</u> Did you think of me at all when you made the decision of where to live?

In every family the parents decide where to make their home, and the children come along. And as I said, Israel seemed to us like the best place for a Jewish child to grow up in.

<u>Son:</u> Except for those that got killed in the army.

In your case, you were just a year old when we came on *aliyah*, in 1961, and we were sure that by the time you were 18 there would be peace. Had I known how long the conflict with the Palestinians would last, I don't know if I would have come. One of our neighbors in Jerusalem who came on *aliyah* a few years earlier with his Israeli-born wife, lost a son in the Lebanese war and never really got over it. It's an awesome responsibility to expose a child to the risk of being killed because you yourself want to realize your ideals. Even doing three years' army service and annual reserve duty after that, while your contemporaries in America enjoy campus life, is a lot to ask for. So you're certainly entitled to question us, even though the answers may not completely satisfy you.

Son: What made you decide so quickly to pack up and leave for Israel?

There was a very unusual job opportunity that presented itself which amounted to a kind of *aliyah de luxe*, with all expenses paid. It was closely related to the work I was doing for the Council of Jewish Federations; involving an American presence in Jerusalem to keep an eye on how tax-exempt UJA funds were being used. What mattered was that it was a job of some responsibility, some room for innovation (or so I thought at the time) and a certain amount of prestige. And that it permitted me to make the move without breaking off my ties with the U.S., leaving me the option of coming back if things didn't work out. I think my parents assumed it was a temporary assignment, which made the parting so much easier. I also flew back to the States on business at least once a year.

Son: And the salary?

That was a minor issue for me at the time. It was agreed that I would continue earning the same salary as I'd been getting at the Council, which was modest by American standards but quite generous by the prevailing Israeli scale. And it was paid in dollars, something highly unusual at the time. So I considered myself lucky. So lucky in fact, that when they offered me a raise a year later, I turned it down. I told Gottlieb Hammer, the Executive Director of the Jewish Agency Inc. in New York (my new employer), that I was being paid enough. Hammer was surprised, and he mentioned it to Dewey Stone, the chairman of the Board of Directors. At the next Board meeting, Stone told his colleagues that it was the first time in his forty years of service in the Jewish community that he heard of someone turning down a raise. I still have the excerpt from the minutes, which Hammer sent me.

Son: It sounds like you were what we Israelis call a *"freier"* (sucker).

I don't think so. I simply felt that I did not want to be placed way above the level of my colleagues in the Jerusalem Jewish Agency, like some colonial official lording it over the natives. You must remember that in those days differences in pay between the lowest and the highest grades were much less in Israel, and the size of the pay check was not an indication of one's importance.

Son: What was the job they sent you to do, precisely?

I won't be too precise, because that would take up most of our time. I've written two books on the subject, and you may want to look at them sometime. One is called, *Chosen Instrument: The Jewish Agency in the First Decade of the State of Israel,* and the other, *Beyond Partnership: The Jewish Agency and the Diaspora.* The term Chosen Instrument refers to an airline or shipping line which a government chooses as its "instrument" on a certain route. The idea was that the Jewish people chose the Jewish Agency as its instrument in dealing with Israel. Now where did I fit in? In about 1960, the U.S. government tightened the regulations whereby money contributed for charitable purposes overseas enjoyed tax exemption, or reduction. From then on, it had to be spent by an American organization, not by a foreign one. The Jewish Agency for Israel, which received almost two-thirds of all the money raised by the United Jewish Appeal, was not an American body. But it had an American branch, called the Jewish Agency Inc. This was reconstituted (mainly by giving it an American board of directors) and put in charge of the entire structure. It became the recipient of the UJA money and entered into a contract with the Israeli Jewish Agency to disburse these funds. So there seemed to be very little change on the ground, only on paper. Except for one other thing: The Jewish Agency up to now had been more or less synonymous with the World Zionist Organization, and its directors (or members of the Executive, as they were called) were representatives of the same political parties which also made up the Israel government. This was also against the U.S. income tax laws, which forbade using tax-exempt funds for political purposes. So the Jewish Agency had to be separated from the Zionist Organization, to conform to those laws. This was going to have additional significance a few years later, after the 1967 War, when Israel started founding settlements in the West Bank and wanted to use the Agricultural Settlement Department of the Jewish Agency to do the job. But it turned out that the American UJA money could only be spent in Israel proper, and so the Agency had to stay out of the occupied territories. Financing the new settlements was turned over to the WZO, which was mostly funded from other sources.

<u>Son:</u> You still didn't tell me how you fitted in with all this.

The Jewish Agency Inc. had to open an office in Jerusalem to supervise the carrying out of the contract, and I was put in charge of it. True, as the official representative in Israel they appointed a man much better known and prestigious than I. He was Dr. Isadore Lubin, an economist who had been a member of President Roosevelt's famous "brain trust." I was to be his deputy. Whereas he visited the Jerusalem office for brief periods from time to time, I stayed behind permanently and helped prepare the reports he presented to the Board in New York.

Chapter Thirty-Two

Five Years with the Jewish Agency

<u>Son:</u> How did they pick you of all people for this job?

I was in a strategic position to apply for it. Or perhaps I maneuvered myself into that position. As I told you, I left Israel in June 1950 determined that I would come back one day. Getting married to an Israeli woman fitted in with that plan, and going to work for the Council of Jewish Federations as their expert on Israel was another step in the same direction. I did research and put out reports on how American Jewish funds were being used in Israel, mostly by the Jewish Agency, but also by other beneficiaries of the community campaigns, such as the universities. The Council had a reputation for objective reporting, rather than making things look good for fund-raising purposes. In fact, one of its main *raisons d'être* was to supply the member federations with the information on which to base their decisions on how to allocate the money they raised. So there was a quasi-academic side to my work, which I managed to get done while studying for a doctorate in international relations at Columbia University. Dr. Lubin himself had a reputation for scholarship and solid research, and he was looking for a deputy with the right qualifications.

It didn't take me very long to understand that if I was going to be overly critical in reporting back on how the money was being spent, I would soon find myself on a plane to the U.S. Even so, I was called on the carpet once or twice by the Agency Treasurer (later chairman), a lawyer from South Africa called Louis Pincus. He was an *ex officio* member of the board of the Jewish Agency Inc., and as such received the reports I'd been sending to New York. But the Jewish Agency in Jerusalem was still an integral part of the party political system in Israel, and they weren't going to let a young whippersnapper from the States tell them how to run things. They had gone along with the reorganization reluctantly, only because there was no alternative. And they also suspected that the Council of Jewish Federations for which I'd been working earlier, was pushing for the reforms because it wanted to see changes in the Jewish Agency structure, and that my loyalties still lay with the Council.

Son: And did they?

Well, I believed in the role of the Council as an impartial reporting agency, which also pressed for more rational decision-making in how philanthropic funds were being spent in Israel. Some of these pressures eventually showed results, but by that time I was no longer with the Jewish Agency, Inc. I came to realize that some of my expectations were naïve and unrealistic. The Council was basically a bureaucratic agency, with a major interest in transparency, or proper accounting for communal funds, whereas the Jewish Agency was an instrument in a historic process, operating on a different level entirely. I could understand that the Agency people were impatient with the Council's somewhat cold-blooded approach, and I sometimes even had a feeling of humility in seeing the tasks they were facing.

Son: What were some of the things you were reporting to which Louis Pincus objected?

Here's an example: At one point I spent a week in Dimona, a so-called "development town" in the Negev to which the

Agency sent a great many immigrants. This was after I had observed how the immigrants were being processed on the ship from Europe. The main criterion for deciding where to send them was the availability of housing in a particular location, regardless of whether there were jobs available for them. At best, they were retrained to work in the building trades, to put up more housing for more immigrants. This made for a lot of unhappiness, and also a waste of valuable skills. As a result, people with some initiative or connections left the development towns for the center of the country, where it was easier to find jobs. These were generally the Europeans, whereas those who stayed behind were the North Africans and other "Orientals." With practically no veteran population as a leavening, some of these new towns remained permanently underdeveloped. But the policy of dispersing the newcomers to outlying areas was really the Government's; the Agency did little more than bring them into the country and contribute a share of the housing cost.

Son: So what *did* most of the money go for?

A very good question. Most of it went for land settlement, or the needs of the agricultural sector of the economy. If the Agency's annual budget was, say, $100 million, as much as $70 million of it went for agriculture. This included subsidizing development of the *kibbutzim*, where relatively few newcomers were being settled, and founding and developing new *moshavim*, of which many were populated by immigrants. A single new *moshav*, which might absorb 50 or 60 families from Morocco, would require investments of hundreds of thousands of dollars, whereas the same fifty families housed in a new town would cost the Agency a fraction of that amount. But turning Jews into farmers was part of the Zionist dream. And the fulfillment of that dream was a major part of the Agency's mission.

Son: I suppose no one foresaw at the time that agriculture would soon become a minor part of the economy.

Or that the kibbutz movement would eventually end up in big trouble, both economically and socially. Actually, at one of the board meetings some of the American members did raise questions about the disproportionate amounts that went into agriculture, and also about the Agency's taking on large debts for developing *kibbutzim* and *moshavim* in years when income from the campaigns was lagging. But, as I said, change came about very slowly. I didn't have the patience to wait, and in January 1966 I quit the job to accept an offer from Brandeis University to direct its branch in Jerusalem.

Son: You mean to say it took you almost five years to realize that you were wasting your time and to look for something else?

That would be overstating it. In the first place, I *did* feel that I was making a contribution, helping to smooth the relationship between American Jewish philanthropy and the Israeli end user. The Jewish Agency was doing quite a remarkable job, bringing in tens, sometimes hundreds of thousands of newcomers a year, even if it involved cutting corners here and there and making mistakes (which became clear with hindsight). It's true that the absorption procedure often involved ignoring individual needs and sensibilities, and treating the clientele *en masse*, which was contrary to modern social work practice. Ben Gurion, who was behind the policy of mass immigration, pointed out that he himself lived in a tent when he first arrived in Palestine, and he saw no reason why those who came after him shouldn't be asked to do the same. This was part of the orientation of his party, Mapai, where the welfare of the group counted for more than that of the individual.

I sympathized with the suffering of the immigrants in the transit camps, the *ma'abarot*, and I felt admiration for their courage and stoicism. The Agency personnel that dealt with them and their problems were mostly untrained; the first school of social work hadn't yet opened. I'll give you a couple of articles I wrote at the time which have more detailed information; you can read them when you have time.

Son: I doubt whether I will. Find the time, I mean.

Suit yourself. One of the articles is about the beginnings of Kiryat Gat, another development town, closer to Tel Aviv, and therefore able to retain a multi-ethnic population which included Europeans. It was designed to become an urban center for the surrounding agricultural region, according to a plan worked out by the Agency's Land Settlement Department, and also to attract industry based on the region's agricultural product, such as sugar beet. Some of the veteran Israelis involved did move there, so it was a good mix. In the article, I deal mainly with the politics of institution building in a new town, which was one of my academic interests. In 1963 I showed off the site of still another new town, Arad, to a New York Times correspondent called Irving Spivak, and I was pleased when his story was given a prominent spot in the paper. In the case of Arad, veteran Israelis were included in the population mix from the start.

But getting back to your question about wasting my time:

At that stage, satisfaction with the job seemed less important than the fact of living in Israel with the family, which was satisfying and even exciting. I would say that, generally, in Israel at the time, the job played less of a role in one's overall life experience than in America, where a person tends to identify unreservedly with his profession. I recall how, during my brief stint on a kibbutz before starting to work on the Post in 1949, I visited Tel Aviv and looked down on the city slickers.

After we arrived in Israel as a family, it took time to find the right apartment. You and Mommy at first stayed with her parents in Tel Aviv, and I put up during the week at a hotel in Jerusalem, where my office was located. We finally decided to move to *Nayot*, which was then called *Shikun Anglo-Saxi*, or the American-Canadian Housing Project. As you know, to Israelis all English speakers are "Anglo-Saxons."

Chapter Thirty-Three

A Yank in Israel

Son: How come you decided to move in with Americans? I thought you wanted to become an Israeli?

I never said that. In the twenty-one years I lived in the States, I had really become an American, and I felt most comfortable with my fellow citizens. The native Israelis didn't accept me as one of them; in the social gatherings I attended with Mommy I often sat in the corner all by myself.

Son: Why do you think that was?

Language was part of it. My Hebrew wasn't that good, and I spoke it with a German accent. Then there's the matter of association: Israelis are very group-minded, and they like to associate with the peer groups to which they belong. It may be their grade school class or the youth movement or the army unit they served in. Unlike Mommy, I was not part of any of this. So most of my social relationships with Israelis were through her. And finally, I became aware that my personality didn't work very well with the Israelis. I was more effective with Americans, who are more easygoing, have more of a sense of humor and don't take themselves as seriously as Israelis do. They are also more civilized in conversation, letting the other fellow talk without interrupting and hogging the floor. You know all that from your own experience; we've mentioned to you that you were more polite and well-mannered when you were abroad.

<u>Son:</u> Wouldn't this have been a good reason to go back to the States?

Not really. There were many other satisfactions in living here that compensated for my outsider status. And then the military victory in the Six-Day War brought about a general euphoria in the country that lasted for several years. It's true: I was convinced from the beginning that the occupied territories would have to be returned before there'd be peace, but that didn't keep me from being caught up in the wave of optimism about the future. The victory really seemed miraculous. One day you sat in the shelter with all the neighbors while Jordanian shells were landing in the garden a few feet away, a few days later the three of us were part of a huge procession winding its way to the *Kotel* (Wailing Wall) in the newly annexed Old City of Jerusalem, where General Dayan had created a vast public square by razing the neighborhood that had blocked access to the Wall.

These were thrilling times to be living in Jerusalem. I enrolled in an Arabic *ulpan* (intensive language course) that met three evenings a week at the Sisters of Zion Convent on the Via Dolorosa. I wanted to be able to speak with our new neighbors in their own tongue. There was no danger in walking through the Old City at night to get to my class. People were friendly to the Israelis; they expected something good to come of all this.

In the previous year I had decided to quit my job with the Jewish Agency, which was then in the doldrums, with almost no immigrants coming in and contributions from world Jewry at a low ebb. Then the war gave the Agency a terrific shot in the arm; Diaspora Jewry showed its solidarity with Israel, and fund raising campaigns broke all records. So my timing in resigning wasn't very good. When I decided to leave, I was actually offered two jobs. The first was as Israel representative of the American Jewish Committee. I had just completed the study on relations between Jews and Arabs in Israel which they commissioned and also published as a book. Their Israel office had the potential for playing an important role in Israel-Diaspora relations, which was my major interest. However, based on my earlier experience, I had reservations about the whole structure of American Jewish community organization, especially as it related to Israel.

The second position was as director of the Brandeis University program in Jerusalem, the Jacob Hiatt Institute. The prospect of being in charge of an academic program for American students was more enticing to me than getting back into Jewish community organization. But it was a difficult choice. I stayed with Brandeis for twelve years, and the rest you know.

Son: There are many things I don't know, about Brandeis and the job you took in Paris afterwards, so this may be a good time to tell me a little more.

Okay. But first, getting back to Nayot: many of the families there were mixed couples, with one of the partners American (or Canadian). So we felt quite at home. With you in mind, we were looking for two things: first, a place with a sense of community; and two, one where you would grow up bi-lingual. We knew that this would be easier in an environment where the neighbors also speak English.

Son: The bi-lingual idea worked out fine, even though I sometimes feel somewhat provincial with a mother tongue that's spoken nowhere else but in Israel What about the community?

Let's save that for later. Right now I'm still explaining why I don't think I was wasting my time during those five years with the Jewish Agency. For the first two years, until 1963, I was kept busy working on my Ph.D. thesis after office hours.

Your room in the Nayot apartment was across the hall from my study, and you heard me pounding away at the typewriter after we put you to bed. It must have been like some kind of lullaby because once, when I stopped typing for a while, I heard you call out: "Abba, why aren't you working?" You were going on three at the time. When I finished the manuscript, I took a leave of absence from my work, and we all flew to New York so I could submit the thesis to my adviser and the faculty committee at Columbia. The process of getting it approved took four months, and during that time you had a chance to improve your English. It was the time President Kennedy was assassinated, and you watched on TV how Jack Ruby shot Harvey Oswald. It made a deep impression, and for weeks afterward you told everybody in sight that "Ruby killed Oswald."

Son: Then back to Israel, I presume, as Herr Doktor Stock. Were you able to put the doctorate to use in some way?

Yes, in several ways. In the rank-conscious Israeli society it added a bit of authority to my Jewish Agency job - or at least I felt that way. Also, I wouldn't have been offered the Brandeis position without the Ph.D. And finally, I began to lecture in the social science faculty of Tel Aviv University. The university had started out a few years earlier as an offshoot of Hebrew University and was still in its early stages. I had hoped to teach international relations, the field in which I got the doctorate, but someone else was teaching that course. So they asked if I could give a course on the *Yishuv* (Jewish community) from Mandate to State. This was not exactly my specialty, but I accepted. A friend who taught a similar course at Hebrew University, Emanuel Guttman, helped me out with bibliographical and other materials. I lectured in Hebrew before 80 students, and was rather proud of myself. But when I took on the Brandeis job the following year, I gave up teaching at Tel Aviv.

Chapter Thirty-Four

Brandeis in Jerusalem

Son: But Brandeis University was also an American Jewish institution, was it not?

Yes, it was. But at the same time, it was an academic one. And the prospect of working with American students as they discovered Israel through political, historical and sociological study was what attracted me. I felt that I had at last found an optimum outlet for my talents, and was also going to make a real contribution to Israel and the relationship with American Jewry. I had quite a bit of leeway in shaping the curriculum, hiring lecturers, planning field trips, etc. Then I supervised students' individual research, some of which resulted in original papers. Through our local guest faculty, men like Professors Yeheskel Dror, Haim Adler and Alan Arian, who were top people in their fields, we developed a high academic standing. Brandeis was the first American university to set up its own program in Israel in 1961, when the Hebrew University foreign student program was still in its infancy. After I took over as director of the program from Howard Sachar, the son of Brandeis president Dr. Abram Sachar, I moved the operation from tiny sublet quarters in the Hillel Foundation to a handsome location on Ethiopia Street, and later to a really spacious building on Maneh Street in the prestigious Talbieh neighborhood. Mr. Hiatt, the Brandeis trustee who had underwritten the cost of the program and also the "key money" for this building, got his name on a plaque and seemed to be quite happy.

There was a committee in the U.S. to which I reported every year, which gave me a chance to visit my parents regularly. The program at first functioned only during the summer and the fall semester, so that I was able to teach a course on Israeli politics at Brandeis in America in the spring. You were not too thrilled about leaving your class in Jerusalem and going to school in Brookline, Mass., and I remember your asking me once reproachfully, *lama sahavtem oti hena?* (why did you drag me here?)

Son: But leaving me aside for a minute, the Brandeis job sounds like a pretty ideal set-up to me.

Yes and no. Like most academic establishments, Brandeis had its share of intrigues and rivalries among the faculty, and between faculty and administration. As a member of the faculty, I was somehow drawn into these, even though I was far away from the campus, or perhaps especially because of that.

In my first year as director we had less than 20 students, most of them from schools other than Brandeis. But then came the Six-Day War, and Israel became fashionable. Applications were pouring in, and in that year, 1967, we had 48 students, which was full capacity. Many came from Brandeis itself, the rest from other schools, and most of them returned home enthusiastic about their experience.

Son: And then what happened?

Once the Institute was successful and popular, the directorship became a desirable post in the eyes of some faculty members. From reports that filtered back to me from the Brandeis campus, I learned that I had to beware even of colleagues whom I had considered my friends.

What made the job fairly secure at first was that the salary was much lower than that paid on the campus. Also, as long as

Dr. Sachar remained university president, I had the feeling that he looked after my interests.

When he was about to retire, he picked as his successor a prominent attorney who had been president of the American Jewish Committee. Morris Abram knew me personally, and he even called me in for a chat about the Hiatt Institute at his New York office before he assumed the presidency. But, sadly, he lasted only a few weeks in the job. He decided to run for senator from New York, and state law obliged him to reside in New York State for six months before the elections. So it was goodbye Brandeis and back to Manhattan.

As the next President of Brandeis the Trustees, with Hiatt as chairman, chose Marver Bernstein, who had been one of the few Jewish faculty members at Princeton at the time I was a student there.

Son: That should have worked out well for you.

It didn't really. It was during his presidency that the Hiatt Institute came to look like an attractive post, and several faculty members began vying for it (behind my back, of course). It eventually went to a cousin of Marver's close associate, a professor of Jewish philosophy who was also the chairman of the Department of Near Eastern and Jewish Studies, with which the Hiatt Institute was then affiliated. The cousin – my successor - was an American rabbi who lived in Jerusalem. It wasn't long before the students were complaining to the University about their new director, and his tenure lasted barely a year. Then Brandeis appointed another director, who also didn't work out, until they eventually closed down the Institute and sent students to the Hebrew University for their junior year in Israel.

Chapter Thirty-Five

Leaving Israel - for a While

Son: When you left the Institute in 1979 you also left Israel. Why was that?

There comes a time in the life of almost every Israeli when he (or she) would like to get away for a while. To be part of the big world again. Breathe new air, see new things. I applied for, and was offered, the job of Director of the European Council of Jewish Communities, with headquarters in Paris. The Council was a creation of the "Joint," the American Jewish Joint Distribution Committee, and was subsidized by it. My earlier experience with the Council of Jewish Federations, and my knowledge of languages must have helped my candidacy, plus the fact that I was known to some of the people involved, including Ralph Goldman, then the head of the "Joint." The main mission of the European Council was to help its member communities learn from one another's experience in the process of postwar reconstruction. It was interesting work, and I learned a great deal about the Jews of Europe while doing it, but that's another story.

Son: Still, why not give me a couple of examples of what you learned?

For one thing, I found that the Jews tend to assume the characteristics of their host people, so to speak, to a surprising degree. Thus the French Jews I dealt with were often quite insular and xenophobic, and I found it difficult to sell them on the need for Europe-wide cooperation. The Executive Director of the *Fonds Social Juif Unifié,* the national body that was our member, once lectured to me, "I have 100,000 Jews to look after in Marseille, and you want me to worry about the 7,000 Jews in Denmark?" I suspect it was only the pressure of the "Joint," which supported the *Fonds Social* financially, that made them maintain their membership in our Council.

Or take the Swiss: They are known to be punctilious about matters financial and, as Heinrich Heine put it, *"wie es sich christelt, so juedelt es sich..."* (as the Christians do, so do the Jews). When we asked the Federation of Swiss Communities for an increase in their annual membership dues, they wanted to know whether the French had already agreed to increase. The Treasurer of our Council was from Zurich, and when he attended meetings in Paris he would submit a bill for his travel expenses right down to the last franc. I was surprised, because in America, it was customary for well-to-do laymen to pay their own expenses, as a contribution to the cause.

From the perspective of Europe, I came to appreciate the strengths of the American Jewish community. The idea of federated fund raising, which unites both the local needs *and* Israel in one campaign, and which was practiced all over America, is a remarkable achievement. But the concept was difficult to implant in Europe, with the exception of France, where it was gradually taking hold. In smaller communities, such as Belgium, the Israeli-focused *Keren Hayesod* campaign invariably took precedence over the financial needs of the local bodies. And its leadership refused to let the fund raising be combined or even coordinated.

To sum up, I'd like to quote from a letter I wrote to you from Paris in October 1980:

"...the synagogue bombing this Erev Shabbat (of the Rue Copernic Reform Temple) was really an atrocious affair: for the first time since the war, this sort of thing was happening in

Europe. The longer I stay here, the more of a Zionist I become. I'm afraid there is only one place for us Jews. It so happened that, on Erev Simhat Torah, I was at another synagogue, and someone telephoned a bomb alert. The hall was evacuated and we stayed in the street for an hour while the police searched the building. They found nothing, and the service resumed. I said to myself already then – I had fled Paris when I was 15 and the Nazis arrived; I didn't come back to let myself be killed by new Nazis.

Chapter Thirty-Six

Three Conclusions - and a Fourth

These conversations came to an end when my son received a fellowship from the Japanese government for graduate studies in design at an art academy in Nagoya.

Son: Now that I'm going to Japan, I can see where our conversations might come in handy there, if I'm asked for some ideological background on Israel. The Japanese, I understand, don't know much about us. And I myself would like to know whether you've come up with some more conclusions by this time about some of the things we discussed.

Yes, I have. But they are still tentative, and I wouldn't want to burden the Japanese with them. Give them the basic facts you're familiar with. And present yourself as an example of the new Israeli.

Conclusion number one: The transformation of the Jews in Israel is progressing to the point where, still in your lifetime, there will be much less in common between them and the Jews of the Diaspora. The conditions created by the sovereign state are simply so different from those of the quasi-religious communities in America, France, England, etc. that the resulting human type will also come out quite different. There has always been something instrumental on both sides in the motivation for maintaining close ties: Israel has been getting financial and political support through the Jewish connection, and the Jews of the world were deriving psychological and emotional benefits from their identification with Israel. This will diminish with the passage of time.

Son: What about the religious ties? Shouldn't those prove to be more permanent?

I don't think so. The formal religious structures involve only about 40 per cent of the Jews in most places. In Israel, the formal structures are predominantly Orthodox. Reform and Conservative congregations, which are the majority in the Diaspora, have had only modest success in Israel; historically, they arose in response to specific Diaspora conditions. As you may remember, I myself was a member of such a congregation in Jerusalem for many years. When I analyzed my motivation, I had to admit it was mainly out of nostalgia and the desire to belong to the social milieu that came with the religious affiliation. Sovereign existence, as I see it now, brings with it the attrition of the religious dimension of Jewishness, to which nearly every member of Israel's secular society is subject. No matter how this is disguised, such as by pointing to participation in the folkloristic aspects of certain religious holidays, or maintaining traditions like lighting the Sabbath candles, there is no denying the overwhelmingly secular nature of mainstream Israeli society. Nor can it be denied that the identification of the religious sector with right-wing politics makes a reversal of this trend unlikely. In the course of time, this is likely to speed up the alienation between the Israeli and the Diaspora-based sectors of the Jewish people.

Another possibility is that the two forms of Jewish existence, sovereign and communal-religious, will continue to co-exist and develop new modes of interaction. A third possible outcome, which no one likes to contemplate, is the decline of the state due to external pressures or inner contradictions, or a combination of both. In that case, the survival of Judaism would again be tied to the Diaspora. For the assertion that Diaspora Jewry could not survive without the state of Israel, no proof is available.

Conclusion number two concerns the Arabs. Not so much the Arabs in Israel as relations with the Arab world. The peace with Egypt has shown that there are no ideological obstacles to normal relations; everything is a question of power, and a readiness to make concessions. Whether Israel will have enough power to force itself on the Arab world without making the main concession they insist on, which is a return to the 1967 borders or lines close to them, is difficult to predict. Once that is agreed to, everything else will fall into place. But then there's the question of whether the right wing elements in Israel, primarily the settlers in the territories, will allow that to happen.

And a third tentative conclusion concerns the hope that a Jewish state would introduce a new and different element into the state system, one that would be motivated by considerations beyond power and interest. I now realize that this is a romantic illusion which stands little chance of fulfilment. Being a state means just that: acting among other states and like other states. Even in biblical times, to be a "kingdom of priests and a holy nation" was a prophetic exhortation, not a reality, and I think it reflected a social and not a political vision. From my reading of the prophets I learned that their visions were a reaction to the ways of their contemporaries and often of their rulers, not a reflection of any reality that we have a right to be proud of. When it comes to modern Israel, I think we ought to be satisfied with being a "nation like all the nations."

Son: Do I detect a note of disappointment here, or even disillusionment?

Getting rid of an illusion, romantic or otherwise, is disillusionment by definition.

But I've tried to preserve my observer stance up to now, which means learning from what one sees and experiences, without taking things too personally. Not that that's always

Ernest Stock

possible. There is so much happening here, even apart from the political arena, so much energy, creativity and sheer vitality all around you, that one willy-nilly becomes involved. For years, no matter how many times I returned from a trip abroad, I always had tears in my eyes when the plane touched down at Ben-Gurion Airport. And it wasn't because of the safe landing.

If there's one aspect of the national revival which I hadn't anticipated, it's the amount of suffering we've caused to the Palestinians as a result of it. I realize that being a state entails a fair amount of *sacré égoisme,* but I still wonder whether we made enough of an effort to alleviate that suffering, by working harder for a peaceful solution when there were opportunities, or by doing more to help solve the refugee problem.

And a fourth and final conclusion has to do with anti-semitism. According to Herzl's scenario, it should have just about disappeared by this time. But his scenario included one precondition which has not been met: that most of the Jews in the world would have been gathered in the homeland. In other words, while we developed into a normal and healthy nation, we would have voluntarily relinquished our status as non-sovereign Diaspora communities. Instead of that, we are determined to have it both ways: benefitting from the advantages of a state of our own while continuing communal life in the *Golah.* Israel *and* the Diaspora. I'm not saying that's bad, or unjustified, but we mustn't be surprised that anti-semitism hasn't disappeared.

I come back to what I told you earlier: that I look upon the fact of being here at such a crucial period as a privilege I would not have liked to miss. It's true, it was a rather rash decision to leave the United States when I did, but I have no regrets. I might even look on the part of my life that I've lived in Israel as a culmination of the other two parts – the European and the American. If there is such a thing as a Jewish people as more than a collection of religiously motivated individuals, then why not be a witness to its defining collective experience, if it coincides with one's lifetime.

Epilogue

In June 2004, only a few weeks before my 80th birthday, I became an Israeli citizen. It was an act more of symbolic than of practical significance, but still, it marked a reversal of a position I'd held for many years.

When I first arrived with my family more than four decades earlier, I "opted out" of citizenship. Instead, my status was that of an *oleh* and permanent resident, with all the privileges and duties of citizenship, except for one: voting for the Knesset.

There were two reasons for my hesitancy. First, I was sent by an American organization (the Jewish Agency, Inc.) which had an interest in being represented in Israel by an American citizen. And secondly, I did not believe in dual citizenship, even though this was widespread among American Jewish immigrants. I looked upon citizenship not unlike as on monogamy. Had I not sworn, on becoming an American in 1943, to give up loyalty to any "foreign potentate"? There was also the remote chance of losing one's American citizenship by becoming an Israeli, especially in the case of a naturalized American like myself. This I was not prepared to risk. Over the years, I found this position of being not quite committed, as it were, compatible with the observer status I claimed for myself, though I sometimes found it difficult to explain this to others. The topic did not come up in our conversations, since my son never asked about it. But the Brandeis students almost invariably wanted to know about my citizenship status. I concluded from their interest that the subject still played an important role for Americans, much more so than to most Israelis to whom it seemed little more than a formality. In recent years, one frequently hears about people who took out passports of their former homeland, such as Germany or Poland, to facilitate travel or to become eligible for compensation. This in addition to their Israeli citizenship, of course.

What, then, has happened to make me change my mind?

In the background, there is the general devaluation of the concept of citizenship to which I've alluded just now. The element of exclusivity has given way, and dual nationality has become a commonplace in many countries. The United States especially has lowered its criteria. Where once the draconian McCarran Act required naturalized Americans to return home once in five years as a condition for remaining citizens, a new Immigration and Nationality Law (Section 322) allows children born abroad to acquire U.S. citizenship by having American grandparents. I could not help but be affected by these developments. My ideological opposition to dual citizenship was being worn down.

Then there was the cumulative effect of the years on self-definition. True, I don't recall ever being asked, "What are you – an Israeli or an American?" Because of my German accent in Hebrew the question was more likely to be, "Are you from Germany or America?" But after a while – after ten years had passed, then twenty, and thirty – I felt more and more Israeli, less American. Once my association with Brandeis University had ended and both my parents had died, my visits to the U.S. became rarer, ties of friendship looser. I recall that, following the 1967 War, I sent a round-robin letter about the event to 80 American addressees; after the Yom Kippur War in 1973 the number of friends and acquaintances with whom I shared the experience had shrunk to twenty.

But there was one determining factor which in the end tipped the scale. After Rabin's assassination and the rise of the Likud to power, I became more and more disaffected with the Israel government's policies. I wanted to express that opposition, also at the ballot box, but I felt myself thwarted by not being a citizen. I always thought that, in Israel as elsewhere, there was something illegitimate about a non-citizen taking part in the internal political debate. Somewhat paradoxically, just at the time I felt the most alienation from the official line, I took the step which expressed the ultimate identification with the country.

A short time later, I travelled abroad with my wife, for the first time as an Israeli.

In meeting strangers and talking with them, I felt the same kind of inner freedom that I had always been aware of in Israel itself, where the element of Jewishness never entered into the relationship between individuals. It may have been my imagination, but what at first appeared as merely a formal, symbolic act, had come to leave its mark on my personality and behavior.